Georg

AN EASTERN CALLING

George Windsor Earl and a Vision of Empire

Ranald Noel-Paton

Ashgrove Publishing
London

For Patricia,
Kirsty, Lora, Hannah and Martha

CONTENTS

•

The photographic sections appear between pages
98-99 and 188-89, respectively.
NLA denotes the National Library of Australia

•

Title page illustration:
HMS *Alligator* and *Britomart* in a storm off Land's End during their voyage to Australia, February 1838. The *Alligator* suffered a split bowsprit (as seen in the illustration) and was forced to return to Plymouth for repairs. From a watercolour by Captain John McArthur who witnessed the incident.

FOREWORD AND ACKNOWLEDGEMENTS

For most of my life I have been vaguely aware of a great, great grandfather named George Samuel Windsor Earl. I knew little about him and the collective knowledge of other members of the family did not amount to much. I had no real interest in correcting this state of affairs until I received a letter dated the 1st of January 2009 from Dr Russell Jones of the School of Oriental and African Studies in London suggesting a meeting.

Russell Jones was a Royal Marines officer in Singapore and Java in 1945 and 1946, and then entered the colonial service in Malaya. After three years of study at SOAS and three years at Leiden University, he became a lecturer in Indonesian and Malay at SOAS and the University of Sydney. It was there that he first came across George Earl as the person who had coined the name 'Indonesia'. In step with his many academic pursuits, Russell had amassed considerable research on Earl with a view to compiling a biography, which, due to other pressures on his time, he never managed to do.

What he proposed at our meeting was either that I might join him in funding both the research and the writing of a biography, or that I might do this myself. Newly retired from full-time business, I could not refuse a challenge like this. I would never have been able to carry it out without Russell's encouragement and extraordinary generosity in handing over to me his research papers and documents on George Windsor Earl.

He also introduced me to two other scholars who had independently built up a great deal of research and knowledge of George Earl: Dorothy Jenkinson, and Professor Bob Reece, of Murdoch University, Perth, Western Australia. Dorothy Jenkinson was a scholar, professional researcher and author. She assembled, over nearly thirty years, a fund of knowledge on George Earl, about whom she knew arguably more than anyone else on the planet. Scholars like her do not need to provide a reason for such an interest. She just happened across his name and developed a wealth of understanding, almost an affection for this unusual man. She most generously gave her research documents and material to me. With her prodigious memory, her sense of humour and her enthusiasm, she was endlessly helpful. Sadly she died in January 2017.

Professor Bob Reece, a historian and academic at Murdoch University in Perth, Western Australia, provided an Australian input along with his expertise on George Earl's Australian career. He has published numerous articles and papers on Earl and has championed him in Australia as an important figure in early Australian history. Bob is to be credited with recently arranging and writing Earl's entry in the *Australian Dictionary of Biography* and the *Oxford Dictionary of National Biography*, neither of which had previously contained his name. He has been continuously helpful, informative and encouraging in my efforts.

It is no exaggeration to say that without the help and support of this triad of scholars, each of whom was determined that George Earl should no longer be a forgotten man, I would not have been able to write this book. I owe each of them an enormous debt of gratitude.

To their material I have of course added my own research. Of Earl's descendants, David Carter, Jennifer Taggart and Tessa Montgomery have been helpful with information and comments; as was the late Pauline Johnston, wife of Brian Johnston. Paul Scofield, Curator of Vertebrate Zoology at Canterbury Museum, Christchurch, New Zealand provided valuable information which he kindly shared with me. Neill and Roberta Giffin in Australia helped with their very useful input. Robert Hellyer, a descendant of William Alt's half-sister, has provided invaluable information on William Alt and his career in Japan. Thanks also to Dr John Holliday who kindly reviewed his fellow doctors' reports from 150 years ago.

My wife Patricia and our daughters, Kirsty, Lora, Hannah and Martha, have all been hugely supportive and, on occasions, long-suffering. They will be in prime position to pass on the story of George Earl to future generations. Kirsty, our eldest daughter, has been the master-enabler in that, with consummate skill, patience and effort, she has translated my writing from manuscript to computer, latterly from her home in Singapore. Both she and her sister Lora lived in Singapore with their families, not far from Mount Erskine where George and Clara Earl lived for a while. Hannah has worked wonders in organising the final narrative and supporting material.

For the most part, biographies are works of scholarship and research. They positively bristle with footnotes and references. I have not attempted to emulate this honoured and respected tradition. What I have tried to do is to give a biographical account of the life of a very interesting and unusual man. This is not a work of scholarship. It is George Earl's story, which has emerged from carefully researched material. Sources are given both in the text and in the Reference section. The reader is able to delve further if he or she so wishes. For the most part, the spelling and punctuation in original documents from the period have been retained.

Finally, I am indebted to my publisher, Brad Thompson, who has also edited the work. He has brought to the task immense skill, interest and investigative energy. His contribution has been invaluable.

– Chapter One –

Roots: The Beginnings

1813-1828

Let us hope that your Children, having a good example set them, & being brought up in the nurture & admonition of the Lord, may thereafter shew in their lives the effect of what they now shall learn.

•

George Samuel Windsor Earl was born at his mother's house, Wildwood, North End, in Hampstead, London, on the 10th of February 1813. His older brother, Percy William, and sister, Elizabeth, were also born there in 1811 and 1817, respectively.

As with all families, lineage provides the backcloth to their lives. Their mother, Elizabeth, came from south Staffordshire, where her family had lived for generations, mostly in a cluster of villages: Baswich, Penkridge, Brocton and Bednall. They all lie between the towns of Stafford and Cannock Chase, an area of gently rolling hills and farming land. Today, Cannock Chase retains much natural beauty, with heaths, woodland (part of the ancient national forest) and rich flora and fauna. Elizabeth was the sixth of seven children of Abel Peploe Sharp and his wife, Mary. Elizabeth was born in Brocton, near Baswich, and was baptised there in 1781. The inscription on her gravestone in the churchyard at St. John's Parish Church, Hampstead, shows that she was 95 years old when she died on the 15th of March 1874; so she was born during 1778 or in early in 1779.

At some stage, Elizabeth and her brothers and sisters moved to London. Migration from country to town was growing apace in the 18th century and it is most likely that her uncle, William Peploe Sharp, was instrumental in their move as he had left Staffordshire for London and had prospered in the capital. William owned a number of properties in the City and held the copyhold of some land and a house, Wildwood, in North End, Hampstead. He and his wife were childless, and after he died in 1808, Elizabeth, who probably was his god-daughter, acquired through his trustees the deeds to Wildwood. She was to remain there for the rest of her long life.

Elizabeth's granddaughter, Elizabeth Alt, described her: 'She was tall and used no armchair until she was ninety. She was a great gardener and spent hours digging etc. She thought the earth was so wholesome. Her language was strong!' Her 1874 obituary, with its somewhat ambitious ancestral claims, appeared in the local Hampstead press and included the following:

> We regret to announce the death, on Sunday last, of Mrs. Earl a lady who we believe was the oldest inhabitant, as she was certainly the longest resident, and the oldest copyholder in Hampstead. She was in her ninety-sixth year and had lived at North-end ever since her childhood. Mrs. Earl claimed collateral descent from Thomas à Becket, Archbishop of Canterbury and James Sharp, Archbishop of St. Andrews. ...Mrs. Earl was, until the past winter in full enjoyment of much bodily and mental power. Last summer she drove to Dulwich, and (some accident happening to the carriage) walked homewards for nearly a mile... Many who read this notice, will recall recollections of a kind and gentle lady, ever courteous and considerate to all, helpful to the poor, full of pleasant reminiscences of Hampstead and its people in days long gone by...

Soon after the death of Elizabeth's uncle and her inheritance of Wildwood in 1808, she met Captain Percy Earl, RN. They were married at St. James Church, Clerkenwell, in June 1809.

Captain Percy was descended from a slightly mysterious line. His roots appear to have been in an area on the Bedfordshire/Hertfordshire border, but there is scant evidence as to his origins. We know from his several wills that his mother's name was Sarah and that she had married his father, also named Percy (variously spelt as Pearce or Piercy), in about 1770, and that he had a brother, Richard. About his father, there is, however, one clue: the name Sundon, a village in Bedfordshire near the county border with Hertfordshire. Sundon Parish records show an illegitimate child who was baptised Piercy Earl in 1746. The parents' names are not given. The name Earl, as perhaps here, was at that time sometimes used as an appellation for an illegitimate child – as George Earl's grandfather seems to have been.

We know nothing of Captain Percy's childhood, nor that of his brother, Richard, although we do know that Richard and his family went as settlers to Swan River, Australia, in 1830. In 1796, Percy entered the Royal Navy as a midshipman. Records show that he served on HMS *Raisonable* under the command of Captain Boyles from August 1796 to December 1797, 'during which time he behaved himself with diligence and sobriety and was always obedient to Command and performed his duty in every respect entirely to my [Boyles'] satisfaction'.

And later:

> These are to certify that the bearer Mr. Percy Earl served as First Mate on board His Majesty's hired Armed Schooner Speedwell from the 29th of October 1799 until the 29th of October 1801 during which time he conducted himself to my satisfaction and is a good Seaman and Navigator. Given under my hand on Board the said Schooner in this 29th of October 1801.
> Commander

Percy left the Royal Navy and during the next few years rose to master mariner, as well as navigating different waters in his private life. He had met, possibly in Bengal, a Mrs Elizabeth Wagner whom he married at St Mary's Islington in 1807. She died the following year giving birth to a daughter, Emma, who also died. From Elizabeth he inherited a trust fund of 15,000 Sicca Rupees (East Indian coins, equal in value to approximately £120,000 today). At the age of seventeen, he had also fathered, illegitimately, a son known as James Hill (sometimes James Hill-Earl) who appears to be the recorded James Percy Hill, born in 1788, illegitimate son of Ann Hill of Fremington, Devon (father's name not given). This young man sailed with him from time to time, but was otherwise out of touch. However, an 1827 codicil to Captain Percy's last will stated: 'I bequeath to James Hill who was seaman with me on board the ship *Aurora* on her voyage out from England to Madras in or about the year 1818, if now living, the sum of £100.' (He did receive the bequest.)

In 1809, at the age of 38, and only a year after the death of Elizabeth Wagner, Captain Percy met and married Elizabeth Sharp. Elizabeth would have been considered, at the age of 28, quite old to marry for the first time but her impressive personality and, no doubt, considerable assets were added attractions for this mercurial, intelligent, ambitious and attractive man. A contemporary miniature portrait of him reveals a firm face, flashing dark eyes and a luxuriant head of black hair.

Their marriage took place at the parish church of St James Clerkenwell, a fine building which at that time had been a place of worship for more than six hundred years. Elizabeth's house, Wildwood, became their home. It would have been the first family home that Captain Percy as an adult had known, where their three children were born, where he died 18 years later, and she 43 years after that. It was situated at North End, a name given to a cluster of houses just within the northern boundary of the parish of Hampstead.

Two contemporary sketches depict a modest yet comfortable family home. In the 1861 Census, two staff are mentioned: a cook and a waiting maid. When the house was full of children and she was on her own, Elizabeth also employed a nanny, a Mrs. Tooley, and probably an additional maid. The location was ideal for a young family. Hampstead was a beautiful and fashionable area and North End was just a mile from the centre of the village with its church, schools and shops. High above the frequently noxious atmosphere of the City of London, it was a much sought-after place to live then, as it is now. Wildwood House was a few yards from Wildwood Corner, which is named in the Domesday Book. A path curved away from the front door a few hundred yards to the Spaniards Inn; Rotten Row led in a straight line through forest and glade to Heath End, and across Spaniards Road lay the great tract of Hampstead Heath proper with its woods, meadows, ponds, and vales. The Earl children from an early age would have found much pleasure from natural pursuits, explorations and discoveries that the area offered.

George Samuel Windsor Earl was baptised on the 13th of July 1813 at the parish church of St John, Hampstead, by the Revd. Dr Samuel White. Dr White was a colourful character, 'quarrelling with all the world', as the poet John Keats observed. (Keats also had a house in Hampstead.) White was also described as 'riveted to the sound and pure principles of the Church of England', which is to say that he was opposed to the Evangelicals then gaining ground. The name Samuel perhaps commemorates one of Elizabeth's ancestors, Samuel Peploe, Bishop of Chester from 1726 until his death in 1752. It is also possible that Elizabeth decided to give her second son the name Samuel after her estimable vicar with whom she had struck up a good friendship. They had both arrived in Hampstead at about the same time, and being newcomers to that civilised and sophisticated society may have brought them together. George was to drop the name in adulthood.

As for the name Windsor, the family tree lists Lord Windsor as George's godfather. However, there is no evidence to support any sort of a link, as the only Lord Windsor at that time was the heir to the Earl of Portsmouth, an unlikely (though not impossible) friend or associate of either Captain Percy or Elizabeth. It is more probable that the name Windsor was selected for its associations, sound and Englishness. As with the later Victorians, families then also had a predilection for ancestral ambitions that were not well founded, and the later compiler of the Earl family tree (believed to have been George's sister, Elizabeth) was no exception. We have already read in Elizabeth's obituary her claimed descent from Thomas à Becket and James Sharp, Archbishop of St Andrews who was murdered at St Andrews on the 17th of May 1679. All this is impressive, but improbable. Naturally, the illegitimacy of Captain Percy's father was not mentioned.

The christening served, too, as a farewell to Captain Percy whose new command, the *General Hewitt*, (sometimes known as the *General Hewart*) was in Woolwich Docks, ready to load convicts bound for Australia. She was a first-class ship of approximately 1,000 tons built in Calcutta in 1812, armed with fourteen guns and owned by the East India Company. A three-decker with a crew of 104, she would be still sailing in the Australia trade in the 1840s. Embarkation began on the 18th of July 1813, and since much preparation was required for the long and arduous voyage, Percy would have left North End a day or so after the christening. George would be two-and-a-half before the captain would see him again.

The *General Hewitt* finally sailed on the 26th of August, on what was to be an ill-starred voyage, from Portsmouth where she was bound for Port Jackson (Sydney) via Madeira and Rio de Janeiro. On-board were some 500 people, including 300 convicts.

The voyage to Madeira proceeded well, although the ship's surgeon, Richard Hughes, had objected to the state of the health of fifteen or so of the convicts before sailing. Nevertheless, he was obliged to accept them as it had been certified by the prison hulk surgeons that all the prisoners were in good health.

After a nine-day stay in Madeira, where the convicts were kept below in hot and humid conditions, the *General Hewitt* sailed for Rio de Janeiro. Within a fortnight a dozen or more of the convicts had come down with dysentery due to, in surgeon Richard Hughes' diagnosis, very wet weather that prevented them (and, presumably, the other passengers) from having regular access to fresh air on the deck. Moreover, during a fumigation of the prisoners' deck, including their bedding, a squall hit the ship and the bedding that was being aired was soaked. It had been heaped together and attempts were made to dry it out, but this was not entirely achievable under the circumstances. About nineteen convicts died on the voyage to Rio de Janeiro and many more were seriously ill.

Nineteen days later, the *General Hewitt* proceeded from Rio on the voyage, during which the prisoners had free access to the deck, to Port Jackson. By the time they arrived there the death toll of convicts for the entire voyage of 165 days had risen to 34, all buried at sea.

Governor Macquarie of New South Wales ordered a Court of Enquiry to examine and report on the conduct of the officers of the *General Hewitt*.

Furthermore, he wrote in 1814 from Government House, Sydney, to Earl Bathurst (HM Secretary of State for War and the Colonies in London) on the matter:

> Having Reason to apprehend from the Sickly State of the Convicts who arrived, and from the alarming Extent of the Mortality during the Passage, that proper Attention had not been paid by the Master and Surgeon [Richard Hughes] of the General Hewitt to the Health and Comforts of the Convicts on board that Vessel, I appointed a Court of Enquiry to Examine into and report on the Conduct of those Officers. The Result of which Enquiry is, that the Conduct of the Commander [Captain Percy] has been highly Culpable in some Instances; Under this Consideration I feel it my Duty to transmit the Proceedings of that Court by the present Opportunity to the Commissioners of the Transport Board, in order to their Adopting such Measures for the Punishment of the Commander as the Circumstances of Case will admit.

In *The Convict Ships 1787-1868* by Charles Bateson, he quotes the following testimony to the Court of Inquiry:

> As a member of the court of inquiry, Redfern [a surgeon] subscribes to the finding that the prisoners had been humanely treated and the prison and hospital carefully cleansed, fumigated and ventilated. But in a special report to Macquarie he stated that these precautions had been neglected during the latter stages of the passage. He also disclosed that the damp bedding had been thrown overboard three weeks before the General Hewitt had reached Rio, and declared that when colder weather was encountered, the lack of the bedding was acutely felt. A passenger, Surgeon John Harris, of the New South Wales Corps, testified to the attention shown the prisoners by Hughes. 'I very frequently visited the prison,' he asserted, 'and never saw any place better fitted up, nor kept in a more cleanly state, and the prisoners had frequent and, indeed, almost constant access to the deck.

Macquarie, remembered today as a first-class governor, was not given to exaggeration and his criticisms carried weight. Personally, he found Percy Earl 'particularly troublesome and refractory', but the deaths did not lead to any court martial, dismissal or disciplinary action, a welcome decision to Captain Earl as he avoided the kind of setback that could profoundly damage a naval career.

The Court of Inquiry judged:

> We are of opinion from the evidence produced before us that there is no reason for supposing a want of humanity or attention on the part of Mr. Earl, Master, and Mr. Hughes, Surgeon of the General Hewitt, towards the Convicts intrusted to their charge, but that on the contrary every attention was paid to keeping the Prison and Hospital carefully cleansed, fumigated and ventilated, and the Comforts put on board for the Service of the Sick were duly appropriated for that purpose.

Captain Percy returned to England in August 1815, still in command of the *General Hewitt*, and resigned his commission. For almost three years he was to be in Hampstead with his wife and family. This was a rare quiet interlude in his generally peripatetic life. The England he returned to would pulsate with pride and confidence after the victory at Waterloo in June 1815 – the years of Napoleonic ascendancy were past and the country could look forward to a new order. Captain Percy, while he was considering his prospects and planning his next move, spent important time with his two small sons, Percy junior and George, who were aged about four and two, respectively, when he had arrived home. This was the only period in their lives that they were to see him at length. His daughter, yet another Elizabeth, was born during this interlude.

But even a happy family life cannot keep a sailor at anchor for long. He joined the East India Company as the captain of the company's ship *Aurora*. She was a splendid three-master of 550 tons, built in Chittagong and launched on the 7th of June 1818. A two-decker sloop at 117ft long, she sailed on her maiden eastbound voyage from London to Madras early in 1819 (with Captain Percy's illegitimate son James Hill-Earl amongst the crew). While she certainly would have sailed in East Asian waters, most of her voyages were between India and England carrying passengers, and cargo of every description. Like most East India Company ships she was stout, if not particularly fast (this was the pre-clipper age). Toughness and reliability were the prerequisites for both ships and crews. Voyages were usually on the same routing: London via Madeira, or the Azores to Rio de Janeiro; then around the Cape of Good Hope and up the Indian Ocean.

These were to be the formative years for George and Percy. They were, respectively, about six and eight when their father had sailed again for the East in 1819. The focus was now on their education and prosperous middle-class Hampstead was a place of mainly private schools. It is probable that as day pupils they first attended Hampstead Parochial School, the

Parochial School of St John, where they had been christened. Founded in 1811, it was very much under the influence of their redoubtable family friend, the Rev Dr Samuel White. The *Rules and Regulations* of the school give a flavour of what was to be expected of the Earl family:

> ...We will do our endeavours to train them up in Virtuous & Religious habits; to make them humble, diligent, & obedient; to inure them to such habits of Order, Industry & Fidelity, as may have a good effect on their conduct through Life; & above all, to make them Read the Word of Almighty God, & practice, to the utmost of their power, a constant obedience of his will which is the only sure principle of Virtue, & the only sure road to happiness hence & hereafter.
>
> ...The Duties which are required of you, are plain & simple, but very important; indeed so important, that, unless you carefully attend to them, the benefits of this Institution will be lost to your children.
>
> 1st Make it your business, in the first place, to see that your Children are ready to attend School at the appointed hours; let them be exact to a minute...
>
> 2nd Let your Children be clean Washed, & combed, & their clothing be as neat & decent as your circumstances will permit; remembering that a dirty Child is a disgrace to its Parents...
>
> 3rd Let it be your most serious concern to set your Children good examples; let them not see anything in your behaviour at home contrary to what is taught them at Church, or at School...
>
> ...It depends more on you, than any one else, what sort of persons your Children will be, when they become Men & Women. They are much more likely to imitate you, than attend to us: – with your assistance, we may hope to train them up in the way in which they should go; that they may not be guilty of such shocking practices as Sabbath breaking, drunkenness & swearing...
>
> This is the hearty desire of us, your friends & well wishers,
> The Committee

Although Captain Percy seems to have been a mercurial character (his granddaughter referred to him in her memoirs as 'irascible and quarrelsome'), he may have displayed different characteristics whilst in command at sea. The following was reported in *The Asiatic Journal and Monthly Register for British India and its Dependencies* (July to December 1819):

> A letter addressed by Lieut. col. J. Garner commanding the 2nd Ceylon vol. bat. to Capt. Percy Earl, commanding the ship Aurora, dated Colombo 5th Jan., after thanking the latter for his kindness and hospitality which rendered the passage to Bengal as agreeable to the officers and men as it could be made, to the great attention to the comforts, and respect to the prejudices of the men, shewn by Capt. Earl, his ship's officers and crew, Col. Garner attributes that happy reconciliation to shipboard evinced by the men of his corps on the present occasion, an effect on the native soldier in India so desirable in a political point of view. Capt. Earl's answer, dated Bombay, 3d. Feb. applauds the good conduct of the men during the passage.

Captain Percy was anxious to be a good provider for his family, as would be evidenced by his detailed and thoughtful wills. He must also have been a dynamic role model for his sons, sailing in command the oceans of the world to exotic places, returning with tales and artefacts from the mysterious East. Because of his frequent long absences, the relationship between father and sons was uncomplicated by close acquaintance. Family fragmentation and lengthy separations were characteristic of many seafaring families. The Empire provided a wealth of opportunity for men to go and seek their fortunes. Many answered the call to serve in the military, the civil service and in trade and commerce. Some wives and children followed, but the East was no place for a European woman and her children. The graveyards of churches throughout Asia bear witness to the dangers, the sickness, the sacrifice and death which all too often occurred when a family accompanied a husband. For the most part, wives and children stayed at home in Britain and endured the travails of separation, and so it was with George's family. He and his brother, Percy William, had an idyllic childhood, notwithstanding their father's absences. They lived in a charming house in a beautiful situation with a mother who, in addition to her other qualities, was a tower of strength. Their upbringing seems to have been happy but was probably strict, particularly when their father was at home as he was between his return on the *General Hewitt* in 1816 and his departure on the *Aurora* at the beginning of 1819.

In the latter half of 1823, Captain Percy reappears in the *Indian Register* as a Bengal resident and is described as 'commanding the Aurora'. It is conceivable that his Bengal residency was necessary to his being able to claim the 15,000 Sicca Rupee legacy which he had inherited from his first wife. At some stage during this period, probably with the help of this inheritance, he had amassed sufficient means to purchase the *Aurora* and become an owner/master. He returned to England where his fortunes waxed and waned. For a short while in 1824, following some difficult trading circumstances during a time of recession in England, he became bankrupt. Fortunately, he was able to manage an early return to solvency by paying around 85% to his creditors in final settlement, and was also able to retain the ownership of the *Aurora*.

George's Hampstead schooling lasted for five years until, in 1824, he was sent at the age of eleven to the Rev. John Stephenson's boarding school at Orpington in Kent. His father obviously decided it was time for George to go to a boarding school to broaden his horizons and experience the benefits such an establishment can provide. Captain Percy had had no formal education himself, but being an ambitious and intelligent man he had formed views on how his sons were to be educated. The school at Orpington was a decent, respectable place. There is no record of the curriculum, but the termly bills covered items like Books, French, Drawing, Dancing and Stationery.

In 1825, when Captain Percy was again in England, he decided to take George (but apparently not Percy *fils*) away from Orpington. His attention had been taken by Wyke House Academy at Isleworth and its headmaster and founder, Dr Alexander Jamieson. He was a distinguished academic and educationalist, and Wyke House Academy was a superior sort of establishment to Orpington.

Dr Jamieson was to became a writer of practical books, mostly to do with mathematics, engineering, mechanical sciences and cartography. One of his better-known works was *A Dictionary of mechanical science, arts, manufactures, and miscellaneous knowledge*. Its contents were described in the subtitle as 'comprising the pure sciences of mathematics, geometry, arithmetic, algebra, &; the mixed sciences of mechanics, hydrostatics, pneumatics, optics, and astronomy; experimental philosophy; the fine arts; agriculture, and its implements; manufactures, and their various processes; commerce and domestic economy; natural history; with biographical and historical notices of eminent men, who have adorned science by their inventions and discoveries'.

Usually at that time, the curriculum for boys attending private schools was a sparse affair and would have comprised for the most part Latin and Greek, Arithmetic and Ciphering, some Religious exercises and a great deal of the disciplines of the English language. Wyke House Academy, however, was more attuned to the contemporary world with its heady mix of industrial development and imperial expansion. Men often set out with the single objective of adding to the pool of knowledge. Expeditions were sent far and wide; no destination was deemed too far or too difficult. The American naval officer and explorer Charles Wilkes embarked on his great journey of 1836 with instructions to 'extend the empire of commerce and science; to diminish the hazards of the ocean.... Although the primary aim of the expedition is the promotion of the great interest of commerce and navigation; yet you will take all occasions... to extend the bounds of science and promote the acquisition of Knowledge'.

Such private schools were not simply places of learning. They were establishments where a boy would hone his wits, his sense of relationship, his independence and the use of his fists. A rather interesting bill sent to the Earls from Wyke House Academy includes the cost of broken windows. George was not averse to trouble, having taken upon himself the unauthorised hiring of a private tutor as mentioned in a letter from Dr Jamieson to Captain Percy's executors on August 29th 1827:

> Dear Sir,
> I have omitted the Spanish master's bill entirely and have written to him to apply himself for it... Besides, it will, I hope, teach Master George a lesson I should like him to learn very soon and very perfectly by heart.
>
> I am Dear Sir,
> very truly
> Alexander Jamieson

Perhaps George had arranged for the private Spanish lessons to be billed to the school. In any case one can catch the gusto of the man who had charge of George's education, although, as we will see, George did not lose his taste for skirting authority.

Early in 1827, the *Aurora* sailed from India on what would be her last voyage under Captain Percy's command. She docked at London on the return voyage towards the middle of May and, now anxious to get home, he travelled on top of a coach in a rainstorm during the hour's drive up to Hampstead from the Docks. The joy of the homecoming to his wife and his sons Percy and George, now aged sixteen and fourteen, respectively, and ten-year-old Elizabeth was not to last. He had caught a 'severe chill' and died within two weeks, probably from pneumonia, on the 5th of June 1827, shortly before his 56th birthday. Details of his funeral expenses show that he was a tall and hefty man: his coffin measured 6ft 3ins and required eight men to carry it down the stairs of Wildwood. He is interred in the burial grounds of Hampstead parish church where the headstone now records the date of his death, and those of his children and of his wife.

His final estate, which included the sale of the *Aurora*, was around £13,000, a considerable sum in 1827, the equivalent today of approximately £1 million. The assets were to be managed by Trustees for the benefit of his wife and children.

In the same month of his father's death, George's time at Wyke House Academy, Isleworth, came to an end after only two-and-a-half years. We do not know if these events were connected; but his formal education was over. Aged fourteen-and-a-half, with the agreement of his mother, and possible instigation and help of his father's friends and executors, he joined the East India Company.

In November 1827, George Earl sailed as a midshipman on the East India Company's *Lady Holland*, one of the old broad-sterned two-deckers that carried many passengers between London and Calcutta. A close friend was later to write that for George, 'the voyage seems to have given him a distaste of a sea-faring life as a profession'. At face value this is a curious observation about a man who became a masterful mariner and occasional ship's captain. But it may be broadly true in that his future voyages on the Eastern seas were to be adjuncts to his main purpose and interests in life. Whatever the case, on his return to England in March 1829, he resigned his commission with the East India Company at the age of sixteen.

– Chapter Two –

The Swan River
1829

...which adventure and procedure on their parts is undertaken with my consent and concurrence.

•

The voyage to India and back on the *Lady Holland* was perhaps a blessing for a very young man recently bereaved of a father. The life of a midshipman on a big vessel was demanding. You had to be fit and strong, and you had to be prepared and able to learn every aspect of sailing a ship, including crucial navigational skills. The *Lady Holland* did not return to London until early in 1829, so the voyage gave George ample time to think about his future. Immediately after his arrival, the sixteen-year-old went home to Wildwood to his mother, his older brother, Percy, who was now eighteen, and his sister, twelve-year-old Elizabeth. Although the house would have been filled with joy over the homecoming, matters would turn without much delay to plans for the future.

Fused with his own sense of ability, his innate curiosity and an overriding spirit of adventure, George had arrived back in England with his confidence established and a determination to embark on a life of gainful adventure. And it was to be the East, in Australia, and not England, where he envisaged his anticipated triumphs.

The England to which young George returned was in the same fevered and troubled state as when he had left. The gaiety and extravagance of the Regency, and the Regent's ascent to the throne as George IV in 1820, were accompanied by a period of commercial turmoil – boom and then finally bust in the recession of 1825. The social fabric continued to change with the continued flow from the country to the cities, from the fields to the mills. Amongst this social upheaval were the soldiers and sailors demobilised at the end of the Napoleonic Wars. There had been little demand for their labour during the previous fifteen years; their pensions were poor and the state of the nation, along with its grace and elegance, contained much poverty and in consequence much crime. Debtors' and other prisons were full; punishments were extreme, with death or transportation even for trivial crimes. Discontent ran high among the poor and even through the middle and lower-middle classes. In the ten years following the peace of 1815, emigration had averaged about 9,000 per annum, but in the subsequent five years it increased to 20,000 per year. For the most part, emigrants went to North America, with only a few to New South Wales, as penal colonies were of little appeal to the *bona fide* migrant. Towards the end of the 1820s, however, the press and other media were awash with reports of the charms and benefits of a new life at the proposed settlement in southwestern Australia:

> The new Settlement on Swan River is in one of the finest climates of the Universe, about three months sail from England, highly suited for the production of cotton, silk, tallow, provisions, linseed, hemp, flax and corn and the culture of the vine.
>
> The country is of an open and undulating character, with excellent soil beautifully but not too much wooded; well adapted for wool growing and the raising of stock. The coast and river literally teem with fish. The shortness of distance between Swan River and the Cape of Good Hope, the Mauritius, the Indian Peninsula, Timor, Batavia, New South Wales, and many other important places, must open a door for commercial enterprise of a vast magnitude.

Western Australia then was largely unexplored. Throughout the eighteenth century, it had only been visited by the occasional ship that had lost its way. The Dutch can lay claim to being the first of the European people to become acquainted with the territory and this was largely by accident. The great, lumbering Dutch ships that sailed for the spice islands to take on cargos of immense value for Europe had to sail east-

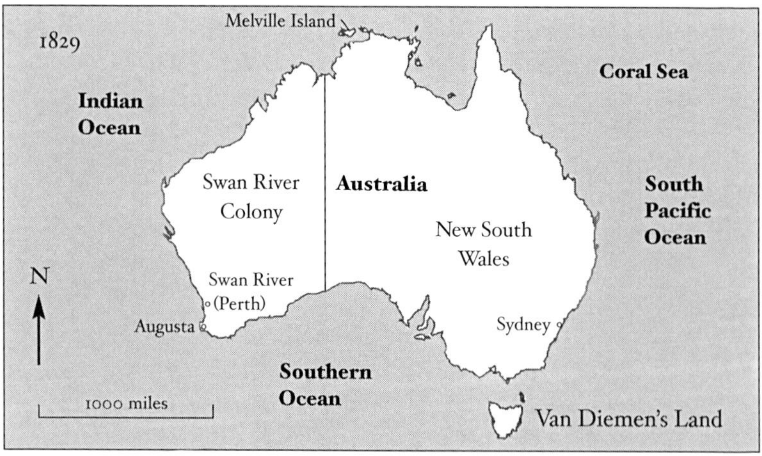

wards across the Indian Ocean with rudimentary navigational equipment. Blown off course by storms and swept along by great seas far to the south of their intended position, many would be wrecked on the reefs and rocks of these western Australian shores – with the loss of entire crews (sometimes of a hundred men or more) and their cargos bound for the Dutch East India possessions.

Occasionally, Dutch search vessels were sent out with the hope of finding some trace of lost ships and men, and so it was in 1696 that Willem de Vlamingh, in command of three ships, was sent to search for the *Ridderschap van Holland* which had left Holland two years previously but had failed to reach Batavia (present-day Jakarta). His search took him further south than was customary for ships sailing from the Cape of Good Hope to Java. He failed to find trace of the lost ship, but he discovered an island as described by W. Charnley in 'The Swan River Venture':

> ...on landing was the most beautiful island he had ever set foot on. And, moreover, thickly peopled by a small furred animal, which he called a racoon – whose meat was very good eating. Seeking a name for this island and perceiving that its furry inhabitants were in appearance akin to the rat – rotte in Dutch – he decided on Rottesnest (rat's nest) and so it remains today. Across from Rottnest, some fifteen miles lay the mainland and white glistening beaches that ran north and south to each horizon, while in the background rose a forest of tall lush green trees. A bare two miles in from the landing, Vlaming [sic] came upon a wide sheet of water. His men were thirsty, but the water was salt. Fresh water, however, was to be got in shallow holes, already scooped out in the sand by men, or by animals. So to Vlaming this was Freshwater Bay, and it is still so today.
>
> Here the Dutch seamen beheld a sight that wise men through the ages had toyed with as a fable – among a hundred other birds of sea and air, they found the fabulous Black Swan of Juvenal. That the water of this wide lake should be salt betokened a connection with the sea; and so during the early days of the New Year, the ships, by careful navigation, were brought round the north of the Rottnest and anchored off the mouth of what henceforth was called the Black Swan river. A company in boats put out, and for some sixteen leagues Vlaming explored this strange silent waterway. But although he found everywhere great natural beauty, there was nothing to interest the hard practical men who were his employers: neither gold, silver or diamonds; not even black men who might be taken and sold as slaves. So, after caging three of the fabulous swans as a gift to Batavia, Vlaming and his ships sailed on.

Decades passed without any further recorded contact with the area. Nearly 75 years later, (then Lieutenant) James Cook sailed into what is now known as Sydney Harbour and by 1778, New South Wales was established as a British colony. Although the Union Jack had been raised on the southern and eastern coasts of Australia, little or no interest was shown in the virtually unexplored northern or western parts of the great continent. However, in 1826, reports reached London that, following a French voyage of exploration, a detailed recommendation was being prepared for the French Government proposing southwestern Australia as a site for a French penal colony.

In London, both the Foreign Office and the Admiralty took this matter seriously, worried that France would claim the territory if the Dutch (who had a prior entitlement) failed to do so. That the Swan River settlement came into being as a British settlement was largely down to the efforts of one man, Captain James Stirling (later Admiral) of HMS *Success*. Stirling was a veteran of the Napoleonic Wars and the war of 1812, and had received his first command at the age of 21 in 1812. After naval and diplomatic work in the Caribbean he was placed on half pay for eight years until given command of the newly built HMS *Success* in 1826.

Stirling's orders were to sail for the northern coast of Australia from Sydney to the relief of the struggling settlement formed on Melville Island some two years before. But he decided, deviously or not, under secret orders from the Admiralty or not, that the imminent arrival of the fierce north-west monsoon would prevent him completing his mission there, and he applied to the Governor of New South Wales, Sir Ralph Darling, for permission instead to explore the Swan River area.

Darling's permission was granted and at the end of January 1827, HMS *Success* sailed from Port Jackson bound for the Swan River, arriving on the 5th of March. Among additional members of his crew were the botanist Charles Frazer, and the artist Frederick Garling. In the course of three weeks the whole area was comprehensively and thoroughly surveyed. Parties from the ship explored the surrounding land on the banks of the estuary and the river up which they travelled 70 miles or so. Climate, soils, vegetation, water, flora and fauna were all examined as far as time allowed; reasonably friendly contact was made with the local people; and accessibility and anchorages were surveyed as far south as Geographe Bay. It was an astonishing achievement, that served to confirm James Stirling's conviction that the Swan River area was ideal for settlement.

HMS *Success* took three weeks to return to Sydney where she arrived on 16th of April 1827. Stirling made his report to Darling and it was a powerful and persuasive document in which he refers to a climate blessed with every sort of benign quality to support trade, agriculture and settlement, as well as a place of rest and rehabilitation for those resident in India. He stressed the benefits of the shortness of voyage between the Swan River and the Indian Archipelago, the Indian subcontinent, and the Cape of Good Hope; benefits also for China shipping outward and inward bound. He emphasised its strategic importance as a valuable and easily defended military and naval station, with an excellent anchorage in Cockburn Sound and a naval strike capability over the Indian Ocean. Interestingly, he also stated that with a settlement on the northern coast as well, the two places 'would probably be sufficient to exclude all foreign intrusion'. Finally, he argued that if England were to fail to claim that part of the western coast, then the French would.

Governor Darling sent this report with a supporting letter of his own to the (War and) Colonial Office in London without delay. James Stirling wrote to Lord Bathurst, Secretary of State for War and the Colonies at the Colonial Office, effectively applying for the post of Governor of the territory should the settlement at Swan River go ahead. This was a bold yet wise move; Governor Darling supported the application for, his other qualities apart, Stirling was the only senior contender who actually had experience of the place. Sydney was full of excited talk about the Western coast, and optimistic reports made their way to London.

HMS *Success* next sailed from Port Jackson on the 19th of May 1827 for the North of Australia, then to Batavia, Penang, Madras and thence to Trincomalee in Ceylon (Sri Lanka). By this time Stirling and many of his crew were ill. James Stirling himself was seriously ill with a stomach ailment and he was invalided to England where he arrived in July 1828. The severity of the illness was such that he was allowed to retire from the Navy on half pay. This enabled him to turn his mind and energies to the Swan River project. He had received no official reaction to his report sent from Australia and to his dismay found that at the end of 1827 both his report and Governor Darling's recommendation had been rejected by the new Colonial Secretary on the grounds of expense, lack of purpose and lack of motive. Even the East India Company had failed to show interest. The case, so carefully argued, appeared to be stillborn.

Stirling grasped at once that the most, and possibly the only, compelling and powerful argument was the threat of another foreign power taking possession of the western coast of Australia from the Swan River base. Following a meeting with Sir John Barrow at the Admiralty, Barrow seems to have renewed his support for this very reason. His influence on the Colonial Office was to be of the greatest importance to the relaunching of the Swan River project.

James Stirling was extremely well-connected and he wasted no time in briefing all those who might be of help to him. One in particular was a fellow Scotsman and very much his senior, Sir George Murray, the Member of Parliament for Perth and an old colleague of the Duke of Wellington. Murray had been appointed Secretary of State for War and the Colonies just before Stirling arrived back in England. Meanwhile, the lobbying and politicking grew in intensity during the summer of 1828. By the autumn, the mood in the Colonial Office had begun to change as it reconsidered its opposition.

The press embraced the cause. The issue of the new settlement entered the public arena and interest was immense, akin to a new gold rush or South Sea Bubble. James Stirling was in continual demand to meet, inform and promote. The City of London, the ultimate hotbed of new capital and entrepreneurial enterprise, threw its weight behind the proposal and wielded its considerable influence on the Colonial Office.

On 5th of November 1828, Sir George Murray sent an official request to the Admiralty Commissioners to dispatch a ship-of-war 'to proceed to the Western Coast of New Holland and take possession of the whole territory in His Majesty's name'. Marines and military troops were readied and the Chatham sloop HMS *Sulphur* was prepared to carry them from England.

Stirling continued with his efforts to publicise the venture so as to encourage greater investment and further settler interest. To the Colonial Office this was welcome news as it made possible the establishment of a new settlement at minimal cost. The means to attract investors and settlers was the Land grant, the building block on which to establish the anticipated fortunes. His Majesty's Government set about drafting the regulations and terms for those seeking to go there. It read in part:

> Although it is the intention of His Majesty's Government to form a settlement on the western coast of Australia, the Government do not intend to incur any expense in conveying settlers or in supplying them with necessaries after their arrival.

And:

> It is not intended that any convicts or other description of prisoners be sent to this new settlement.

The main hurdle for immigrants was the need for capital, both to travel and to acquire land. The Colonial Office was swamped with letters of enquiry from those seeking particulars. For every successful candidate able to raise funds or eligible to participate in one of the emigrant arrangements which were available, there were many who were turned down.

Meanwhile, Senior Civil Officers were appointed and the Colonial Office chartered the 440-ton *Parmelia* to take them, their families and stores to the new land. Stirling was appointed Lieutenant-Governor of the new colony. It had taken him only five months from his return to England to accomplish his mission. During that December and before his appointment as Lieutenant-Governor, the Admiralty dispatched the ship of war HMS *Challenger*, under the command of Captain Fremantle, to take formal possession of the western coast of Australia in the name of His Majesty. This was the ultimate sign of commitment.

There was no time to be lost. The *Challenger* having sailed, the *Parmelia* could not be far behind. To prepare her for departure was a gargantuan task. The passenger load consisted of the civil establishment and their families and servants. This was effectively the Government and administration of the new colony. In addition there were a number of specially appointed trades people with particular skills. There were about 80 passengers, including James Stirling, his pregnant wife Ellen and their four-year-old son. In addition to passenger baggage, the cargo comprised building materials, government stores, equipment and tools of every kind, plants and seeds, livestock, as well as the rations for the voyage. When she sailed there cannot have been a square inch of unused space. They faced at least a four-month voyage, with a break at Cape Town.

Stirling had to supervise this entire operation as well as spend time at the Colonial Office finalising, in so far as was possible, the regulations and detailed arrangements concerning the governance of the colony. He will have been mightily relieved when the *Parmelia* finally left London Docks on the 24th of January 1829, followed shortly afterwards by HMS *Sulphur* and her detachment of the military guard from the 63rd Regiment.

* * *

During the third week of February 1829, the outbound *Parmelia* with her load of pioneers had passed the East Indiaman *Lady Holland* with midshipman George Earl on-board, inbound from Calcutta. Perhaps for a moment, somewhere off the Azores, they were in sight of each other. At any rate, it was soon after George had returned to England that he began to consider a future in the new settlement at Swan River. The attractions were manifold: new settlers would receive grants of land in proportion to the amount of capital to be invested in the land as assets; thus £3 so invested brought 40 acres. Land grants would be made by the new colony's administration to settlers in order of arrival, once all requirements had been met. The climate was fine, the soil rich, and the natural resources abundant. This was a chance to pioneer a path to great prosperity. There was, no doubt, much discussion among the Earl family about Swan River in the first half of 1829 until the decision was reached to seize the opportunities offered.

On 28th of July 1829, George's mother, Elizabeth, wrote to Mr William Thompson and Mr John Pryce, the trustees of her late husband's estate, at Dunster Court, Mincing Lane, London.

> Gentlemen,
> I request and authorise you agreeably to the Will of my late husband to advance to my son Percy Wm. Earl and to my son George Samuel Windsor Earl the sum of Five hundred pounds each, for the purposes of their outfits, investments, passage and monies on their intended procedure to the new settlements on the west coast of Australia which adventure and procedure on their parts is undertaken with my consent and concurrence.
>
> I remain, Gentlemen,
> Your much obliged
> E. Earl

This is the first evidence that George's elder brother Percy had decided to join him as a settler in the new colony. Moreover, the boys' uncle, Captain Percy's brother, Richard, and his family were to emigrate to there as well. As it happened, George made all the arrangements for himself and for his brother, who was not known for effort if he could avoid it. On the 4th of August 1829, George signed a contract with Mr John Fenwick, owner of the ship *Egyptian*. The contract, in part, states:

> ...that the said ship shall receive on board in the St Katherines Docks all the goods that Mr Earl may be disposed to ship and shall on the 20th August inst. sail and proceed wind and weather permitting to the Cape of Good Hope and Swan River. Mr Earl engages to proceed as Cabin

> Passenger for which he is to pay sixty pounds and for three or more steerage passengers, twenty five pounds each, the goods to be at the rate of freight that shall obtain at the time. The said owner binds himself in the Penalty of One Hundred Pounds in case the ship does not sail on the 20th August wind and weather permitting.
>
> John Fenwick

To prepare quickly and fulfil the detailed requirements to set off for the other side of the world to start a new life in an as yet unestablished colony was a prodigious task. The contract for his sailing was signed on the 4th of August, his mother's letter to the Trustees authorising payment of funds was dated only one week beforehand, and the entire consignment of his goods and property was to be on-board the *Egyptian* by the 16th of August. Invoices from suppliers were: £25-9-3 from J. Aken, Ship Chandler, Wapping, on the 8th; £31-1-1 from Lacy and Witton, Gun Makers and Sword Cutlers, Bishopsgate Street, on the 14th; £155-19-4 from Richards, Wood & Co, Edge Tool & Sword Manufacturers & Wholesale Ironmongers, London & Birmingham, dated the 16th of August.

The invoices that Earl received from the suppliers detail hundreds of items: guns (rifle, fowling piece, French pistols), knives and swords; spikes, nails, tool, plough shares, splitting wedges, sledgehammer, barrow wheel; all sorts of kitchen equipment and household goods; conceivably everything that a settler would need over the following year or three. The last major expenditure before departure was for £29-18-6 for packing and baling the cargo which comprised 75 packages. The full manifest for their cargo on-board the *Egyptian* was signed by her Captain William Lilburn and concludes, 'And so God send the good ship to her desired Port 27th of August 1829'.

The departure was then delayed. This gave George time to contract services from one Thomas Jones who was listed as his servant. On the 29th of August 1829 an agreement was signed:

> ...Between Thomas Jones at the age of thirty two years and upwards, of Guildford in the County Montgomery of the one part and George Samuel Windsor Earl of Hampstead in the County of Middlesex of the other part witnesseth that in consideration of the covenants hereinafter entered into by the said [GSWE] the said Thomas Jones doth by these precents contract and bind himself with and to the said [GSWE] faithfully to serve the said [GSWE], his Executors, Administrators and

> Assigns, as a general servant on the Settlement on the Swan and Canning Rivers or elsewhere in Australia or Van Dieman's Land, and to make himself generally useful in the service of the said George Samuel Windsor Earl.... for the term of seven years to be computed from the time of Landing at the Colony.

George was to pay for Jones's passage (in steerage class) and his father, Walter Jones, would also travel, independently, on the *Egyptian*. Now that the frantic business of organising every detail of the entire consignment was complete, He had extra time to make his farewells to friends and family. It must have been an exciting and happy time for the sixteen-year-old. Although the risks were high, communications minimal, medicines primitive and absence was at best for years, at worst forever, the Earl family were well acquainted with such things. George's mother and little sister, Elizabeth, must have been sad at the boys' going, yet it was accepted in the family that such was the necessary price of enterprise.

George had prudently taken out two insurance policies, one for £500 and the other for £200, from the same underwriter. Both policies contained the following paragraph which enumerated some of the then potential hazards of sea travel:

> Touching the Adventures and Perils which we the Assurers are contented to bear, and do take upon in this voyage: they are, of the Seas, Men of War, Fire, Enemies, Pirates, Rovers, Thieves, Jettisons, Letters of Mart and Counter-mart, Surprisals, Takings at Sea, Arrests, Restraints and Detainments of all Kings, Princes, and People, of what Nation, Condition, or Quality soever, Barretry of the Master and Mariners, and of all other Perils, Losses and Misfortunes that have, or shall come to the Hurt, Detriment, or Damage of the said Goods and Merchandizes and Ship, &c. or any Part thereof.

The *Egyptian* weighed anchor by the middle of September, sailing south-westerly into the strong equinoctial winds. She was a British-registered vessel of some 400 tons, not dissimilar to the other ships bringing settlers to the Swan River at that time. With a crew of about 30 she would have carried about 150 passengers and their cargo. Including a two-week stopover at the Cape of Good Hope, the normal journey time was about four-and-a-half months. (James Stirling's ship the *Parmelia* had left London on the 24th of January and arrived at Garden Island, off Fremantle, at the beginning of June 1829.)

Many of *Egyptian*'s passengers, inexperienced with life on-board ship in rough seas and suffering from seasickness, no doubt rued the day they set foot off dry land. She was heavily laden with every sort of passenger and cargo; livestock both in hold and on deck; accommodation by today's standards appalling for steerage class, bearable for cabin class. Steerage-class accommodation was below deck in dormitories of berths laid out end to end, with a few steerage cabins for families. Here or on deck the steerage passengers would have spent the time. Cabin-class accommodations were aft and under the poop deck. At least George and other cabin-class passengers messed with the captain and officers; steerage passengers had to fend for themselves, having brought on-board basic provisions for the voyage.

On a crowded ship, boredom was the main problem. There was little room for exercise and little to do. As they headed south, the winds abated and the weather grew steadily warmer. Her route took her past Madeira to the Cape Verde Islands where they almost certainly would have stopped for a few days, a welcome respite for play and replenishment. Then after bobbing through the Doldrums, they crossed the Equator with the usual celebrations before the winds picked up and carried them towards and then down the coast of Brazil. They stopped at Rio de Janeiro for several days before setting off south-easterly across the South Atlantic. The trade winds carried them through sun-filled days, violent tropical storms, under velvety-black night skies lit by starlight and glorious sunsets left in their wake until they reached in early December the aptly named Cape of Good Hope.

This stop at Simonstown provided a much-needed break of about two weeks, where spirits and bodies were revived and minds set for the long and often dangerous haul across the southern Indian Ocean. In Cape Town, George purchased some sheep, although his knowledge of sheep and farming in general was negligible. But, with the optimism of youth and aided by books to read on the journey, he no doubt imagined a prosperous outcome to all his endeavours.

On the 13th of February 1830, just after George Earl's seventeenth birthday, the great journey was over. The *Egyptian* dropped anchor off Fremantle and the *Fremantle Journal and General Advertiser*, dated 27th of February 1830, reported that the passengers, showing their appreciation of Captain Lilburn's command during the voyage out, presented him with a silver cup and a snuffbox. It added, no doubt with pleasure, that the vessel had 'landed a very respectable class of settlers'.

James Stirling's 'village' at Freemantle on the Swan River. Drawing from 1829.

– Chapter Three –

Landfall and Thereafter
1830-1832

...His talents lay in a scientific, linguistic and ethnological direction.

•

Stirling and the first settlers had arrived on-board the barque *Parmelia* on May 31st 1829, eight-and-a-half months before George's arrival, and anchored near Garden Island, in Cockburn Sound, just off the mainland. Stirling proclaimed the Swan River Colony to include all territory westward of Longitude 129° E. He moved quickly to establish Fremantle, at the mouth of the Swan River, as the port town. As for the capital, Stirling strongly felt that it should be inland in a place of natural authority and easily defendable. Several sites were considered before Stirling selected an area below Mount Eliza and named it Perth, which to this day is the site of the capital city of Western Australia.

Within a few months of Stirling's arrival, thirteen ships arrived carrying some 1400 passengers and their cargo. It was a rustic sight that greeted them. Fremantle looked like a shanty town, consisting mostly of tents of various sizes, a few wooden prefabricated buildings shipped out from England, and crude livestock pens for the animals that had survived the journey (and hadn't escaped on landing). Stores, cargos and personal effects were in rough shelters overseen by their owners. Men, women and children went about their business in an atmosphere of mostly joyful shambles; an *omnium-gatherum*; a medley of people who for the most part were thrilled to have arrived safely and anxious to set about building their new lives.

New arrivals made the twelve-mile journey up the river to Perth to enter their names in the Register and therefore receive permission to live in the colony. Land claims were also registered there, although this was not a straightforward process and there was considerable unhappiness with delays encountered. Moreover, the first-come, first-served policy had led to large quantities of prime land being allocated early on. By the end of 1829, six weeks before George Earl's arrival, 525,000 acres had already been granted. This was to become a lasting problem for the new Governor, who also had not been entirely even-handed in looking after the interests of his family and friends.

The granting of land had been a controversial issue from the start. Various syndicates and individuals like Thomas Peel, a relation of the then Home Secretary, Sir Robert Peel, had, amongst others, applied for vast acreages of land and Thomas Peel was eventually granted 250,00 acres. For the rest, there was application, negotiation, interpretation, discussion, speculation and consternation aplenty. Violent arguments took place and there were also threats of duels. In her biography of James Stirling, Pamela Statham-Drew writes:

> To ease the threatened land shortage, Stirling was forced to intervene. He sensibly decided to limit the amount of land any one settler could take in the Swan region to 1000 acres, remaining entitlements to be taken either in the interior or to the south, where early exploratory missions had discovered more suitable land.

George Earl made the trip to Perth, applied for land and returned to Fremantle to await the arrival of his brother. Percy and his bonded servant, William Colvin, landed on the 25th of February 1830 on the *Protector*, just two weeks after George's arrival. Percy, and his new business partner, Wallace Bickley who was on the same voyage, were prepared to invest somewhat more than George under the applicable terms so while George eventually was allocated two hundred acres on the 19th of March 1830, Percy and his partner were to receive six hundred acres. A document in the Western Australia Archives refers to George Earl's two hundred acres as being 'opposite Perth', and an obituary of 1865 refers to his attempt to establish himself in 'the sandy tract of the lower Swan'. Taking literally the 'opposite Perth' pointer, this suggests the area on the south bank of the river, today bisected by the Canning Highway and known as South Perth.

It would have been around the end of March 1830 that George and his brother/Bickley took possession of their land. Earlier reports of the overall quality of the soil were misleading. Rich, alluvial soil was abundant on either side of the Upper Swan, but on the lower tracts of the river it was limited to a narrow strand along the banks. Inland of this narrow strand, the soil was sandy and generally of low quality, covered by grasses, scrub and eucalyptus trees which favoured this type of soil. The chances here for crop cultivation were to prove limited.

George began his work: ground was cleared; buildings erected from the cut wood, both for accommodation and the storage of all his goods and equipment; sheep put out to graze; plans made for tilling the soil and growing produce. In these tasks, George was helped by his man, Thomas

Jones, the sturdy Welshman fifteen years his senior, from Montgomeryshire. Even with help, these were difficult undertakings for a young man who knew nothing about farming other than what he had read, and who had little or no experience of country life. Indeed, nearly three-quarters of the immigrants had come from urban lives in Britain.

In common with the other settlers involved in crop-raising and animal husbandry, the timing was unfortunate in that the Southern winter had begun. This lasts for approximately three months until early September. Winter in name only, it is a period of wind and rain with temperatures from 40° to 60° Fahrenheit, cool enough to limit agricultural growth and dampen spirits.

After the glowing, not to say, inspirational, reports in England of the new land, and after an arduous journey of four or five months, many settlers found Swan River far below expectations. In his pamphlet, *Eating and Drinking at Early Swan River Colony*, Professor Bob Reece writes:

> Seventeen ships arrived between June 1829 and late 1831 bringing passengers and supplies, but thereafter the number dramatically declined due to jaundiced reports of the colony's progress (or rather, lack of progress) that had been received in Britain from disillusioned early arrivals. Prices of all imported foodstuffs consequently rose and this, together with the shortage of coin, caused considerable hardship for a time. The two imports that provided the settlers' staple diet during those first few years were flour (often rancid and weevilly) and saltpork and beef – the former coming from the wheat fields of England and the latter from the pastures of south-eastern Ireland. Irish pork exported from Cork and Waterford had fed the early British settlements in North America and the slave colonies of the Caribbean as well as the British army and navy during the not so distant Napoleonic wars. It had also been, of course, the standard shipboard fare, together with the ships' biscuits (known as hard tack) of the passenger vessels which disembarked these early hopefuls on the beach at Fremantle, Garden Island and other places to the north and south...

During the 9,000-mile voyage from Britain, many of the less well-to-do settlers more dependent on basic rations suffered persistent stomach and bowel upsets from their diet. Also, the high salt content of the preserved meat, together with the absence of fresh vegetables, caused diseases such as scurvy and dysentery. On arrival at the Swan River they discovered that it might be two or three years before farming could produce the livestock, cereals, fruits and vegetables of their normal diet. However, the traditional remedy for trying times, strong beverage, could be easily acquired. Professor Reece quotes from *Two Years At Sea*:

> The cheapest and most readily available alcoholic drink at seven shillings a gallon was West Indian Rum, of which many of the indentured servants availed themselves in Fremantle's makeshift grog shanties to the point of abandonment. From all reports, it seems that drunkenness was extremely common across all classes during the first eighteen months, reflecting the severe problems of dislocation and adjustment to a new environment, which was a far cry from the verdant land of milk and honey that James Stirling had invoked in his first reports. In one celebrated incident, a young lawyer and two medical friends whose 'fine personal appearance' earned them the title 'the pride of Fremantle' despaired of success after exhausting their modest capital, sold their instruments and tried to drink themselves to death, one of them lying in the open and hiding his head in a canvas bag for some days before he was rescued.

In contrast to the overblown accounts that appeared in the newspapers and periodicals in England in the early 1830s (some claiming that the settlers were in a state of near starvation and that the colony had been abandoned), most of the settlers at the Swan River made strenuous and sober efforts to achieve success.

George Fletcher Moore, a Northern Irish immigrant who had arrived in October 1830, and who was to occupy a number of official positions in the colony, made a plea on behalf of the colony (that also, perhaps, captured the spirit of colonial enterprise in the popular imagination):

> When Great Britain, from the superabundance of her treasures and her population, is sending forth her tens of thousands to lay the foundation of future kingdoms, to plant her standard, establish her religion, her laws, her language, and her commerce, in distant territories, Western Australia, we trust, will not be among the least favoured and least vigorous of her offsets.

George was certainly not one of the least vigorous, but that first winter must have brought him little but dismay. Throughout the area there were atrocious gales, heavy rain and flooding during July. Crops and vegetables were destroyed and buildings damaged. Illnesses such as scurvy and dysentery were common. Cattle and sheep died from an unknown disease which, as discovered later, was caused by their eating certain poisonous plants that grew naturally in pasturage. Even George Earl with all his ambition and optimism must have despaired as his plantings failed and his sheep died. He had invested a considerable sum in tools and equipment; he had land; but did he have the ability or the patience? Had he chosen the right path? Was the Swan River area the opposite of a land of opportunity? Brother Percy had clearly lost interest or the will to continue, for it is recorded that on the 11th of January 1831, ten months after his arrival, he sailed from Fremantle on the ship *Eagle*, for Hobart, Tasmania, where he arrived on January 30th.*

* * *

During the latter months of 1830, Earl also had decided to move on. He relinquished the claim to his two hundred acres of land, sold what he could of what was left of the equipment brought out by him from England, and agreed the termination of the indenture contract with Thomas Jones. George must have felt that he was in a very difficult situation, both materially and personally. He had lost almost all of the assets he possessed and faced the possibility of having to return to England with, so to speak, his tail between his legs.

Salvation of a sort now came from another direction. Near to the time when George arrived at Fremantle, Governor Stirling's attention had been drawn in his quest to find new and suitable land to allocate to new immigrants to the area around Geographe Bay and Port Leschenault, some 100 miles to the south of Perth. Stirling personally surveyed the land and had been greatly impressed. But, he had also heard reports from whalers and sealers of fine country at Cape Leeuwin and Flinders Bay, a further 100 miles to the south. Following the arrival at Fremantle in mid-March 1830 of the *Warrior*, bearing some prosperous and well-connected individuals, the Governor found good reason to make an expedition down the coast to Cape Leeuwin. Of the new arrivals from the *Warrior*, one in particular caught the attention of Governor Stirling.

Sir John Molloy was a hero of the Peninsular War and the Battle of Waterloo. He had been recommended as a settler to the Secretary of

* Percy Earl's partner, Wallace Bickley, was later granted 4,000 acres in the Avon Valley east of Perth and eventually prospered after spending fifteen years in India. He returned to the Perth area in 1851, and in 1872 became a member of the Western Australia Legislative Council.

State for the Colonies by the General Commanding-in-Chief, Lord Hill (later the first Viscount), who had known him well during the campaign. Stirling saw in Sir John Molloy an ideal candidate for Justice of the Peace and Resident Magistrate of a new settlement.

The Governor wasted no time in organising the expedition. The brig *Emily Taylor* was commissioned and prepared, and she sailed on 29th of April 1830, escorted by HMS *Sulphur*. On-board were the Governor, some advisers, Molloy and his wife, Georgiana, and the two other individuals from the *Warrior*, Messrs Turner and Bussell, plus servants and indentured men.

The intention, all things being favourable, was to leave most of the party at the settlement, which was to be called Augusta, after a daughter of George III. The two ships arrived in Flinders Bay on 2nd of May. Four days were spent surveying the area and the party was reported to be well pleased. In the ships' boats they entered Hardy Inlet and surveyed the banks of what was immediately named the Blackwood River. Its banks were covered with good timber, plenty of water was available, and there appeared to be good soil along the hilly land by the estuary. The settlers' freight and baggage was offloaded from the ships and tents were put up on the sands of the estuary's sheltered shore. Then the *Emily Taylor*, bearing the Governor, returned to Fremantle, leaving HMS *Sulphur* and her crew for a few days to help the settlers establish themselves.

Sir John, as the Resident Magistrate, oversaw the allocation of land plots to those in the party who were entitled. There were initial grants to enable houses to be built and other accommodation needs to be met. Ground clearance parties had to be organised and put in hand. This was hard graft. The beautiful appearance of the whole area disguised the fact that the dense, high timber was of wood (mostly Karri trees) so hard to cut that it blunted saws, dulled axes and blistered hands. The undergrowth was thick scrub, difficult and prickly to deal with. Time was of the essence, as the Southern winter was on its way with rain, and cold winds blowing straight from Antarctica. Recently cleared ground had to be prepared for pasture and garden, and seeds planted. At the back of their minds, they knew how isolated they were and how self-sufficient they had to be. Supplies from the Swan River could not at first be relied upon, and until their presence was known there would be little or no passing shipping. After ten weeks or so, HMS *Sulphur* returned with supplies and to relieve the detachment of soldiers who had been helping with the initial work. The small settlement had fish and game aplenty, but for all other goods and supplies they depended on vessels coming down the coast from Fremantle, as there was not yet any passable overland route.

In spite of hardships, while not exactly prospering, they certainly endured successfully at first. Word of Augusta and the progress being made there was heard in Fremantle and Perth. Reports were favourable, perhaps inaccurately so, but they caught the attention of young George Earl. Although we have no record of his arrival in Augusta, his name is included in a list of Land Assignments for Augusta dated December 1830, so he must have arrived some weeks in advance of that date. He was assigned two parcels of land almost immediately on his arrival. However, having no family and living in a single man's quarters somewhere nearer the main settlement, George had no real incentive to clear the bush and build a new home. But he had staked his claim and the option was real.*

What he did with himself in Augusta for the first nine months of 1831 is a matter of conjecture. He had had his eighteenth birthday two months after arrival. Discounting the presence of a few children, he was the youngest settler and there will have been any amount of work available. Being an educated man, he probably made himself useful around the Resident's Office. Such activity may be the reason for Lady Hasluck, in her biography of Sir John Molloy's wife, Georgiana, to refer to George Earl as 'a shadowy figure of clerkly attainments'. More accurately, he was genuinely a jack-of-all-trades. *Inter alia*, he helped the Surveyor's Office in October 1831 make a plan of the town-site and also performed the duties of pilot, harbour master and clerk-of-the-peace. It followed that on the 4th of November 1831 Sir John Molloy wrote to the Colonial Secretary in Perth.

> Sir,
> I beg leave to acquaint you that his Excellency [Governor Stirling] has been pleased to appoint Mr Earl to act as my clerk until further orders with a salary of £3 per month & permission to draw one free ration from the store the date of his appointment... to take place from the 1st November. I have the honour to be,
> Sir, Etc. JM

* Both plots were resumed by the Government on the 24th October 1834, number 69 'for ecclesiastical purposes', and no 23 'GE quitted the colony'. It was not until 1979 that plot no. 69, no church having been built on the site, began to be developed. Number 23 Trigg St., as it now is, has only recently had a house built on it, having been left untouched for the 185 years or so since George had stood there, gazing to the sea at the very occasional sailing ship coming into the Bay.

This was his first appointment and brought with it the not unreasonable stipend of £36 per annum, bearing in mind that Sir John Molloy himself drew only £100 per annum. Throughout that year, as Clerk to the Resident Magistrate, George was no doubt kept busy in that settlement 200 miles from what is even today the most isolated capital city in the world.

But by February 1832 Augusta was in crisis. A letter written on the 29th of February 1832 by Sir John Molloy to the Colonial Secretary in Perth described the situation:

> Sir,
> I beg to acquaint you that, from the non-arrival of any vessel at this port, no opportunity has presented itself to the settlers to lay in any stock of provisions.... in the present extremity Mr. Earl has undertaken to navigate the Eaglette, a boat which has been lent by Mr. Middlemas for the purpose, to proceed to the seat of Government, I beg you would be pleased to lay before HE this statement.

George carried news of acute shortage, of the seriousness of the situation and the need for urgent action to relieve the settlement. The *Eaglette* was probably an open 18ft or 20ft cutter, single-masted and with a bowsprit, just the sort of general-purpose little boat that a settlement like Augusta needed for inlet, harbour and river activity. George sailed this craft, certainly by himself, the 200 miles or so in shark-infested waters up the dangerous and windswept coast. His training as an East India Company midshipman no doubt served him well, but it was nevertheless a brave mission. The only reference George himself ever made to this exploit was five years later when he wrote: '...for during a residence of two years and a half in various parts of Western Australia, I was often engaged in marine excursions, and have traced more than 200 miles of coastline in an open boat'.

When George arrived in Fremantle in March 1830, he found that only two ships had arrived there during the previous six months. Local supplies were running short, and although ships and supplies were expected from New South Wales, no one knew when they might arrive. Moreover, no ship was available to carry any supplies to Augusta even if they could be spared. The population of the main part of the colony was now a little over one thousand and, while people were generally more settled, until harvests stabilised there was a general air of insecurity. It was not until the end of May 1832 that the *Sulphur* arrived from Sydney bearing her vital cargo. She had called at Augusta en route to relieve them and she brought a welcome lift to the spirits there and in Fremantle and Perth.

George was to spend a few months in Fremantle while he considered his next move. Having left Augusta after a stay of just over a year, he decided not to return. Perhaps his working relationship with Sir John had given George an insight into the future, or lack thereof, of Augusta. It was to be several years before the Augusta settlers, having decided themselves that the settlement was not viable, abandoned it and moved north 80 miles or so towards the Vasse River and Geographe Bay, the area found most agreeable by James Stirling, near where today the City of Busselton stands.

George Earl had made a reasonable success of his time in Augusta; certainly it was a stable period after the debacle at the Swan River. Perhaps perceiving that settlements in Western Australia would not flourish in the foreseeable future, he was set on seeking opportunities elsewhere. Still believing that the East held promise, he rejected the option of returning to England, and on August 5th 1832 he sailed from Fremantle on the British-owned schooner *Monkey* for Batavia (present-day Jakarta) in the Dutch colonies.

Years later his granddaughter, Phillis Alt, was to write of this time in his life: 'He went to Australia first at the age of fifteen [he was sixteen] taking with him his patrimony which he soon sank. He took out sheep with him but was not successful in that venture. His talents lay in a scientific, linguistic and ethnological direction.' It would be these talents that would largely set a course for the rest of his life.

Cartoon from 1830 of the Swan River Colony.
Lower-right text: *Water Unfit For Use*.

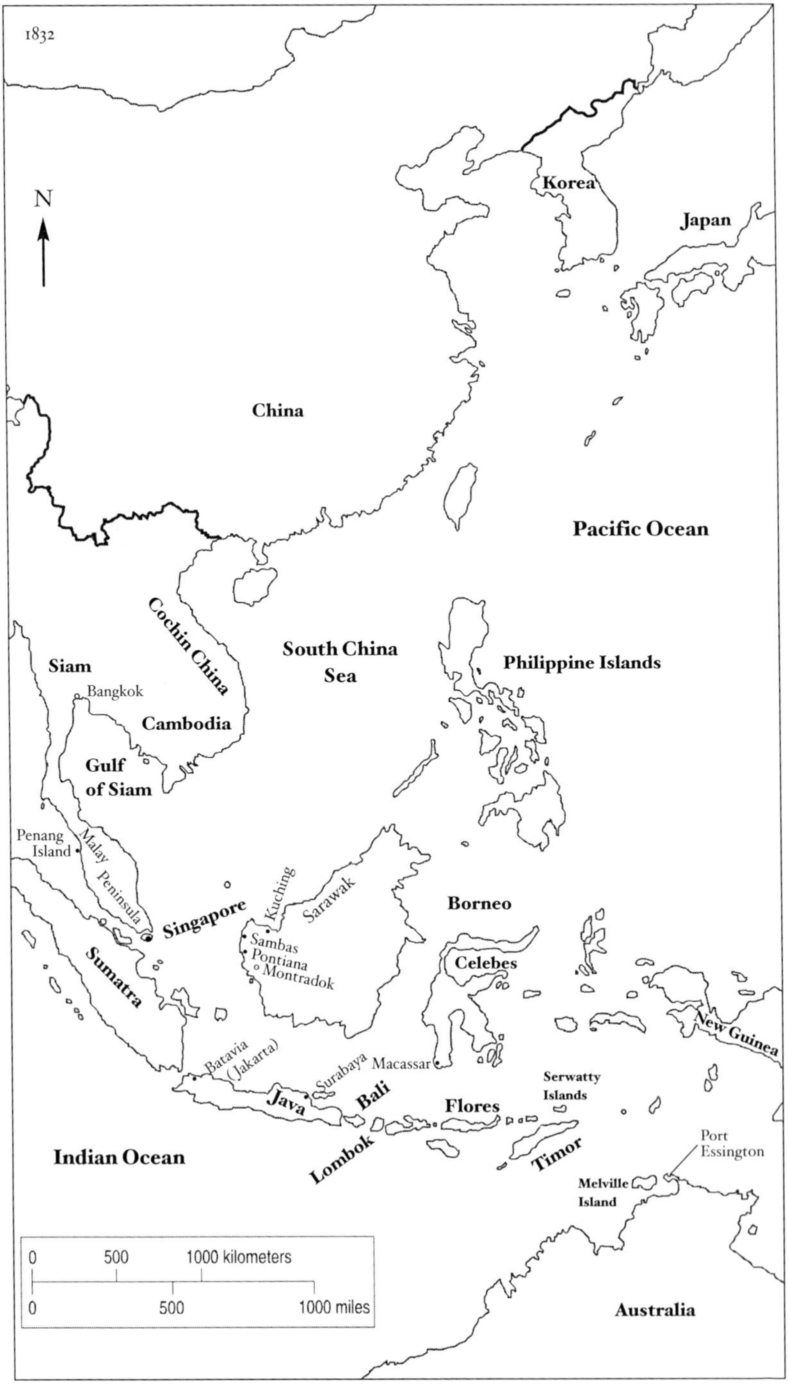
1832
N
China
Korea
Japan
Pacific Ocean
Cochin China
South China Sea
Philippine Islands
Siam
Bangkok
Cambodia
Gulf of Siam
Penang Island
Malay Peninsula
Singapore
Kuching
Sarawak
Borneo
Sambas
Pontiana
Montradok
Celebes
Sumatra
New Guinea
Batavia (Jakarta)
Surabaya
Macassar
Serwatty Islands
Java
Bali
Flores
Lombok
Timor
Port Essington
Melville Island
Indian Ocean
0 500 1000 kilometers
0 500 1000 miles
Australia

– Chapter Four –

The Eastern Seas

1832-1833

...I embarked for Java, on board the Dutch schooner Monkey and sailed in the evening.

•

When George Earl sailed from the Swan River in August 1832 he had had, by the age of nineteen, the experiences of midshipman, immigrant, settler, failed settler and government clerk. Since going to sea in early 1827, he had spent less than a year in England and, as would soon become apparent, he was now committed to the desire of making a success of himself in the East.

The *Monkey*, bound for Batavia, was owned and captained by Walter Pace and crewed by natives from across the East Indian region. Pace and George Earl were the only Europeans on-board and George travelled as a crew member, effectively acting as first mate. Also, it was on this voyage that George began keeping a detailed journal of his travels and started his learning of the Malay language, the 'Lingua Franca' of the maritime population of the Archipelago.

Pace had previously captained the *Medina*, a standard ship of the England-Australia trade and owned considerable acreage in the Swan and Avon districts. A prosperous and educated man, with much knowledge of commerce in Eastern waters, he was an ideal mentor for George who later wrote of the voyage that: 'I was fortunate in having ample employment, for... I proposed to remain two or three years in the Indian Archipelago...'*

They arrived in Batavia, the capital of the Dutch Empire in the East on the north coast of the island of Java, on the 2nd of September 1832, after a month's sailing. Earl wrote of his first impressions:

> The objects that met my view on our way to the town, were by no means calculated to give a favourable impression of the place. We first overtook a boat carrying three sick Europeans to the hospital, and a little farther we passed a large lighter, in which a number of native convicts were

*See Chapter Sixteen with regard to the wide variety of names used for this area.

> busily employed in clearing the mud from the bottom of the river. Many of them were heavily ironed, and being nearly naked and covered with mud, had a very unprepossessing appearance. A short distance below the town, a large alligator, of a light brown colour, was floating in the centre of the river devouring some garbage. He did not deem in necessary to move out of our way, and we passed close to him without interrupting his meal.

The departure of the *Monkey* was to be delayed by adverse monsoon conditions, so George spent 25 days in the town. He observed that the population was approximately 100,000, mainly made up 'of Malay extraction, being either the slaves, or the descendants of slaves of the Dutch, and are much inferior in every respect to the true Javanese'. The Chinese formed a large merchant class between the natives and the Dutch, and whom George thought industrious but terribly exploitative of the natives. The British traders, in excess of 200, were the most influential private merchants, 'although the rate of duties to be levied on British goods has been fixed by treaty, they [the Dutch] have not hesitated to raise them to such an amount as to act as almost a prohibition'.*

Trading relations between Britain and the Dutch in the East at this time were highly contentious but non-belligerent. When Napoleon subjugated the Netherlands in 1811, Britain had seized the Dutch possessions in the Indian Archipelago. Sir Thomas Stamford Raffles had been appointed Lieutenant-Governor of Java in 1811, and worked to make that island the centre of an eastern insular Empire. In all probability he would have succeeded had the island not been restored to Holland in 1816 under an 1814 Treaty. Raffles' five-year governorship had been a conspicuous success due to his policies of efficient, honest administration, encouragement of trade, establishment of fair taxes and dues, and the minimising of bureaucracy. When the Dutch re-established themselves in the Moluccas (then generally known as the Spice Islands), they were to bring in a complex system of rules, permits and levies in the hope of severely restricting British trade and commerce throughout the region. Conversely, British traders continually sought ways to circumvent the Dutch restrictions.

Although Batavia's trade and importance had been diminished by the emergence of Singapore as a free-trade entrepôt, it was still a busy port

* Most forms of slavery in the Dutch East Indies were abolished in the 1850s, and all forms by 1910.

and the Dutch moved to replace lost China (and China Sea) commerce by increased profiteering in their own possessions. Earl observed:

> Of the three articles most in demand for European consumption, coffee, pepper, and sugar, the two former are entirely monopolized by the government, and heavy penalties are inflicted on those cultivators who dispose of their produce to private individuals. The price paid by the government for these articles is extremely low, and they are afterwards sold at greatly advanced prices to the merchants. This system has been found so oppressive, that frequently the natives, driven to desperation, destroy their own plantations, preferring beggary to such severe taxation for the support of a government which only seeks to enrich itself, and proves utterly regardless of the welfare and prosperity of those who are subjected to its rule. These acts are always visited with severe punishment, but they are nevertheless of constant occurrence.

Commerce in Batavia was only accomplished under the duress of the climate:

> The unfavourable nature of the climate of Batavia is well known, and it is justly dreaded, not only by Europeans, but by the natives of the island [Java] themselves. Why the Dutch should have fixed upon this spot for their seat of government, when so many others are to be found on the island in every respect superior, it is impossible to say, unless they chose it in the expectation that its climate would deter strangers from visiting it, or in remembrance of the sites of their native cities. The town being situated in a swamp, near which large tracts of mud are left uncovered by the receding tide, the noxious exhalations arising from them cannot fail to be highly injurious to the human constitution. The prevailing fever, which has prematurely carried off thousands of Europeans, is intermitting, and the only remedies yet discovered are of such a violent nature that the constitutions of the few who survive are generally destroyed.

The dreaded malady 'highly injurious to the human constitution' was malaria. Its connection to the mosquito was not yet understood, and indeed, the word malaria is from the Italian *mal'aria* (*mala aria*); literally 'bad air'.

Earl thought that the Dutch colonial organisations (although not the Dutch people in general) pursued 'unwise and oppressive' policies in their

Eastern colonies, and he felt he would 'be guilty of great injustice to the natives' not to explain 'their position with regard to their rulers', including the following:

> The vicinity of Batavia is so dreaded by the natives, that the government is obliged to resort to conscription to keep up a sufficient number of fishermen for the supply of the city, the unfortunate creatures being drafted from the different towns on the north coast of the island, each of which is compelled to furnish its quota. During the time that they are obliged to remain at Batavia, the pernicious nature of the climate always causes a great mortality among them.

On the 27th of September 1832, at the end of the dry season, the *Monkey*, under Captain Pace and First Mate George Earl, sailed for Surabaya on the 400-mile journey, arriving there on the 11th of October. The *Monkey* was in need of extensive repairs and Surabaya, in addition to being a busy trading port with a secure anchorage, was famous for shipbuilding and repair. But in particular it had a society of almost cosmopolitan charm despite its modest size, and enjoyed a salubrious climate in comparison to Batavia.

George lodged in a large house overlooking the quay. His mornings were generally occupied by visiting the Chinese and native parts of the town and also the shipbuilders' yards. He wrote: 'I had by this time acquired a tolerable knowledge of the Malay language and therefore was enabled to derive much amusement from my conversations with the natives.' He spent his evenings chiefly at the residences of an English merchant whose hospitality had made his home the place for the European community, including both British and Dutch, to rendezvous. Here the contacts and conversation provided Earl with rich material for a man deeply committed to ongoing self-education. Whilst in Surabaya, George took the time to observe not only the geography, but also the people of all classes and their customs. He noted:

> Among the lower classes of Javanese a nuptial ceremony is rarely performed, the mere fact of a man and a woman living together constituting the marriage. Neither is polygamy practised by them, for the men often find one wife too much for their domestic comfort. The females are never secluded, except by the descendants of Arabs, and two or three fanatical chiefs; indeed they enjoy a degree of liberty perhaps unequalled in any country in the world. The necessaries of life are to be procured

> so cheaply, that the women, who are even more industrious than the men, find no difficulty in supporting themselves, and consequently feel quite independent, and at liberty to act according to their inclinations. As no ceremony is required for the marriage, of course none can be necessary for the divorce, and when the parties are tired of each other, they separate and form new connexions. Women of two or three and twenty may sometimes be seen living with their fourth or fifth husbands, without any great odium being attached to them on account of the frequent transfer of their affections.

And on the Javanese as sailors:

> The Javanese are decidedly an agricultural people, nevertheless four-fifths of the crews of ships navigating the Archipelago are composed of them. The Malays, although addicted to maritime pursuits, are rarely to be found on board ships conducted by Europeans, and the few that I have met with were far inferior to the Javanese, both in seamanship and steadiness.

Nevertheless, he added:

> It is said of English sailors, that they 'earn their money like horses and spend it like asses', and the saying is equally applicable to the Javanese. When they receive their wages, they think of little else but getting rid of them, and all their money is soon laid out in finery and sweetmeats.

After five or so weeks in Surabaya, Earl set sail back to Batavia on the *Mercury*, a Dutch ship, commanded by a Scotsman, Captain Brodie. She was a fine vessel, a 350-ton brig that had been chartered by the Dutch Government to carry salt and specie to settlements on the south coast of Java, calling at various points and finishing the journey back at Batavia. He bade a fond farewell to his friend, Captain Walter Pace, who was to remain in Surabaya until the *Monkey*'s repairs were completed. George wrote: 'On the 10th November 1832 I took leave of Captain Pace who had contributed to render my voyage in his schooner one of the most agreeable which I had ever made.'

As the monsoon was against them they had a long passage of six weeks back to Batavia. It was not time wasted; he became well-acquainted with the operations of a country (local) vessel like the *Mercury*, the trade, agriculture and circumstances of the Javanese settlements and countless other matters which he was to later describe in *The Eastern Seas*. Of particular fascination was the performance of Wayang theatre which Captain Brodie organised during the *Mercury*'s call at Cali Pujang, an important coastal town. Wayang (or Wyang) theatre is acknowledged as a highlight of Javanese culture.

Earl wrote of the [leather shadow-]puppets representing the legendary, mythical creatures which depict and explain the relationship between Heaven and human society: the age-old contest between the pure and refined and the rough and uncivilised, and, in a religious context, the strife between good and evil. The puppets were works of art handled with consummate skill by the puppeteers who made full use of silhouette and reflection; special lighting and shadows on-screen; music and dance where every note, movement and gesture carries meaning. Traditionally, a performance lasted a whole night, starting just after sunset and continuing without a break until dawn, with much food, moving about and general entertainment being enjoyed by the audience.

The *Mercury* arrived back in Batavia on the 23rd of December. With the unpleasantness of that place still fresh in his mind, Earl was anxious to spend as short a time there as possible. Not even the traditions of Christmas, always somewhat diminished in the tropics, tempted him to extend his stay. He was now determined to reach Singapore as early as possible, as he was thinking of a return to England. About to celebrate his twentieth birthday, he had not been home for three and a half years. Perhaps a bout of homesickness had afflicted him as he had lately been 'very unwell'.

Earl embarked on the Dutch ship *Theodora* and sailed from Batavia on the 27th of December 1832, bound for Singapore. He was fortunate to have a Captain Collins as a fellow passenger, an Englishman who for several years had commanded a British Government ship in the Straits of Malacca. George remarked: 'He was an intelligent seaman and I was able to gather much more information from him about the Straits Malays.' Throughout these voyages, George would absorb from any knowledgeable person information about culture, language, customs, dress, housing, agriculture, food, wildlife, geography, etc. His writings read as part journalism; part travelogue; part anthropology; part sociology; part political; and are imbued with a lively and analytical perspective rendered in clear prose. His fascination with the characteristics of the various races is clearly demonstrated as are his likes and dislikes – contempt for Bengali and Malay seamen, fierce criticism of the Dutch and Mohammedans – admiration for Java and the Javanese.

Earl sharply observed:

> The genuine Arabs are often high-minded enterprising men, but their half-caste descendants who swarm in the Archipelago, comprise the most despicable set of wretches in existence. Under the name of religion they have introduced among the natives the vilest system of intolerance and wickedness imaginable, and those places which they have gained an ascendancy, are invariably converted into dens of infamy and piracy. In Java, although they have succeeded in rendering their religion paramount, they have been unable to introduce the bigotry which has caused the ruin of all the Malay states, the feelings of the natives being directly opposed to anything approaching the fanaticism which forms a distinguishing mark of too many of the followers of the prophet.

It is with conviction that he wrote:

> Before taking leave of the beautiful island of Java, and its interesting inhabitants, I cannot help expressing a wish that we may hereafter become better acquainted with them. The conduct of the British towards its Indian subjects has not always been of the most meritorious description, but during our occupation of Java, the colonial government was administered by one who well understood and appreciated the character and disposition of the natives. The measures pursued by the late Sir Stamford Raffles, the governor, are indeed beyond all praise, and both as a statesman and a philanthropist, he stands unrivalled. He is remembered by the natives with feelings little short of adoration, and the illiberality of the government to which they are now subjected, only tends to make them the more regret the misfortune which deprived them of a father and a friend. The name of Sir Stamford Raffles is, perhaps, almost unknown to nine-tenths of the people of England, but scarcely a native of Java is to be found who does not remember some anecdote relative to the kindness and consideration with which the people were treated by him during his most popular administration, of a country very unadvisedly relinquished to a selfish and barbarous tyranny. It is impossible to contemplate this interesting country without feelings of the deepest indignation since from neither Holland nor England has it received justice. The reckless and ungenerous manner in which the natives of Java were delivered over to their former oppressors, without a single clause for the security of better treatment in future, after having during several years been permitted to consider themselves British subjects, has rendered

> our occupation of Java very destructive to the happiness of the people. The advantages which they experienced under the mild and beneficent policy adopted towards them, contrasted with their present misery and degradation, render their condition intolerable. They feel it with tenfold force, striving at intervals, though in vain, to free themselves from a yoke which has become too heavy for them to bear. Thus, many of the natives of the interior, though naturally of the mildest and most docile disposition, goaded to desperation, rise year after year in arms against their tyrants, losing life or liberty in a hopeless struggle for independence.

The *Theodora* made passage up the north coast of Sumatra past various Dutch settlements, the tin mines of Banka, through the 100-mile-long strait that separates the island of Banka from Sumatra. The journey, with the monsoon against them, had been a long grind of 40 days, almost four times the duration of the same journey he would make in the future. Shortly before arrival at Singapore she went aground on a reef, a reminder of the ever-present dangers of those waters, but luckily was refloated on the next tide. The approach to Singapore in February 1833 lifted his spirits, for this was his first visit, and he wrote:

> The ship was soon at anchor in the Roads, and after breakfast I got into one of the numerous Malay sampans which surrounded it, and in the course of five minutes had entered the creek, and landed on the commercial wharf. If the Roads had a bustling appearance, that of the town was even more so. The wharfs were absolutely crowded with natives from all parts of India; vast numbers of Chinese labourers were dragging bales and boxes out of the merchants' warehouses and putting them into boats, where they were received by kling boatmen from the Coromandel coast. At the landing-place the Malay sampan boys (who resign the laborious employment in the cargo-boats to the klings) were plying for hire; and on stepping on shore I was received by an obsequious Madras dubash, who offered to conduct master to any part of the town to which he might wish to go.

Earl arrived in Singapore, so-named from the sanskrit *singa* (lion) and *pura* (city), on the 7th of February 1833 with a letter of introduction to a Dr José d'Almeida, whom he knew simply as 'a Portuguese merchant from Oporto'. This was rather like a young man today arriving in London with a letter of introduction to the Duke of Westminster and thinking him a country gentleman with a house in town. As Dr d'Almeida was a man of great quality, great wealth and great influence, how was it that George had this letter? It might have been given to him in Western Australia before he left, perhaps by Sir John Molloy or indeed by Governor Stirling himself (as a gesture after Earl's single-handed sail and on learning of his departure from that colony?). It might have been given to him by Captain Walter Pace. We don't know, but there is another possibility.

In 1764, a spinster lady named Welcome Dalmeida 'was admitted to the copyhold of (in other words, bought) a cottage and several pieces of land at North End'. In 1792, William Sharp (George's mother's uncle) 'was admitted in succession to Welcome Dalmeida to a cottage being at Wildwood Corner otherwise North End'. This then is the property which George's mother inherited. There may well have been some connection, some family friendship or other between William Sharp and Welcome Dalmeida which in turn was known to the Earl family Trustee, William Thompson. Thompson may have been aware of the wider d'Almeida family and when preparing George for his departure in 1829, among other things he may have given him a letter to Dr José in Singapore. One can imagine him saying: 'who knows, it may come in handy'. This of course is surmise; the fact is that he had a letter of introduction, and letters of introduction were a *sine qua non* of gaining hospitality, help and initial acceptance in the 19th century where one was not known.

José d'Almeida had been a surgeon on a Portuguese man-o'-war. While passing through the Straits in 1820, he was immediately attracted by Singapore's position and prospects. He decided to settle and by 1824 the name José d'Almeida appears amongst the names of landholders. On his lot on Beach Road, Kampong Glam, he built one of the finest houses in Singapore. As a doctor, he set up his dispensary in a street in Chinatown which became known as d'Almeida Street (today called Temple Street) where he rapidly attracted a large clientele.

The story has it that his commercial empire was based on a completely fortuitous event. Two large merchant vessels, one Portuguese and the other Spanish, respectively bound for Macao and Manila, had arrived in Singapore. Unfortunately, their slow eastbound passage had meant that they now could not complete their journeys because of the start of the northeast monsoon. Confronted with a delay of four months or so, they decided to sell their cargoes in Singapore, and consulted Dr d'Almeida who agreed to take their cargoes and dispose of them as their agent. This he did, mostly at auction, and the venture was highly successful. Thus the firm of José d'Almeida & Sons was launched and had grown into a major trading emporium, famed throughout the East.

Dr d'Almeida was immensely popular in Singapore's European society (the local entrepreneurs held lavish society functions which the local civil servants were unable to afford to do) while at the same time his medical background and his charitable activities gave him great access to the Asian community and its traders. He must have taken a shine to young George Earl because he immediately invited him to stay in his house on Beach Road, with its fine views over the waters and anchorages of Singapore. This was the start to what would become a long friendship.

With his entrée to the world of the economic and political elite of this thriving city, George Earl soon abandoned his plan to return to England. He had suffered some sort of ill health and wrote: '...the indisposition which had caused this determination [to return to England] having passed away soon after my departure from Batavia'. Within a month he was to ship out again to the islands of the Indian Archipelago, but this time as a trader. If he was suffering any lingering disappointment from his failure at Swan River, his spirits were now fully revived and, as he celebrated his 20th birthday, a bright future beckoned.

Harbour and town of Singapore, view from the Governor's House.
Engraving from a drawing by Louis Le Breton, late 1830s.

– Chapter Five –

Captain Earl

1833-1834

However, I am proud to say that I have got on entirely by my own exertion.

•

It is unsurprising that a young man like George Windsor Earl found Singapore stimulating and exciting: it was a booming trade centre in an exotic part of the world as well as the headquarters for British interests in the entire Eastern region. Moreover, he had gained access to and acceptance in the higher circles there. He wrote:

> Singapore is situated on an island at the southwest extremity of the Malay peninsula, near the narrowest part of the strait which affords communication between the China Seas and the Bay of Bengal. Equidistant from Calcutta and Canton, the most important commercial cities in eastern and western Asia... [A]nd, in addition to an extensive commerce carried on by Europeans, the native traders, encouraged by the perfect freedom from duties enjoyed there, flock from all parts of the East, while the manufactures of Hindustan are there exchanged for the rich productions of the Indian archipelago. ...The port is visited by vessels of all nations, and the flags of Great Britain, Holland, France, and America, may often be seen intermingled with the streamers of the Chinese junks, and the fanciful colours of the native prahus.

Great Britain, whose trade with China had grown rapidly in the second half of the eighteenth century, sought to expand its Dominion in India. In so doing there was a need to provide safe ports of call on the trade routes for its merchant and naval fleets to replenish, refit and revitalise.

In 1818, Lord Hastings, Governor-General of India, had given approval for Sir Thomas Stamford Raffles, in spite of the displeasure of the Dutch and the wariness of the British Government, to establish a trading post at the tip of the Malay Peninsula. Raffles had been appointed Lieutenant-Governor of Bencoolen (Sumatra) in 1817, where his administration was characterised by his trademark philosophy and policies: abolishing forced labour; improving agriculture; declaring it a free port; reforming the civil service; regulating the currency; and expanding education. Many of these reforms were opposed by the powerful Javanese princes, and Raffles took firm and sometimes violent action against them.

Raffles landed on the all but uninhabited island of Singapore in January 1819. On the 6th of February 1819, a formal treaty was signed with the rulers of the island, granting control to the East India Company. In this, he was aided by Major William Farquhar of the EIC who was the Resident (Governor) and Commandant of Malacca, where the fluent Malay speaker and engineer had excelled. Raffles spent almost five months in the initial work of setting up the city, and then appointed Farquhar as the first Resident of Singapore to fulfil the plans and instructions as drawn up by himself. He then returned to his post in Bencoolen having seen the population of the island rise to some 5,000 during that short period. Although Raffles and Farquhar were to fall out – principally over Farquhar turning a blind eye to some forms of slavery and his property development policies – and the latter replaced in 1823, Singapore proved rapidly to be a prize settlement, and within three years its trade had exceeded that of Penang, the other major British settlement in the area that had been established in 1786.

In 1824, Singapore's status as a British possession was formalised by two treaties – first, the Anglo-Dutch Treaty of 1824 by which the Dutch withdrew all objections to the British occupation of Singapore and second, with the two rulers, Sultan Hussein of Johor and the Temenggong, Abdul Rahman, who ceded the island outright to the British on favourable terms.

Singapore's strategic location enabled it to soon become a natural entrepôt for trade with China and the islands of the Indian Archipelago. Along with the other two British settlements in the area, the island of Penang (including Province Wellesley) and Malacca (on the Malay Peninsula, north of Singapore), the Straits Settlements was established in 1826 under the control of British India (East India Company), and in 1832 Singapore became the centre of government for the three areas.

Singapore's founding and subsequent ethos were largely down to the vision and firm resolution of Sir Thomas Stamford Raffles. In 1823 he had declared: 'Let the principles of British Law be applied not only with mildness but with a patriarchal kindness and indulgent consideration for the prejudices of each tribe as far as natural justice will allow but also with reference to their reasoning powers, however weak, and that moral principle which however often disregarded still exists in the conscience of all men.' Furthermore: 'Let all the native institutions as far as regards religion, ceremonies, marriage, and inheritance be respected where they may not be inconsistent with justice and humanity and injurious to the peace and morals of society. Let all men be considered equal in the eye of the Law.'

Raffles consistently outmanoeuvred the Dutch in the area and enabled the creation of what was to become one of the jewels of the British Empire in the East. However, much controversy came with his actions and achievements including strenuous opposition from some within the British Government. When he returned, ill, to London in 1824, Major Farquhar raised severe charges against him in the Court of Directors of the East India Company. Farquhar was unable to discredit Raffles but after Raffles died (a day before his 45th birthday) in 1826, his estate of £10,000 was paid over to the EIC for costs that he had incurred, mainly in Bencoolen.*

* * *

On the 10th of March 1833, George Earl set sail on the *Reliance* under the command of Captain Burgess. This was a schooner of 140 tons that had been chartered by a Robert Hunter, an English merchant, based in Bangkok and trading to Siam. Hunter and Burgess were good examples of the sort of buccaneering, high-octane, reasonably amoral hawker/dealer to be found at that time all over the East. The *Reliance* was well-armed with four twelve-pounder carronades and four long brass guns, plus muskets and small arms, and was well manned with 20 Javanese sailors. Such precautions were necessary for sailing in those dangerous, pirate-infested waters. Her cargo consisted of rice and 30 chests of opium, and Hunter anticipated a considerable profit from the voyage.

The schooner headed north-westerly up the Gulf of Siam, passing islands and trading points where attempts to sell the cargo proved unsuccessful, although George found Mr Hunter 'a most agreeable companion'

* In addition to his political activities, Raffles had a great interest in botany and zoology. He was the first president of the Zoological Society and the London Zoo. He also wrote a history of Java and made careful studies of the indigenous tribes there. His personal life was marred with much sadness. His first wife died in Java in 1814. He remarried in 1817 and they had four children. In the six months between July 1821 and January 1822, three of the four died in Bencoolen – Charlotte, a month short of her fourth birthday; Leopold 'the handsomest and most princely little fellow that ever lived', aged two years and four months; and little Stamford, aged 17 months.

who 'possessed much information of value' about the Archipelago. The conclusion was reluctantly reached that only the opium was well-suited to the present market and that the most profit from it could be had in Siam. Great caution was required as its importation was strictly prohibited there.

They anchored some 40 miles off Bangkok in shallow water, and Hunter and Captain Burgess set off for the city in the ship's longboat. George was left on-board the *Reliance* for a week before setting off himself up the river to Bangkok where he found his way to Robert Hunter's base. In *The Eastern Seas* he was to describe in colourful detail the events which accompanied this visit: the appearance, dress and mannerisms of the people; the 'junks, boats and floating houses, jumbled together in glorious confusion'; the assemblies which they attended, and so on. But their business did not proceed well. George had to return to the *Reliance* after only a short time in Bangkok, leaving Hunter and Burgess in the city.

It was two weeks before the two rejoined the vessel, having finally disposed of the opium. George observed: 'the drug happened this year to be very cheap in China and many of the junks from Canton had brought two or three chests each, which completely spoiled his market'. They set sail on the 26th of April and arrived in Singapore Roads on the 2nd of June 1833, having encountered various further vicissitudes on the voyage south. Hunter did manage to sell the rice en route, although at a much lower than anticipated price. Twelve weeks had elapsed, full of interest for George, making it a most valuable experience. By this time he was able to speak Malay fairly fluently and so was able to talk easily to all and sundry. But the venture had not turned out so well for Robert Hunter.

Earl had received another invitation from Dr d'Almeida to stay at his house, which was readily accepted. It was extraordinarily generous of the Doctor, as it provided George with a base for a full nine months. During this time, encouraged by d'Almeida and others, he worked on his languages and carried out much research on the islands of the eastern Archipelago; their climates, geology, fertility, crops, animals and, of course, their inhabitants and customs. D'Almeida and circle were of great help in this research, and after the relatively lengthy and highly beneficial stay, Earl embarked on the 28th of February 1834 on the most remarkable of his many voyages.

Word had reached Singapore that an independent Chinese colony inland from the west coast of Borneo sought to establish a regular commercial link with Singapore. This colony, thought to be several thousand strong, was primarily working the gold and diamond mines of the Sinkawan-Montradok region between the two Dutch ports of Sambas and Pontiana. The Chinese were forced to trade through the two Dutch ports and in consequence were paying very high duties. A group of Singapore businessmen, mostly prosperous Chinese, decided to investigate this potentially profitable new market. This project had the mark of Dr d'Almeida to it. Only he would have put together such a group, chartered a ship and seen to the appointment of the 21-year-old George Windsor Earl as captain.

The *Stamford* was a British schooner of some 80 tons, not large but well suited to the task and especially to the coastal waters of Borneo which were then very little known. The *Singapore Chronicle* for the 6th of March 1833 gives her cargo for the outbound voyage as 'ten koyan of salt, forty pikul of Swedish iron, one corge of Java tobacco, twelve corge of chellopans, twelve chests of Benares opium, fifty bundles of coarse paper, three corge of iron pans, and a hundred boxes of tea'. The crew consisted of 35 Javanese sailors and eight Chinese, two of whom were businessmen/interpreters. Two of the Chinese were elderly and habitual opium smokers. Captain Earl forbade opium-smoking on the voyage and for a couple of days he observed the two who 'looked the very picture of woe'. On the third day they 'appeared to be comparatively reconciled', and Earl thought he had broken their habit only to find later that they had 'taken to chewing the drug'.

This voyage to Borneo's west coast was not only pioneering, but dangerous, as the *Stamford* was sailing into contested territory. That an independent colony (of some 30,000 Hakka Chinese) within the Dutch sphere of influence had made a trade approach to Singapore carried no weight with Batavia. The *Stamford* made the coast on the 7th of March 1834. After one false start inland, George took the longboat with twelve well-armed men for the three-mile journey inland to Sinkawan. Shortly after arrival they received a warm welcome from the Chinese population, multi-gun salutes to mark the occasion, and a reception held at the Court House. However, the head of the *cuensi* (Magistrates) was, because of the Dutch, fearful of allowing George to travel to the interior and suggested that Earl wait for permission from the Chinese governor at Montradok to proceed.

Earl returned to The *Stamford* and for reasons of safety, decided to leave her at anchor there. He, with four men and a Chinese clerk, set out in the schooner's gig for Sambas some 30 miles upriver, and arrived there on the 13th of March. George described the town as presenting 'rather a mean appearance', and the houses 'very miserable, being all of wood, and covered with plank or attap leaves; many are built on floats in the river, moored to large posts'.

There was a friendly meeting with the Dutch Resident, Mr Rumswinkle, who nevertheless informed George of instructions from Batavia that no commercial intercourse would be allowed with the Chinese territory from Sinkawan, but only from Sambas. A few days later, Earl met with the rájá to see if matters could be circumvented and his trip hastened:

> The rájá was, to appearance, about fifty; but, as he was an inveterate opium-smoker, he might have been several years younger. He was tolerably well informed for a Malay, and was very inquisitive respecting the English, I being the first one that he had seen. He said that, in the event of a war between England and Holland, which was then expected, the Dutch would retire from Sambass and Pontiana to Batavia. After about two hours' conversation I departed, without coming to any terms about the opium, as he said he required to sleep over every affair of importance.

Earl brought the *Stamford* up to Sambas on the 15th of March 1834. He was eventually able to sell some opium and 'After a great deal of trouble' obtained permission from the rájá to dispose the remainder of their cargo at Sinkawan. The *Stamford* left Sambas and arrived at Sinkawan on the 18th of April where a letter awaited Earl from the Chinese governor inviting him to visit the capital Montradok. This was a great surprise; for although the Chinese wanted to open up trade with Singapore, it was widely known that they allowed neither European nor Malay to travel into their territory. The most important task of the mission could now begin. George, writing with real verve, takes up the tale:*

> I got up at day-break, and commenced the journey immediately... I was accompanied by six of the *cuensi* men, each of whom carried a large paper umbrella and a long tobacco-pipe, my two Chinese interpreters, and two *kúlís*, for carrying the baggage. We were all on foot, for there are no horses in the country, and, if there were, the roads are of a nature that

* This text is taken from an address that Earl was to give to the Royal Asiatic Society in London on July 4th 1835 and differs from that covering the same journey as later printed in *The Eastern Seas*. This earlier text, perhaps, points us in the direction of Earl's conversational style and displays a flair for narrative drive.

would prevent their use. The first five miles of our journey were in an easterly direction, through a swampy jungle, the path in many places being upon trees, that had been felled for the purpose, and laid length ways, their ends touching each other. They were quite round, and very slippery, and did very well for the bare feet of the Chinese; but, before the first mile had been completed, my feet slipped from under me, and I had the opportunity of trying the depth of the mud, which was considerably higher than my knees. I was pulled out by the united efforts of three Chinamen.

After crossing the swamp, we ascended a rising ground, and a sudden turn of the road brought to view one of the finest prospects I had ever seen... Immediately below us lay a large valley in the state of the highest cultivation, covered with villages and cottages; and the Sinkawan river, here about fifteen yards wide, winding through it. The south-east side was bounded by some high woody hills; but to the north-east, the ground was gently undulating, as far as the eye could reach... After a delightful walk through the valley of about three miles, crossing the river several times, we arrived in the town where we were to breakfast, at eight o'-clock. The street through which we had to pass was crowded with people, many of them women; who, stepping aside, left a small space in the centre for us to pass through to the court-house. From the curiosity and surprise of these people, I am convinced most of them had never seen a European before...

A few miles past the town we crossed several trenches about three feet wide, and from three to fifteen feet deep; which, to my surprise, I found were exhausted gold-mines. I had expected that the mines were on the hills to the south-east of the valley...

We continued crossing the trenches for about six miles... and the distance between them being sometimes not twenty yards, and at other times nearly half a mile. We then struck to the south-east, over a number of hills covered with trees, the valleys between them being generally cultivated, till one o'clock, when we descended the last hill, and had a view of the whole of the valley of Montradok below us...

We arrived at Montradok at three o'clock, having walked about thirty-five miles. I was very tired... I might have been carried, if I had liked, on a kind of bamboo sedan... but I did not like to acknowledge myself tired, more particularly as I had joined in the laugh against my two people [the interpreters], both of whom were knocked up before they had proceed half-way... They did not arrive in Montradok till two hours after me.

I passed through the town, which consisted of only one street, about three-quarters of a mile long, to the governor's house... His excellency, with the *cuensi*, met me at the yard-gate, though it was raining hard, and honoured me with a salute of three guns, one of which kept fizzing for about five minutes before it went off... He did not understand a word of Malay; so we were unable to converse till the interpreters came, for which I was not sorry for, as fatigue had by no means impaired my appetite; and I had plenty of time before their arrival, both for an attack on the good cheer, and to change my clothes, which were drenched with the rain that had been pouring down for the last half-hour.

...The Chinese here are all of the tribe that forms the lowest class about Canton; and, I believe, are of Tartar origin. They are as dark as Malays, and very spare in the body. This, however, may be owing to their way of living; for most of the women – that is, those born in China – are the reverse... They have great liberty here, quite as much as females in England; and I could perceive, in more than one house, that the 'grey mare was the better horse'.

There seemed to be little distinction of rank; for the *kúlís* who carried my baggage sat down to eat at the same mat with the governor, and frequently dipped their chop-sticks into the same dish: but he always sat at the upper end, and never had occasion to rise to procure *samshú*, which was in general poured out by women, who always eat with the men.

The governor was the only man to whom I saw any respect shewn, and I think this was owing more to his abilities than to the dignity of the situation he held. To the *cuensi*, or representatives, little or no respect is shewn. The form of government approaches very near to the republican.

...Indeed, he is the only man I saw who had any ideas beyond the common affairs of life; and I was told by one of the *cuensi* of Sinkawan, who was rather more gifted than his compeers, that he was afraid the settlement would go to wreck if anything should happen to the present governor...

The gold-mines that are at present worked lie about four miles, in an easterly direction, from Montradok... The veins are very small, and near the surface, being seldom deeper than fifteen feet, and in general considerably less. The ore is procured by digging with spades and mattocks, the soil which contains the metal being carefully taken up and removed in close baskets to the place where it is washed. This is done in the dry season, and nearly all the male population are employed in it. ...The bulk of the soil is removed by turning a strong stream of water through a large wooden trough, in which the whole is put; after which the remainder of the soil is removed by washing in smaller vessels with the hand. It is altogether a very tedious work.

The washers smoke an enormous quantity of opium; and, when I visited the washing-place, I saw a great number of them lying on the platforms erected for the purpose, some smoking through a bamboo, others, who had finished their debauch, lying in a state of unconsciousness, neither sleeping nor waking. On seeing this, I was inclined to regret that by far the most valuable part of my cargo was composed of this pernicious drug; but I had a kind of consolation in knowing, that, if I had not brought it, they would procure it by some other means; for it is become, with many of them, so absolutely necessary that they cannot live without it.

...The gold is in general very small, being, for the most part, as fine as sand; and I never saw a piece heavier than a sixpence. The dust belonging to the *cuensi* is always better cleaned than any other; and, when it is put up in tials or packets, they stamp a mark on the paper envelope. The punishment for adulterating the dust thus marked, or for forging the stamp, is no less than cutting off the right hand of the offender, which is done immediately on conviction.

The forenoon after my arrival was spent in examining the gold-mines and washing-place in the neighbourhood; and I returned to the house about noon, when I found all the *cuensi* from the neighbouring districts, and one from the more distant ones assembled. After deliberating for about a half hour, they all came into my room, when the governor told me that they had agreed to open the trade...

Having arranged every thing before night, I determined to return to the coast at daylight next morning, much against the wish of my kind host, who was making preparations for a play, and other entertainments; but as a report had arrived that a number of Lanun* prahas had been seen on the coast, I felt very anxious to be on board the vessel; as, in the case of an attack from them, we should have to trust to our own exertions alone...

George Earl and his party left Montradok at the break of day and walked through torrential rain during the morning on what he described as the 'fatiguing and unpleasant' journey back. He continues:

* These probably would have been Sea Dayaks, indigenous to Borneo. Lanun is the Malay word for pirate.

On approaching Sinkawan, I was rather alarmed at hearing great guns fired at intervals near the mouth of the river, expecting that it was the pirates that I had heard of at Montradok attacking the schooner; and I was well aware, that had that been the case, it would have been impossible for me to get off to her, for neither love nor money would induce either the Chinese or Dutch cruise-práhus [patrol boats] to put me on board. On arriving in Sinkawan, I found my boat waiting for me; and the cockswain informed me, that a fleet of about a dozen Lanun pirates had appeared in the offing in the morning, but had passed to the southward without coming near the schooner, although they lay to, about two hours, apparently deliberating what they should do... I went on board immediately; and as the sea-breeze was setting in, got a spring on a cable to bring her broadside to bear seaward, in case they should come in the evening, but I saw no more of them. They probably mistook me for a Dutch man-of-war schooner, and they seldom meddle with each other.

...The second day after my arrival on board was the day appointed for the sale of my cargo... On the day appointed we met at the *cuensi*'s house, and the crowd of expectant purchasers was large enough to gratify the most ambitious vendor. After a considerable time their names were all put down, and the quantity they wanted of each article opposite their respective names... This was the only plan that could be adopted to prevent one of these disturbances which so frequently happen... [i]f any person was suspected of an endeavour to monopolise any article, particularly opium, he would run great risk of losing his life.

In the evening, I took the schooner to one of the Lamúkatan islands, about ten miles from Sinkawan, where wood, water and stone-ballast could be procured in abundance, leaving a Chinese at Sinkawan to weigh the gold-dust [from the sale of cargo].

On the 1st of May [1833], having completed our wood and water, we returned to Sinkawan, where I found we should be obliged to wait some days for the gold-dust, all of which had not arrived from Montradok. At last, after nearly a whole day's disputing, we came to a settlement... After settling the different accounts, the *cuensi* made to sum total five hundred reals less than it really was. I could see in a short time that they were determined to cheat me out of it; so I got up to prepare to set off before dark, having been told in the morning, by a man born at Batavia of Chinese parents, to keep a good look out at the mouth of the river, as several bad characters had come into town that day, who might take advantage of the narrowness of the river to intercept me when going off with the

> gold-dust… nor could I help thinking afterwards of the manner in which the secretary delivered me the box of gold-dust, when I took leave. 'There,' said he, 'there is your gold in the hands of your own people; whatever happens to it now, I call you all to witness that I will not be responsible.' In reply, I merely told him that I was able to take care of it; and should it come to the worst, that I had two men's lives in my hand, alluding to my double-barrelled gun… I knew the people well enough to be aware that they would not attack us, when they saw we were prepared to resist. I had fourteen men well armed with muskets in the boat with me, ten of whom stood up facing both ways, while the other four pulled down the river…
>
> By six o'clock I was on board, and got underway immediately for Singapore; never in my life feeling more pleasure at leaving a place.

On the 4th of May 1834 the *Stamford* sailed from Sinkawan and, after a relatively long passage across the China Sea of 'light airs and calms', arrived in Singapore on the 15th May. Her inbound cargo consisted of ten baskets of tobacco and twenty-eight kati of gold dust. This amount of gold was the equivalent of about 31lbs (today worth about £500,000 at a price of £1000 per ounce).

This expedition had occupied almost three months. It was both successful and profitable, but hopes of regular trade between Singapore and Sinkawan were not to be fulfilled, although a regular trade between Singapore and some parts of Borneo was to be instituted later that year. The Dutch, ever protective of their own trade and interests, insisted that the Chinese settlements in western Borneo trade only through their own ports at Sambas and Pontiana. They stiffened their blockades and enforced their monopoly.

After a week or so in Singapore, the *Stamford* sailed again, under George's command, for Malacca and Penang. This was a standard coastal trading voyage from which he returned in the middle of July. On the 23rd of July 1834, George wrote to the family Trustee in London, Mr. William Thompson:

> My dear Sir,
>
> I wrote to you about twelve months ago and expected to hear from you, but as there are several Freetraders at Batavia no doubt shall have a letter by one of them. I had a letter from my brother about a fortnight ago and find he has married; and also quarrelled with my mother; indeed I had heard of it at Penang about a month before from Mr. Nairne, a merchant

there recently arrived from England where he was acquainted with my mother; he did not speak very highly of Percy's prospects. I have been the last eight months in command of the Stamford, a vessel belonging to Singapore, trading mostly to Borneo and the Pedir coast. In the course of a few months I propose joining Messrs. Almeida & Son in a small ship for which they are now treating, in which case I will go into the Bali trade, taking opium and China goods from here to Bali, exchanging them for rice to sell in China and then return from China with tea and cassia for Singapore.

I believe I came in for the remainder of my property last February. I propose drawing for about £200 but should like to receive some communication from you first.*

I should like to go home but if I do I shall lose twelve months perhaps more and go to a great expense. I am happy to say that I am in a fair way of doing well as I have excellent opportunities of trading, and a little increase of capital will be a great help. When I left Swan River I was almost penniless so you cannot expect that I am very rich. However, I am proud to say that I have got on entirely by my own exertion. There are many of my father's old friends here but although I was acquainted with several they did not know who my father was till Mr. Reid came out with whom I believe you are well acquainted.

I really am afraid Percy is doing no good for himself. He is no sailor or I would propose his coming out here but then again he is married. However he is old enough to take care of himself though I assure you it gives me great uneasiness.

My mother may think it unkind in me not coming home to see her so perhaps you will be so kind as to explain to her that if I leave the country I shall lose time and money and perhaps on my return find difficulty in getting a ship.

Many thanks, my dear Sir, for the kindness you showed me in England for which, depend upon it, I shall never be ungrateful. A few lines from you occasionally would give me great pleasure and show me that I am not yet forgotten. Remember me to Mrs. Thompson and the children and believe me my dear Sir

Yours sincerely, Geo Earl

*The children of Captain Percy were to receive £1000 [approximately £88,000 today] each at the age of 21, or in daughter Elizabeth's case earlier, if she married with the approval of her mother and the trustees.

This was a mature letter from a 21-year-old far from home. It exhibits a wider concern for the family, a modest (but self-aware) sense of pride in his achievements, a grasp of the world, and no doubt it would have pleased both his mother and the Trustees that George, if not Percy, was making true progress.

At the beginning of August 1834, Captain Earl sailed on the *Stamford* on what was to be his final trading voyage, this time to Java. They were to have a close brush with piracy which, though a traditional, if pestilent, profession in the South China and Java Seas, was an increasing threat to Singapore trade. The main perpetrators were the Dayaks from Borneo and their area of activity stretched as far as Mindanao in the southern Philippines. The pirates' prahus, quite substantial vessels, would cruise these waters especially during the south-easterly monsoons, plundering both offshore and onshore. Their spoil was merchandise of all sorts, and in the case of the Dayaks, a fair amount of human heads. Any Europeans captured would be murdered and the Native crews sold into slavery. The *Stamford* had a skirmish with a fleet of these pirate boats. Earl wrote:

> The Malay pirates absolutely swarm in the neighbourhood of Singapore, the numerous islands in the vicinity, the intersecting channels of which are known only to themselves... whence they can pounce upon the defenceless traders, and drag them into their lairs to plunder them at their leisure. Square-rigged vessels are generally allowed to pass unmolested, for the pirates, who are as cowardly as they are cruel, rarely attack craft of this description, unless they have received authentic information from their spies at Singapore that they may be taken with facility.

Earl was certain of the remedy for such danger and its eradication. He observed: 'A visit from one of the British men-of-war stationed in the Straits of Malacca, and the expenditure of a few charges of powder and shot, would effect this desirable object.'

The *Stamford* returned safely to Singapore at the end of October 1834. It seems likely that while he was away, correspondence arrived from England, the contents of which concerned him greatly. The ideas for the future Earl had set out in his letter to Thompson were superceded and he made plans to return to London.

This must have been a difficult decision. His prospects in Singapore were very favourable and he clearly loved life in the East, of which he was fast becoming an authority. Earl had been approached by some Chinese merchants to command an expedition to the north coast of Australia in order to collect Trepang* and tortoiseshell, but had declined the offer in the belief that no lasting benefit could be derived from this trade without a permanent settlement there under the protection of the British Government.

Opportunities were coming his way. However, he had now been away from home for more than five years, almost a quarter of his life: he wanted to see his mother and she needed to see him, perhaps concerning his own family's business. Thus, Captain George Earl bade adieu to colleagues and friends and sailed for England in December 1834.

Macassan Prahus, Raffles Bay, 1839. Lithograph by E. Lassalle from a drawing by Le Breton.

* Considered a great delicacy by the Chinese, Trepang or bêche-de-mer is a sea-slug. For generations the Malays had sailed on the north-west trade winds to the Australian north coast, fished for the sea-slug which they then cured in the sun on the beaches before sailing back on the southeast trades to barter their cargo in China for silks, tea and other luxuries. It was a very profitable business.

– Chapter Six –

INTO THE FRAY

1835-1836

...with a singleness of purpose which enabled him to make enemies as well as friends.

•

George Earl's voyage to England was uneventful, if one can ever so describe a journey of 80 to 90 days half way around the world by ship – across the Indian Ocean to Cape Town, thence up the South Atlantic, past the islands off the West African coast, all regular ports of call for those in the Eastern shipping trade. Using the trade and prevailing winds to best advantage, the ship was in time to be blown up the Channel by the March Westerlies. Earl had celebrated his 22nd birthday during the voyage and his arrival home in March 1835 after the 10,500-mile journey was to prove a demarcation in his young life.

His homecoming to Wildwood was not like those of his father with the latter's bluster, baubles and bangles. Here, to his family, was a new person, almost a stranger. His mother was of course overjoyed to see him, her favourite son whom she had wanted so much to return. A boy when he had left five years before, she now saw an attractive, maturing, confident young man, full of energy, with considerable intellect and fine conversation spiced with accounts of his recent experiences and travels.

Elizabeth was now in her fifties and shared the house at North End with George's brother, Percy, and their sister, Elizabeth. Elizabeth was ten when her father died and twelve when she had last seen George. She was educated at home and by all reports was a quiet, intelligent girl. But there was a sadness: she was physically handicapped, though seemingly not seriously so and she was to spend the whole of her life at Wildwood, except for the short time that she was married. George found again a sister, now seventeen, and their reunion was to be the start of a close and trusting relationship as adults.

It was the behaviour of George Earl's brother, Percy, which seems to have been the major reason for George's return from Singapore. Percy and George had not seen each other during the four years since January 1831 when Percy sailed from Fremantle to Tasmania on the *Eagle*. Their mother, no doubt concerned about Percy, had wished for George to return home and he, possibly reluctantly, agreed. Percy had steadily accumulated an unsatisfactory curriculum vitae, including recently marrying without his mother's approval. He had sunk a considerable amount of his patrimony into the partnership with Wallace Bickley. Their land at the Swan River was not productive but, as we have seen, the initial difficulties there were enormous. Like George, he had lost his money. He broke his partnership with Mr Bickley and set off for Hobart, Tasmania, in the hope of finding better pickings. In this he was unsuccessful and a year later he had returned to England.

Initially staying at North End with his mother and sister, Percy quarrelled about money and property and had moved away from the family home. He had few realisable funds, although he had received £1000 from his father's estate in 1832, and was not employed. Another cause for argument was his marriage to a widow just 16 or 17 years old, Ann Ellen Howe Eustace (née Tucker), on 20th of July 1833. Why Elizabeth Earl disapproved of the match is not precisely known, but it may have had something to do with religious matters. Subsequently, Ann appears to have been disowned by the Earl family because, whilst Percy is named on the Earl family headstone in Hampstead Cemetery, there is no mention of Ann.

Shortly after they were married, Percy and Ann moved to France where their first son, another Percy William, was born in 1834 and christened in Le Havre. Ann's uncle, William Tucker, was a noted gentleman-naturalist, and it was no doubt under his influence and tutelage that Percy adopted the discipline. France was the place to be at that particular time as the science of Naturalism there was experiencing a burst of interest and support. However, the family was back in England by the middle of 1835, as Percy faced a lawsuit that July for £700 that he had borrowed but not paid back.

Percy was still dreaming up ventures. He also continued to badger his mother for money from his father's estate to which he considered he was entitled. This drew a stern letter from one of old Captain Percy Earl's executors on the 6th of December 1835:

> In reply to your letter, I am sorry to find that you have been so imprudent as to lose all your money. When the son of a departed friend brings such difficulties upon himself you must be aware it creates very unpleasant feelings. Your expedition to Canada will be about as prosperous as the one to Sidney. Before I consent to things being done, as regards property under my Trust, I must have a detailed account from my friend Mr Thompson who is more acquainted with the nature of affairs than I

> am. It runs in my mind that you have already received all that belongs to you. I cannot think that you will attempt to deprive your mother to relieve yourself.

George attempted to mediate between his brother and their mother, and this could have been neither pleasant nor painless. Although there are few records of Percy and his affairs, he seems to have been volatile, bad-tempered and unpredictable, rather like his father but without the old captain's seafaring or financial abilities.

At the end of April 1836, Percy, Ann and their baby son sailed to New York from Liverpool on the *Florida*, and in August 1836 Alfred Huntley Earl was born in America. Before leaving England, Percy had sold outright the remainder of his future inheritance for the sum of £750, and it is probably this transaction to which the trustee referred in his letter.*

Not much is known about their travels during the following two years or so, but in late 1836, the 25-year-old Percy and his family were in Cleveland, Ohio, where he had set up a reading room, although this appears not to have been a success. The family was back in England by early 1838, soon with three children as Elizabeth Rosa Earl was born on 9th of April 1838 at the Quadrant, Regent Street, London.

Nevertheless, as we shall later see, after a string of failures Percy was to reinvent himself as a naturalist, and having showed every enthusiasm and determination in doing so, was to achieve a certain distinction.

* * *

After his arrival home in March 1835, George Earl initially directed his energies to letting it be known to interested parties that he had recently returned from the East and possessed information of a pertinent nature about an area of the world that was attracting increasing attention. After he had left Western Australia in 1832, Earl witnessed during the ensuing two and a half years the politics of the Archipelago, the policies and felonies of the Dutch, the continuing interest in the region by rival nations, and above all the growing prosperity and influence of Singapore

* Under the terms of old Captain Earl's will, his wife, Elizabeth, received £2000 outright and a further sum of approximately £6800 was held in trust for the three children, to be paid on either the remarriage or death of Elizabeth. Percy's share was diminished by the £500 he had received for the Swan River emigration (as was George's share), so the net amount of Percy's future inheritance was probably calculated at around £1750.

as a free-trade port. He knew that the Archipelago, its seas and islands, were rich in natural resources and populated by intelligent, enterprising, entrepreneurial people eager to improve their lives by trade and commerce. The resulting prospect which formed in his mind was that of a second Singapore, strategically based on the Australian northern shore and trading with the islands to the north and China, as well as to the populated areas of Australia's eastern coast. Perhaps an added attraction was that the area was not under the dominion of the East India Company, that behemoth which then ruled over 20% of the world's population and which maintained a prickly relationship with its charge, Singapore. Although he was not the first to have such thoughts for this new and substantial trading area, George Windsor Earl, the 23-year-old budding ethnologist, now also set his sights on becoming seriously involved in the politics of Empire, perhaps in emulation of the career of his hero, Sir Stamford Raffles.

In what was to become nearly a three-year process, Earl busied himself in London putting himself about; knocking on doors; seeking out interested people and organisations and developing alliances; badgering the (War and) Colonial Office; ascertaining and tracking down those to whom he might be of use towards achieving a new settlement in Northern Australia. In particular, he was to establish important relationships within the Royal Geographical Society and the Royal Asiatic Society. Both were influential organisations as their leading members then had the ear of Ministers, senior civil servants, and the good and the great. Barely three months after his return, Earl addressed the Royal Asiatic Society on July 4th 1835 with his impressive paper, 'A Narrative of a Voyage from Singapore to the West Coast of Borneo, in the Schooner Stamford in the Year 1834, with an Account of a Journey to Montradok, the Capital of a Chinese Colony in possession of the principal Gold Mines'.

Earl also had begun work on the material collected during his travels which would be published in 1837 as *The Eastern Seas*. Largely self-taught, he was now fluent in French, Dutch, German and Spanish, as well as Malay and some of its dialects, including Buginese and Bajau. The historian F. J. Allen described him thus: 'one sees Earl in 1835 as a young, intelligent and capable man, dogmatic and with a singleness of purpose which enabled him to make enemies as well as friends'.

On April 23rd 1836, Earl wrote to the Colonial Office to enquire if the Government had any plans for the formation a new settlement on the Australian north coast. The reply was firmly negative. Undeterred, a month later he wrote to Lord Glenelg, the Secretary of State for War and the Colonies, and included his first published stand-alone work, a pamphlet unambiguously entitled, *Observations on the Commercial and Agricultural Capabilities of the North Coast of New Holland and the Advantages to be Derived from the Establishment of a Settlement in the Vicinity of Raffles Bay*. The first part of the pamphlet dealt with the earlier attempts to establish settlements in the region and the reasons for their failure. Then, a case was made for commercial trading in general, the benefits of such a port for merchant shipping navigating the treacherous Torres Strait. Finally, Earl highlighted the strategic value of such a settlement for the protection and furtherance of British interests in the area. This time the Colonial Office merely thanked him for his correspondence. The *Asiatic Journal* commented on the pamphlet: 'The observations and suggestions of Mr. Earl, being the fruit of local experience, are valuable. He has personally conversed with commanders of Bughis prahus, who have been to New Holland and Raffles Bay.' It might be noted that at this time Earl had not yet set foot in Northern Australia.

* * *

The establishment of a new settlement crucially depended on the support and coordination of the great offices of state. In the case for Northern Australia, these were the Colonial Office, the Admiralty, the Treasury and, initially, the government and parliament. Advocates within these great offices formed varied alliances with supporters from the 'secular' side – the learned societies, organisations such as the East India Trade Committee, the press, and knowledgeable individuals such as George Windsor Earl. By the time Earl joined with these voices there had already been a considerable history of lobbying, politicking and disputation.

An initial survey of the Northern Australian coastline had been carried out by Matthew Flinders, the great navigator and explorer, in 1803 when he made the first circumnavigation of Australia. Further and more detailed surveys were undertaken from 1817 to 1822 by Captain Phillip Parker King, the pre-eminent Naval Hydrographer. But given the disruptions created by the Napoleonic Wars, the provocative (to the Dutch) founding of Singapore in 1819 and the tensions leading up to the 1824 agreement between Britain and Holland, there was little consensus among the various interested parties as to the importance of and potential for development on the north-eastern coast of Australia.

William Barnes, a seasoned trader between Sydney and the Moluccas, met with Lord Bathurst, Secretary of State for War and the Colonies, in

London in 1823. Barnes maintained that the Dutch were stealing a march on Britain by involving themselves in the lucrative trepang/bêche-de-mer trade that originated in the Gulf of Carpentaria. Lord Bathurst was deeply unimpressed. Undeterred, Barnes then urged, unsuccessfully, the Colonial Office to establish a trading port in the area in order to exchange British manufactured goods for the bêche-de-mer. The East India Trade Committee, representing the 20 or so largest trading houses in East Indies and Australia, had also been meeting with Colonial Office officials, and in December 1823 the Committee produced a report urging Lord Bathurst to authorise a settlement at Port Essington for commercial and strategic reasons. It should be noted that William Barnes was acting as an (undisclosed) agent for one of the trading houses.

Nevertheless, the report convinced Lord Bathurst that action should be taken in case the soon-to-be-completed Anglo-Dutch Treaty might cause a future obstruction, and he agreed in January 1824 that Britain should take possession of an area in the vicinity of Port Essington. The report from the East India Trade Committee was passed to Sir John Barrow, the Second Secretary at the Admiralty, and he agreed, although not necessarily for the reasons stated in the report, on Britain's need to stake a claim on the north-eastern coast of Australia. Barrow had been appointed to his position in 1804 and was to serve in it for 40 years. An ardent imperialist who thought that the East India Company put profit over patriotism and Empire, he was to play perhaps the most important single role in the development of Australia as a colony.

What followed was more than a decade of political and physical struggle to establish a permanent settlement on the north-eastern coast of Australia.

In August 1824, HMS *Tamar* and the transport *Countess of Harcourt* under the command of Captain (later Sir) James J Gordon Bremer, accompanied by the colonial vessel *Lady Nelson*, sailed from Sydney bound for the Cobourg Peninsula. When they arrived at Port Essington, Captain Bremer was unable to find a sufficient supply of water so, after taking possession of the territory, sailed on west to Melville Island. He did record, however, that Port Essington was, in his opinion, one of the most beautiful stretches of water imaginable.

It was a considerable party that landed on Melville Island in September 1824. Apart from a detachment of Marines on HMS *Tamar*, there were on the other two vessels two officers and 24 men of the 3rd Regiment, a medical officer, commissariat officer, two storekeepers and 42 convicts. Water having being located, they threw up a stockade to which the name

Fort Dundas was given. Bremer sent a glowing report to London of the initial progress made and indicated a bright future for the settlement despite there having been serious conflict with the local Aborigines. The optimism was precipitate; in the three years that Fort Dundas was to be occupied, no regular traffic would occur from Bughis or Malay ships plying the seasonal trepang/bêche-de-mer trade. In fact, there was to be no significant trade of any sort as the trading companies who had lobbied for a settlement adopted a 'wait and see' policy before committing their resources and also quibbled about the site chosen. Navigation into the port was tricky: the soil was poor; the natives hostile; two supply boats (the *Lady Nelson* and the brig *Stedcombe*) were sent to other islands to obtain fresh supplies and never returned (their crews murdered by pirates); the settlers were after a while indifferent, listless and undernourished; the island was malarial and, after the November 1824 departure of Captain Bremer, the leadership poor.

In 1826, the Colonial Office, having received widely conflicting reports of the conditions and progress at Melville Island, decided to relieve the settlement just two years after its founding. The task was given to HMS *Success* under the command of Captain James Stirling. A year and a half later, after his two exploratory visits to the Swan River, Stirling sailed from Port Jackson (Sydney) in May 1827 bound for Melville Island. There he found the previously optimistic commandant, Major John Campbell, dispirited in the face of disease, death, violent weather, crop failures, lack of supplies and violence between the settlement and the Aborigines. Campbell had earlier written about his concerns to Governor Darling in Sydney (who then passed them on to London), and Darling soon began to look on settlements in the north as no more than a drain on resources.

Although Stirling had been instructed to found a new settlement on Croker Island he decided that the adjacent Raffles Bay was more suitable. There, Fort Wellington, was established in June 1827, with the men and equipment moving across from Melville Island early the following year. In September 1828, Captain Collet Barker became the Commander at Fort Wellington and through his establishment of better relations with the natives and growing knowledge of the local conditions, the new settlement slowly began to flourish.

Stirling also had been carrying out a covert mission for the government to ascertain the intentions of other rival powers in the region and the potential for further British settlements in Australia. He concluded that the Swan River was where the new, coastal Australian settlement should be and that anything which could be achieved by way of strategy on the north coast could just as effectively be accomplished from Perth. Given the distances involved (more than 2,500 miles by sea) from Perth to the Cobourg peninsula, Stirling's conclusion is perplexing. However, overall imperial policy towards Australia was yet unformed and, as an ardent supporter of the Swan River, he may have had in mind the limited government resources available to subsidise distant colonies. It was Stirling's assessment that would be heeded in London.

In spite of the improvement in circumstances at Raffles Bay (of which London was ignorant), the decision was taken to abandon the settlement. After this decision was taken, the Admiralty then received in April 1829 a report from Captain Laws RN of HMS *Satellite* concluding that the adverse reports from both settlements were the result of misrepresentation, wilful or otherwise, of the actual conditions. After arriving in the area in September 1828, Laws became to believe that the authors of the reports had been affected by the isolation of their postings and by the ignorance and inexperience of their circumstances. Laws may have been exaggerating when he reported that the climate there was healthy and superior to other tropical areas occupied in the region by Britons, and that the soil was fertile for tropical agriculture. In any event, his recommendation not only that was there a need for the two settlements, but also that Port Essington additionally be developed came too late, and Fort Wellington at Raffles Bay was evacuated in August 1829.

After much effort, expenditure and loss of life, the north coast was abandoned. The whole affair was a complete muddle but it is easy to forget the immense difficulties caused by isolation, distant communications, lack of local knowledge and lack of experience. These first brave attempts at settling the northern coastline had ended in failure but this had not dampened the spirits of small but influential and vocal groups inside and outside the government in favour of a new settlement. By 1834, the debate had again begun in earnest.

On the 12th and 20th of May 1834, Major John Campbell, who had been the highly critical commandant at Melville Island, was invited to address the RGS and he gave a long account comparing the geography, climate, plant life, animal life, military value, commercial potential and native population of Melville Island, Port Essington and Raffles Bay. Campbell made, in no uncertain terms, the case for a new settlement in the area, and recommended Port Essington for the site, as it 'forms altogether one of the finest harbours in the world. There is no harbour yet known (Port Jackson excepted) to be compared to it in the whole extent of Australia...' An analysis of Campbell's addresses appeared in *The*

Athenæum. Campbell concluded his remarks with a lengthy quote from John Crawfurd's 1820 *History of the Indian Archipelago* which called for 'a great emporium' in the area. In part it read:

> There ought to exist the most unbounded freedom of commerce and settlement to persons of all nations and religion; and a pure and impartial administration of a code of laws, suited to the state of such a colony, and adapted to the peculiar character of its varied population, should form the most important branches of the administration. A moderate impost on external commerce – which that commerce well protected should certainly afford – with the sale of public lands, and an excise on vicious luxury, would afford a sufficient revenue to defray the expenses of government and the charge of public works.

However, the offices of state, with the exception of the Admiralty, were not enthusiastic for Campbell's proposal, given the failures at Melville Island and Raffles Bay. But the optimism expressed in Laws' report of 1829 had not been forgotten.

* * *

When George Earl had written in May 1836 to the Colonial Office 'on behalf of a few friends', it seems that this was at the urging of some members of the Royal Geographical Society, and as such may date the initiation of his serious involvement with some of those advocating a new settlement.

Through the remainder of 1836 he cemented relationships with some of the principal members of the RGS, most notably Sir John Barrow, Sir Francis Beaufort, the Hydrogapher of the Navy (and he of the eponymous wind-force scale), and Captain (later Rear-Admiral and Hydrographer of the Navy) John Washington. Captain Washington had been a member of the RGS since its founding by Sir John Barrow in 1830, and became the Society's Secretary in 1836. A polyglot (French; Italian; Spanish) like George, the two were to have a warm personal and professional relationship during the ensuing years. Washington was also, at 36, the closest in age to the 23-year-old George. (Barrow was 72; Beaufort, 62.)

Earl continued at Wildwood working on the final draft of what was to be published in early 1837 as *The Eastern Seas*, and probably had completed the work as originally conceived before the end of 1836. But he was to later add material (as an Appendix) in support of sharply renewed activity by the advocates for the creation of a new settlement and entrepôt on the north coast of Australia. As a sign of his growing relationship with the Admiralty, George was commissioned to assist the Hydrographic Office in updating charts and sailing information on the Arafura Sea, that body of water between Australia and New Guinea.

Earl, who perhaps had been looked on by the Colonial Office in early 1836 as an upstart or mouthpiece at best, or an adventurer at worst, was, as 1836 turned to 1837, poised and positioned to take a notable role in the fight for a new settlement.

View in Raffles Bay, frontispiece engraving, after a drawing by Captain P. P. King, from his book *A Narrative of a Survey of the Intertropical and Western Coasts of Australia* (*Volume I*).

– Chapter Seven –

The Case for a New Settlement
1837

...he alone possessed the experience and first-hand knowledge to pursue the venture to which he now turned; the establishment of the third British emporium on the north coast of Australia. Jim Allen in *Port Essington.*

•

In November 1836, the Royal Geographical Society received a letter from two young army Lieutenants, George Grey and Francis Lushington, offering to explore for the RGS, 'a portion of Australia which has never yet been visited by land or sea', by which they meant the west of the continent. Their plan was to strike inland from the Swan River settlement and discover, as the RGS' Minutes described, 'some great river, which might conduct into the very heart of Australia', or, conversely, to start in Van Dampier's Land in the north-west. This was very much to the purpose of Second Secretary of the Admiralty and now President of the RGS, Sir John Barrow, who promised the support of the Society and urged Grey and Lushington to approach Colonial Office' head, Lord Glenelg, for financial support.

In late November, Barrow (with Beaufort, Washington and the geologist, Roderick Murchison, at the RGS) also wrote to Lord Glenelg, endorsing the proposal and pointing out that despite Britain's possession of Australia for more than a half-century, much of it remained unexplored. Also, the spectre of rival foreign expeditions was raised and it was deemed that, 'it would be a most humiliating mortification to witness the tri-coloured flag, or that of the stripes and stars, waving on Dampier's Land'. They further recommended a detailed survey of the Torres Strait, that narrow (approximately 90 miles wide), treacherous and strategic sailing area between Cape York on the far north-eastern coast of Australia and New Guinea, as being vital to the economic success of Sydney. It was implied that the Admiralty would perform its part of these activities from its own funds.

Although there was a theoretical threat that the Dutch might form a settlement on the south coastline of New Guinea from which they could control traffic through the Torres Strait and that the Americans and the French were rumoured to be interested in the unprotected northern shoreline of Australia, it was difficult to ascertain if there existed any real and present threats. Up to that point the Dutch, although anxious to protect their holdings in the region, had avoided outright aggression or expansion that could lead to open hostilities and the Americans were no colonialists. French ships, often posing as scientific expeditions, had long been present in the area, but they had made no serious attempts to claim land or create settlements, although unfounded rumours to the contrary circulated after the French naval officer and experienced explorer of the region, Dumont d'Urville, had met in London in 1837 with Francis Beaufort and John Washington. It was the contemplation of an unknowable future that had brought uncertainty and wariness to some in the British establishment.

Additionally, it was a widely-accepted contemporary belief that there existed a vast, as yet undiscovered, inland sea in Australia and that major rivers flowed from it to the coast where settlements could be founded to spur commerce and provide bases from which to protect the sea lanes. The abandonment of settlements at Melville Island and Raffles Bay more than seven years before was still seen by some, and most definitely by Sir John Bremer, as a strategic mistake.

For Bremer, this proposed expedition was but a piece of a larger design – that of surveying the entire coastline of the continent and the creation of a ring of fortified settlements around the circumference of Australia and thus all but ensuring its absorption into the British Empire. Lord Glenelg, a fellow imperialist who also shared Bremer's sceptical view of the East India Company and its ultimate loyalties, agreed to support the proposal. Neither man wished to see a private company prevail in Australia. On the 6th of January 1837, Glenelg endorsed the general plan and petitioned the Treasury for Parliamentary approval for a grant of £1000 to the RGS, which was soon agreed. However, this was but the start to further, often contentious, negotiations that were to follow on into early 1838.

* * *

> On the exactitude of the minutest details of Hydrography must always depend the safety of Commerce and Navigation. ...It has been well observed, that 'the man who points out, in the midst of the wide ocean, a single rock unknown before, is a benefactor of the human race'; and scarcely less so is he, who, after careful examination, is able to decide that a rock or shoal, which appears on a chart, is either misplaced, or has no existence. ...It may also be noticed that many practical observations are still desirable on the prevailing winds and currents, and more

particularly on tides, of which there are various peculiarities among the islands and along the different coasts of the ocean, concerning which, facts and observations are still wanting, for establishing one general theory that shall be found applicable to every part of the Globe.

Every accession, therefore, to hydrographical knowledge,—a real danger discovered—a fictitious one demolished—of a peculiarity ascertained—must be of great importance to navigation, and a fit object for promulgation by the Society.

So wrote Sir John Barrow in 'Observations', a proclamation at the beginning of the first issue of *The Journal of the Royal Geographical Society of London* in May 1831. (The piece had been read before the Society the previous year.) Indeed, hydrography was the first listed of the aims of the Society, 'whose sole object should be the promotion and diffusion of that most important and entertaining branch of knowledge, Geography'. And, as the Admiralty and the RGS saw it, hydrography was the very foundation of not just physical knowledge but also the lynchpin for military advantage and the development of colonies and trade for the Empire.

As a part of the support for the new expedition, George Earl's hydrographical work on the Arafura Sea was read before the RGS in February 1837; but he had also been busy in other spheres. In that same month Earl had a member's paper (having been elected in January 1836) read at The Royal Asiatic Society, just a few days before his 24th birthday. His letter, 'Sketch of the Island of Borneo', concluded with a modest paragraph extolling the island as a good market for 'British produce and manufacture', but there was no mention here, perhaps in keeping with the ethos of RAS, of any grander design. He had also submitted a number of papers to Captain Washington at the RGS: 'Remarks on the Fittest Season for Exploring the Coasts of Australia'; 'Observations on the Colonization of North Australia'; and two translations of Dutch articles: 'Narrative of a Voyage along the S.W. Coast of New Guinea, in 1828' by J. Modera and 'Voyage through the Southern, or little known part of the Archipelago of the Moluccas, &c.' by D.H. Kolff. All of the above subsequently appeared in the respective Societies' journals. 'Remarks on the Fittest Season...' was published under the revised title: 'Opinion on the Best Time for Exploring the Coast of Australia'. In 'Observations on the Colonization of North Australia', Earl noted presciently that Bowen Strait, some 25 miles north-east of Port Essington, and lying on the mainland opposite Croker Island, might prove the best site for a settlement than Port Essington, as it was much more accessible to ships and slightly closer to the nautically dangerous and potentially strategically valuable Torres Strait shipping lanes.

As the plans for the expedition developed at the RGS, Grey and Lushington became aware that they were being subordinated within a larger set of goals. The RGS and, by extension, the Admiralty, were now pressing for a joint expedition with the Colonial Office for a survey by land *and* sea to include a detailed survey of the Torres Strait and a survey of the northern and western Coasts of Australia. John Washington wrote to Glenelg and questioned the experience of Grey and Lushington and their ability to cope in a harsh environment. Barrow wanted them to be an inland adjunct to his main purposes.

In February 1837, Lieutenant George Grey wrote to Lord Glenelg's Permanent Under-Secretary of State for the Colonies, James Stephens, of his and Lushington's dissatisfaction at their loss of control of their expedition. Since many went out into the Empire for gold, glory or Gospel, Grey showed the colours when he wrote that, 'whatever celebrity or success might attend the expedition, would attach to the vessel and not to us'. A tussle between the RGS and the officers, with the Colonial Office in the middle would continue for the next couple of months.

In early April, Barrow and Beaufort wrote to Glenelg that nothing less than Britain 'resuming formal possession in His Majesty's name' of land would deter the Dutch or others from potentially claiming sovereignty over vast areas of Northern Australia. They argued that the whole northern coast should be claimed and singled out the area to the east of the Cobourg Peninsula and Cape York as especially important, the former because of its large rivers and fine ports and the latter as the key to the Torres Strait and thus the security of the trade between Sydney and India. Glenelg was persuaded by the argument (which also called for a settlement manned by marines under the command of a naval officer) and for the time being dismissed the objections from Grey and Lushington.

* * *

In April 1837, Earl made another approach to the Colonial Office by writing to Lord Glenelg and enclosing the proofs of the Appendix ('Observations on the Commercial Resources of the Indian Archipelago') to his forthcoming book, *The Eastern Seas*. The piece emphasised his earlier arguments to them that Northern Australia could be an outstanding area for British mercantile enterprise; the land rich for agriculture and laden with raw materials; an able and ample labour force available from the wider area; the location ideal for the creation of a second Singapore, trading not least with the islands to the north eager for British manufactured goods; a bulwark against the commercial aggressions of the Dutch as well as British settlements bringing rescue services and the order of law to the area and precluding other powers from an occupation that they surely must desire. George also called for the appointment of a roving Commissioner for the greater area ('possessing conciliating manners and with a knowledge of the Malay language') to liaise with the natives. (Perhaps he had someone in mind for the post.) Glenelg's reply was neutral but certainly not dismissive. However, if the advocacy made little impression, it no doubt added to the growing clamour surrounding the question and marked George Earl as a voice of some merit in the matter.

Further pressure for action now came from different sources. A group of Scottish shipowners made representations to the Colonial Office after the wreck in the previous year of their ship, *Stirling Castle*, on a coral reef off the east coast of Australia. Lurid (and exaggerated) tales of murder and savagery by the Aborigines appeared in the Australian press and subsequently in London. Earlier, in August 1834, the barque *Charles Eaton* sank in the Torres Strait. Shortly after the wreck, a party from the British ship, *Augustus Caesar*, found debris from the *Charles Eaton* and the remains of fire and charred human bones on Double Island, but no trace of any survivors. Five of the crew had safely made it to Timor where they were initially held in captivity but the fate of the other 27 was unknown. Appeals were made to the Admiralty in London and two rescue missions were sent, under Glenelg's recommendation, in 1835, from Sydney and Bombay respectively. There had been a recent outcry in the press when seventeen European skulls, presumed to be from crew and passengers of the *Charles Eaton,* were discovered (forming part of the decorative border of a tortoiseshell effigy) on the Murray Islands (Torres Strait) in late 1836.

The shipowners' request to Glenelg was that there should be a string of protective settlements around the coast from Moreton Bay to Port Essington was financially impractical. However, in June 1837, the Colonial Office would write to advise the Scottish shipowners that the Government would take steps to ensure the 'increased security of the lives and property of HM Subjects in that quarter of the Globe'.

Glenelg continued to be the man in the middle of the tussle for primacy between Lieutenants Grey and Lushington and the Admiralty/RGS. Finally, Grey wrote to Glenelg and threatened to withdraw the officers' services because of the meddling in the aims of the expedition. Glenelg gave way, took the expedition under the auspices of the Colonial Office, and the two lieutenants sailed on HMS *Beagle* from Portsmouth bound for Australia on the 5th of July 1837. Grey and Lushington* had served well as a catalyst for the Admiralty's and the RGS' larger plans.

* * *

It was following the publication, in May 1837, of *The Eastern Seas; or Voyages and Adventures in the Indian Archipelago in 1832-33-34; Comprising a Tour of the Island of Java–Visits to Borneo, the Malay Peninsula, Siam, &c.; Also, an Account of the Present State of Singapore, with Observations on the Commercial Resources of the Archipelago* (to give it its full title) by George Windsor Earl M.R.A.S., and its subsequent success that established Earl's position as a prominent authority on the region.

The Eastern Seas, published by Wm. H. Allen and Co. totalled some 473 pages, plus maps, and was dedicated to Dr José d'Almeida ('whose kindness and liberality are so widely acknowledged'). It was at its publication the most wide-ranging and detailed contemporary study available of this region covering the Dutch Empire based at Batavia; Java; Sumatra; Singapore; Siam (Bangkok); the Malay Peninsula; Borneo, and the Chinese goldmines at Montradok. The wealth of information offered included particulars of hydrography, geography, agriculture, fishing, fauna, natural and mineral resources, peoples, languages and dialects, manners & customs, colonial practices and mercantile opportunities. The final three chapters were devoted to Singapore. Added to the original typesetting of the main text was the 40-page Appendix, a proof of which Earl had sent to Lord Glenelg in April.

The Eastern Seas was widely reviewed and, for the most part, enthusiastically received. *The Monthly Review* of July 1837 commented:

> ...we may not very far miss the mark, in the way of a general index to his powers, when we say in a single sentence that he has done his observations and feelings great justice by distinctly bringing out much of the manners, character, and capabilities of the numberless tribes which inhabit the eastern islands – many of them almost like amphibious creatures, being at home upon the sea, as well as when upon the land – and by happily contrasting the mild, peaceful, and industrious natives of the interior of several of the places visited, with the restless and unscrupu-

* They reached Hanover Bay, off North-Western Australia, on December 3rd 1837. Their party travelled south, and then east. As it was the rainy season, rivers were swollen, and this was taken to indicate that a vast inland sea believed to exist was yet to be discovered.

> lous population that swarms on the shores and along the rivers of the Indian Archipelago – thus affording, we believe, a fuller and clearer view of the physical and moral features, as well as the capabilities of the vast regions referred to, than has ever been before made public.
>
> ...the facts it contains are important, valuable and of pressing concern – and doubtless they will be felt by our government and the commercial community of the country as eminently entitled to regard and immediate consideration. ...a volume of greater value, merit, and mark, than any belonging to the same class of literature that has been published for a long time.

The *Naval and Military Gazette* wrote: 'The author is an intelligent traveller, upon whose accuracy the utmost reliance may be placed.' *The Spectator* thought: 'The distinguishing character of Mr. Earl's unpretending book is reality and distinctness.' In addition to matters geographical and ethnological, *The Eastern Seas* touched upon the political, economic and moral realities of the region. As noted before, Earl argued strongly against what he considered depredations of the Dutch Empire, the deleterious presence of Arab traders and the Islamic religion, and the slavery and piracy prevalent throughout the archipelago. *The Athenæum* of May 27th 1837 (the day before Victoria's coronation) carried a substantial and positive review of the book which in part read:

> A pleasing account of the Indian Archipelago was given to the public, a few years ago, by Mr. Crawfurd.* But that, which was not critically correct, did not afford a nearer view of the insular communities and their singular manners; nor did it point out their political tendency, or commercial capabilities. These defects are, in great measure, supplied by Mr. Earl – whose volume contains much that is novel, communicated in an unaffected and agreeable manner.

Given the somewhat encyclopaedic nature of *The Eastern Seas*, Earl was criticised on some details. In January 1849, *The Chinese Repository*, printed in Canton, found that, 'his representations of things in Siam [are] greatly exaggerated', and his dates with regard to events in Bangkok 'strangely inaccurate'. An extended and somewhat erroneously nit-picking review that appeared over two December 1837 issues of the *Singapore Free Press*

* John Crawfurd (1783-1868) had a long and illustrious career in the East as a surgeon, senior civil servant, linguist, orientalist, geographer, author and ethnologist.

bemoaned the lack in the text of 'hair-breath scapes... accidents... savage beasts' or love adventures with 'brown nymphs of Polynesia' in Java, Borneo or the Malay Peninsula. The review also noted:

> [Earl's] speculations as to the existence of an inland sea in Australia, is ground which we do not feel ourselves at home. It is certainly a very interesting subject of inquiry, and to many of his readers will perhaps be more so than any other portion of the volume. To the author's plan for establishing a settlement on the northern coast of New Holland, to be an emporium for the trade of the more eastern islands of the Archipelago, we shall probably on some other occasion take an opportunity to revert.

In their piece, the *Monthly Review* quoted the following passage from the Appendix to *The Eastern Seas*, drolly noting, 'with the hints thus thrown out':

> The commercial rivalry of the Americans, however, is very different in its nature from that of the Dutch, and is carried on in a spirit worthy of an enterprising nation. As their commerce receives the greatest attention from their government, their rapid advances in the Archipelago may be easily accounted for. A political agent is constantly employed in visiting the various countries in Asia, and in making arrangements by which their merchants can carry on a traffic both with credit and advantage.*

It is not unreasonable to imagine that George Earl saw himself as an ideal candidate to fulfil the role of 'political agent' for the region, based in the proposed entrepôt on the north coast of Australia. This would be a plumb position for a 24-year-old, but there was more work to be done as, by mid-1837, neither the expedition nor the proposed settlement had as yet been agreed to between the great offices of state.

Unsurprisingly, little further progress would be made until the end of July 1837, as the monarch, William IV, had died on June 20th. His death triggered the dissolution of Parliament on the 29th (the last time Par-

* Earl probably had in mind Edmund Roberts who was appointed (in an undercover capacity) as Envoy Extraordinary to the Far East by President Andrew Jackson. Roberts' 1837 book, *Embassy to the Eastern Courts of Cochin-China, Siam, and Muscat*;... was to appear posthumously as he had died of dysentery at Macau in June 1836 whilst on his second mission to the region.

liament would be dissolved for such reason), and a general election was called for July. The Whigs, lead by Melbourne, narrowly defeated the Tories under Peel, thus largely preserving the continuity of senior office holders. At the end of July, the Admiralty (Barrow and Beaufort) and the Colonial Office (Glenelg) felt that it was time to seek funding approval from Parliament via the Treasury. The Chancellor of the Exchequer, Thomas Spring-Rice, was approached and considerable emphasis was put on the eventual commercial potential of the enterprise, if only to persuade that the proposed settlement would be relatively inexpensive to fund. The Treasury was also informed that the expedition was ready to sail.

Spring-Rice was, however, unwilling to ask Parliament for the funds which were estimated at £1465 for the senior personnel. He cited the relatively recent failure to establish a viable settlement at Melville Island and probably thought it unlikely that Parliament would or should approve the funds. Although the requested sum was relatively modest, the Government had recently suffered serious financial pressure, paying out some 25% of the entire budget (an amount greater than all expenditure for the armed forces) in 1836 alone to compensate the losses of British slaveholders due to the Slavery Abolition Act of 1833. Although this percentage would drop to about 7.5% (roughly equivalent to the Admiralty's entire budget for the year) in 1837 (and rise to 12% in 1838), the final cost of this compensation was at that time unknown and Government commitments were being carefully scrutinised.

Spring-Rice was adamant in his opposition, dismissing counter arguments from Barrow and Earl, but this did not stop plans of the senior players now strengthened by the return from China of another enthusiastic supporter of the project, Captain Sir James Gordon Bremer. With the agreement of Lord Minto, the First Sea Lord, to whom Barrow reported, it was deemed that Parliamentary approval was not required for 'warships in commission', and that the initial establishment of a naval station in the Northern Australia could be funded in the first instance through the Admiralty's normal budget without reference to other offices of State. Spring-Rice, now no longer in control of any purse strings, was obliged, by mid-October, to drop his initial opposition.

In January 1838, Barrow submitted his final plans for the expedition to the Colonial Office for approval, but there were now to be further objections raised when the Treasury also had sight of the plans. Captain Bremer, who was to be in command, had been instructed to pursue a policy of encouraging significant emigration and colonisation in the chosen area. The Treasury was determined not to find itself having to fund unknown liabilities in the future that would no doubt be incurred in the establishment of a new colony, and made its objections known to the Colonial Office. The Admiralty's plans had to be amended in light of the Treasury's (via the Colonial Office) dictate that the expedition was to 'distinctly understand' that there was to be no 'permanent settlement of Her Majesty's Subjects at the Port selected', and that the site's *raison d'être* would be limited to protecting sea commerce that passed through the Torres Strait and acting as a refuge for those who met disaster at sea in the greater area. And yet, there were those that hoped such policy would be in place but temporarily.

The expedition was to embark during February 1838. The Royal Marines would garrison the settlement and there were to be three civilian adjuncts including George Windsor Earl as linguist and draughtsman. The Admiralty's Hydrographic Office had published in November of 1837 *Sailing Directions for the Arafura Sea; compiled from the Narratives of Lieuts. Kolff and Modera, of the Dutch Navy* by Earl. There would have been an element of prestige for him to have this published under his name – the Hydrographic Office was the world's leading authority for charts, sailing directions, tide tables, etc. The work (which would be read before the RGS in February 1838) may have gone some way along with *The Eastern Seas* to solidifying a place on an enterprise which he had tirelessly promoted for almost two years. Moreover, on the 30th of September 1837, Sir Gordon Bremmer had written to John Washington at the RGS to argue for Earl's inclusion in the expedition, calling him 'so able and scientific a person'.

Although the rather grander position of roving 'political agent' that Earl undoubted sought had not come to fruition, his enthusiasm was in no way diminished. Any present obstacles erected by dissenting voices in the Government could and would, as he saw it, be overcome to achieve a second Singapore somewhere on the shores of Northern Australia.

– Chapter Eight –

Journey to a New Settlement

1838

...the ship's guns were making the woods echo with a royal salute.

•

After the debates, the arguments and the lobbying, George Earl was at last a member of the expedition to Northern Australia. Although the roles of linguist and draughtsman hardly did justice to his knowledge and experience, he now had an official position and salary to underpin his plans for his future in the East. HMS *Alligator*, a 28-gun warship, and the accompanying HMS *Britomart* swung at anchor in Plymouth Harbour in February 1838. They had been refitted and prepared for the long voyage to North Australia and were now ready to sail. George, on-board the *Alligator*, wrote to his friend Captain Washington at the Royal Geographical Society on the 19th of that month:

My dear Captain Washington,

The Britomart came out of dock today, and I believe we shall sail on Wednesday or Thursday. I will not fail to attend to your suggestions respecting the measurement of heights, and you shall have every Geographical particular I can collect. I think I know all the points in which you will be most interested. I have been shockingly idle since I have been here, but as soon as I am well settled down on board, I shall work hard at [the translations of] Kolff and Modera, and hope to have it all completed for Mr Parbury by the time we reach Rhio [Rio de Janeiro].

I have been pumping the Captain of a Dutch Indiaman lately arrived from Batavia and find that one of the sons of the present King of Holland is making a tour of their possessions and one of the results of his trip has been an order to survey the port of Cali Pujang, on the south coast of Java (a sketch of which is given in my Indian Archip.) with a view to its being opened to traders.

A number of negroes have been purchased by the Dutch on the west coast of Africa, at about £10 per head who are now on the way out to Batavia, where they are to act as soldiers in the war against Sumatra. Mynheer will burn his fingers if he don't take care.

The vessel mentioned by Kolff to have been cut off at Bali appears to have been a fine schooner which arrived out of Melville Island after the Lady Nelson had been cut off at Timor Laut, and was taken up by the Government – she sailed, and like the brig, was never afterwards heard of. Sir Gordon [Bremer] has no doubt that the brig was the Lady Nelson – the word 'dak-black' of which I gave the literal translation viz. slates, proves to have meant shingles, a quantity she had on board for the government buildings.

Ever yours truly,
Geo. Windsor Earl

The day this letter was dated, both ships sailed from Plymouth. It was cold and miserable, wet with a north-easterly wind strengthening to gale force as they set off down the English Channel. Not long afterwards the *Alligator* suffered a split bowsprit and was forced to return to Plymouth for repairs whilst the *Britomart* sailed on. Under the command of Captain Sir J. J. Gordon Bremer, the *Alligator* carried a detachment of 25 marines commanded by Captain John McArthur RM.* This body of men was to largely comprise the garrison of the new settlement. In addition to George Earl, there were two other civilians on-board; James H McArthur, acting storekeeper (and son of Captain McArthur), and John Armstrong, botanist, gardener to the new settlement and botanical collector for the Royal Gardens at Kew.

On the 10th of March, the *Alligator* set sail again and subsequently met up with the *Britomart* which had waited for her at Tenerife. Together they then sailed for the Cape, via Rio, where they stayed for a week or so, revictualling and repairing. Sailing on from the Cape, the two ships split up for the long voyage across the southern ocean. The *Britomart* proceeded straight to Sydney while the *Alligator* called at the new colony at South Australia (Adelaide), arriving in Sydney at the end of July where the vessels hove-to together. There they were joined by HMS *Beagle*. Sir Gordon Bremer called on the Governor of the colony, Sir George Gipps, to present his credentials. He also handed over the dispatch from Lord

* The spellings of his surname in letters, official documents and newspaper reports vary (he was not himself consistent) and include Mcarthur, Macarthur, M'Arthur and MacArthur. 'McArthur' has been used in this book except when appearing in print otherwise at the time. George's surname occasionally appears in print and official documents as Earle.

Glenelg at the Colonial Office which advised of the appointment of Captain Bremer by the Lords Commissioners of the Admiralty 'to establish a post on the northern coast of Australia'.

Given the isolation of the new settlement it was vital that basic infrastructure quickly be put in place. Instructions by Captain Bremer were given for the issue of all stores required and for the supply of ordnance. This was a major undertaking. Including the *Beagle*, which was to plan her surveying duties from a base at the new settlement, five vessels and some 300 people had to be provided for through a period of up to eighteen months. Materials included six prefabricated houses framed in wood and weatherboarded; tools and equipment of every sort; tropical fruit trees and seeds from the Botanical Gardens in Sydney; a wood-framed and weatherboarded church to seat 300 gifted by the Lord Bishop of Australia; hospital equipment, barracks, storerooms; every sort of suitable stores, medicines, clothing, textiles; and, finally, cows, sheep, pigs and poultry. The large 450-ton barque *Orontes* was hired to complete the little fleet, which comprised the *Alligator*, the *Britomart*, the *Orontes* and the *Beagle* along with the schooner *Essington*, which was intended to be based at the new settlement and used for trade throughout the eastern archipelago. Each ship was packed to the gunwales.

It was already late-July 1838 when the *Alligator* and *Britomart* arrived and it was essential that the expedition made it to the north coast before the north-west monsoon set in. Sydney was abuzz with talk and conjecture, not all of it positive, about the expedition and its future. George Earl, working as a sort of unofficial PA to Captain Bremer, was involved in almost every aspect of the planning. On the 16th of August, he wrote again to Captain John Washington at the Royal Geographical Society.

> My Dear Captain Washington
> We arrived here on the 21st of last month, after an excellent passage from the Cape, and if fortune favours us as it has hitherto done, the best results must be expected from our enterprise. I enclose you a few scraps of information concerning South Australia, by far the most agreeable part of the continent that I have hitherto seen, and trust you may find them useful. Mr Stephenson, the late Governor's private secretary, has promised me that he will communicate all information possessing geographical interest that may subsequently come to light there, and as several exploring expeditions are in contemplation, we may at length expect something concerning the neighbouring country. ...As the carpenters do not proceed very quickly, I fear we shall not leave this place before the

middle of next month. I do not think that any mechanics will be taken with us, which I am much rejoiced at for I am convinced that the less we have to do with this hot-bed of vice, the better it will be for us.

I cannot tell you exactly what will be our movements after leaving here, for although Sir Gordon is very communicative with me, he does not state explicitly his intentions, nor do I believe he himself has decided as to what part we shall settle in. ... Point Record, in Port Essington, appears to be a favourite spot. ... I hope, however, that the 'Britomart' or some other vessel, will be sent up to Singapore before the end of the year, as all the Bughis who come down the coast of Australia would then be found there, and they could be informed of the settlement. Information that I have received here from an intelligent friend just arrived from Singapore confirms me in my opinion that we should have a number of Bughis among us as settlers the very first year, provided that they were informed of the state of affairs in time.

...With the exception of Sir Gordon Bremer, Captain McArthur, and Lieut. Priest, his second in command, not a soul among us appears to care much whether we succeed or not, indeed, from the expressions of some I would be inclined to think that they were unfavourable to it, or rather to the nature of the service. They will certainly be long separated from civilized society. However, we have the right men on our side, that is those who are going to remain.

The translation of Kolff is completed, and will be forwarded to Messrs Parbury by their brother, who is a merchant here. If you are good enough to see it through the press, I trust that you will not have much trouble in revision.*

I have lately learned that the Dutch settlement at Fort du Bus on the SW coast of New Guinea has been abandoned, this event occurring about 12 months ago. The natives have been very troublesome. It appears certain that this port, which should, according to the views of their government, have been placed near Cape Valch, was intended as a foil to Raffles Bay, or, as a Dutch captain in the navy expressed himself, to check-mate it.

* Lt. D.H. (Dirk Hendrik) Kolff had written perhaps the first comprehensive account of the Arafura Sea during his voyages on the vessel *Dourga*. George's translation was to be published in 1840 under the title: *Voyages of the Dutch Brig-of-War Dourga, through the southern and little-known ports of the Moluccan Archipelago, and along the previously unknown southern coast of New Guinea, performed during the years 1825 & 1826*.

The trade of the Arafura islands has increased wonderfully since Kolff was there. I am informed by the master of a Dutch ship just arrived here, that no less than thirty square rigged vessels sailed from Java last year, from Timor and the adjacent islands. A few years ago the trade did not give employment for more than five or six.

Pray do not fail to write to me by every opportunity, though it should be only a few lines. No one on hand has received any letters from home through the Admiralty, but I trust some will arrive before we leave.

Yours very sincerely,
George Windsor Earl

PS I have written to you from Teneriffe [sic], Rhio [Rio] and the Cape. I trust you received them all.

On the 17th of September 1838, the *Alligator* and her accompanying vessels set sail and rounded Sydney Heads into the open sea. George wrote: 'The ship was quite a Noah's ark. Cows, sheep, pigs and poultry were quartered between the guns, and a number of giant kangaroo-dogs were incessantly stalking about the decks, trying to discover if there really existed any spot where they could lie down for five minutes without being trodden upon.'

Eight years later, in his book *Enterprise in Tropical Australia*, George was to recount his impressions of that voyage from Sydney to Port Essington.

I will now proceed to describe our voyage along the north-east coast of Australia, which proved to be one of the most agreeable that I ever remember to have made; and if I enter somewhat into detail, I trust that the circumstance of this portion of the continent being very imperfectly known, even in New South Wales, will prove a sufficient excuse. On leaving Sydney, after running a few leagues off the land, a course was steered for Smoky Cape, two hundred miles to the northward of Port Jackson, the first point of rendezvous for the ships in case of separation... Two other merchant-ships, which had sailed in company with us to take advantage of our convoy through Torres Strait, were lost sight of soon after leaving Sydney, so that on arriving off Smoky Cape on the 23rd, the Orontes was the only ship in company. We hove to here for fourteen hours, but the *Britomart* and her consort not making their appearance, we once more stood along the coast to the northward...

On the 24th we saw a little sloop in shore under sail, near the mouth of a small river, apparently hove-to until the tide should have risen sufficiently to permit her to enter. We fired a gun as a signal for her to communicate with us, but she popped in over the bar, and in a few minutes was out of sight among the windings of the river. She was probably bound here for a cargo of cedar timber, but we thought at the time that she might be employed in smuggling spirits, a system that was carried on to a very considerable extent upon different parts of the coast.

The banks of this river, which we subsequently learned was called the Macleay, are clothed with dense jungles, the timber being of a description superior to that of Australian trees generally. The great demand that existed at Sydney for building materials had induced parties of labourers to settle upon the banks of this, and of some of the neighbouring rivers, where they led a life similar to that of the log-wood cutters in the Bay of Honduras, occupying themselves in felling the trees and preparing the timber for exportation in the numerous coasting craft that were employed in the trade. The elevated table-land in which these rivers take their rise had lately become a favourite resort for newly-arrived settlers, the pasturage being very luxuriant.

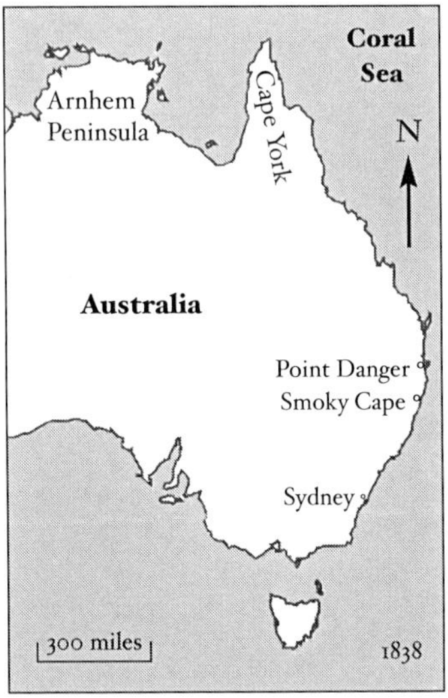

By the 1st of October we had not succeeded in advancing further than Mount Warning, a fine bold mountain, three hundred and fifty miles to the northward of Sydney, owing to almost constant foul winds having rendered it necessary to tack repeatedly; and as the current set strong with the wind, the ship, on some days, scarcely gained an inch of ground. In the afternoon we communicated with the Pocklington, a whaler, which was returning to Sydney, owing to the typhus-fever having broken out on board, and carried off the captain and several of the crew. The chief mate of this vessel, who had had much experience on the coast, recommended to the boarding-officer that we should stand off the land, when the strength of the current would be avoided, and a very fair chance afforded of meeting with a favourable wind. We did so, and in twenty-four hours fell in with a fine southerly breeze, to which we squared the yards, and set all studding-sails, and were soon sailing merrily along for Break-sea Spit.

This singular reef extends for about twenty miles out to sea in a northerly direction from Sandy Cape, where the east coast of Australia terminates, the land beyond it stretching away in a north-west direction towards New Guinea. The Spit was thus appropriately named by Captain Cook; indeed, this able navigator has almost invariably applied very striking names to those spots near which the seaman would have to exert especial vigilance, while he has reserved the more fashionable appellations of those whom he delighted to honour for parts where a distinctive title would not be particularly required. Thus, Mount Warning forms an excellent land-mark for avoiding the reef that extends out to sea from Point Danger, one of the very few obstructions to navigation that are found upon the eastern coast, and other cases are constantly met with. When the traffic upon the north-east coast increases, which will probably soon be the case, since the settlers are rapidly extending themselves in this direction, a light-house will become necessary upon the end of Break-sea Spit, and a dreary enough abode it will prove.

We had now fairly entered the limits of the south-east trade-wind, and the breeze was light but steady from the eastern quarter. In the morning, after passing Break-sea Spit, we found ourselves again near the main-land, and were now within the Great Barrier Reefs. Our course henceforward for more than a thousand miles lay close along the coast, through seas studded with islands and shoals, but as smooth as the waters of an inland lake; for the Barrier Reefs, like a mighty sea-wall, break off the swell of the ocean, and waters within are undisturbed, except by the short ripples raised by the breeze that blows over its surface. During the 7th and 8th, we were passing through the hundred islands of the Northumberland and Cumberland groups, but the breeze was too steady to admit of our stopping to examine them. The Percy Islands attracted especial attention, owing to their being covered with pine-trees *(araucaria excelsa)* which are stated to be exceedingly well adapted for jib-booms and top-masts. The glimpses that we had of the main-land, while passing through this archipelago, presented many striking views. The mountain range which extends along the coast here approaches close to the shore; the lofty pines which crown its summits, and which from their appearance we judged to be the same with those found at Norfolk Island, giving the scenery quite an Alpine character; that is to say, a portion of it, for the dark and luxuriant vegetation at the base of the range; which told tales of tropical heats, by no means served to keep up the delusion.

But it was during the night, with the bright moon shining upon them, that these mountains appeared in all their glory. I remained on deck this evening until past midnight, leaning over the hammock nettings, watching the land as we glided smoothly past, and wondering whether I should ever live to see these shores occupied by a busy people. When I went below we were passing Cape Upstart, a bold, frowning promontory. Captain Cook, who saw it during the day, says that it 'affords but a barren prospect'; which may probably be the case, but now, in the clear moonlight, with its rugged outlines softened by distance, its appearance was truly beautiful. On the morning of the 10th, we passed within the Barnard Islands, and now, for the first time, saw natives, five of whom appeared upon a hill near the shore. Three of their number, perhaps old men, remained sitting upon the ground watching the ship, but the remaining two occasionally started up, and rushed to and fro past each other, jumping in the air, and waving green branches, apparently to attract our notice. After continuing these active exertions for some minutes, and when seemingly almost frantic, they would sit down so suddenly that it appeared as if they had thrown their heels high up in the air, and pitched plump down upon their latter ends. These strange antics were repeated at intervals for more than an hour, and the singular finale was looked forward to by us with great anticipation. The poor creatures were, perhaps, inviting us to land. Some passing navigator may have treated them with kindness, and made them anxious to renew their acquaintance with strangers. Their performance was evidently some ceremony; perhaps a dance of welcome. The abrupt termination is a peculiar characteristic of both the songs and dances of the Northern Australian natives. The former always end with a high note, which makes it appear as if the singer had been suddenly cut short in his performance; but the effect is striking, and rather pleasing than otherwise. The dances, again, terminate when the action and excitement are at the highest pitch, and, so sudden is the transition from frantic exertion to calm repose that it appears almost magical.

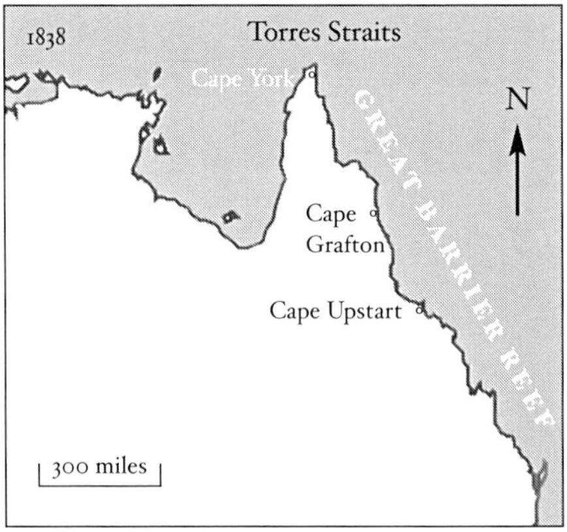

While yet in sight of our eccentric entertainers, the tackles were got up on the yards and the decked boat hoisted out and rigged, after which she sailed in company with the ships. Probably the natives, who were watching us, looked upon this proceeding on our part with a feeling of surprise equal to that with which we had regarded their strange evolutions.

...Throughout the day two high mountains, the Bellenden Kerr range of Captain King, were in sight, but the summits were often enveloped in clouds. I find noted in my journal that the highest of these is 6,500 feet high, but, unfortunately, I have not noted down my authority, which I very much regret, as the general height of the mountains on this coast has since been a subject of discussion. The impression on my mind is, that this calculation of the altitude was the result of observations taken by our excellent surveyor Mr Tyers, but upon this point I cannot speak with certainty.*

In the evening we anchored for the first time. Our voyage had hitherto been continued during the night, but a similar course of proceeding could not now be persisted in, owing to the numerous dangers that lay in our route. We were now six hundred miles within Break-sea Spit, and five hundred miles of difficult navigation yet remained before we should be clear of the Straits. Our anchorage this evening was within the Frankland Islands, but we arrived too late to visit them before dark.

...We commenced getting under weigh before daylight on the morning of the 11th, and a strong party of men was sent on board the 'Orontes' to assist the crew in purchasing her anchor. In the forenoon we passed through the narrow but safe channel which separates Fitzroy Island from Cape Grafton [near modern-day Cairns]. This spot will probably attract attention when the coast hereabouts is occupied. The island is about five miles long; hilly and clothed with wood; fresh water is found convenient to the beach. The channel between it and the main, is about three miles wide, and affords excellent anchorage, while the most direct route for ships passing this way lies right through the roads. These circumstances coupled with the apparent great fertility of the adjacent parts of the main-land, will probably lead to this being the site of one of the first settlements made upon the coast, and certainly it must prove a very delightful residence. Ten minutes' walk from the beach leads to the

* George's own observations, and those of the 'excellent surveyor Mr Tyers', from a boat at sea level were not unreasonable. The height of Mt. Bartle Frere, to which George probably is referring, is 1622m, roughly 5000 feet.

summit of the hills which traverse the island from north to south; and here may be enjoyed the healthy breeze from the Pacific, together with a view, both to landward and seaward, such as very few parts of the world present.

We did not anchor this evening until eight o'clock, when three miles to the southward of the Low Islands. Throughout the following day we were running close along the land, and saw many natives on the beach. Two, who were fishing in a canoe, pulled for the shore as the ship approached them, and hauled their boat up; but beyond this they did not appear to take the slightest notice of us. In the evening we anchored near the Hope Islands...

The channel now became narrow and intricate, owing to the Great Barrier Reefs here approaching very near to the coast. During the night we continually heard the roaring of the breakers on the outer reefs, and had reason to be thankful that so firm a barrier interposed between us and the swell of the Southern Ocean.

On the morning of the 12th the wind was light from the southward, and our progress was not very rapid. We were now on classic ground. To seaward, lay the Endeavour Reef, upon which the ship that first explored these coasts was thrown during the night, and only saved from total wreck by the energy and skill of the ablest of navigators. Within us, Cape Tribulation, a bold and lofty headland, rose abruptly from the sea, forming the most prominent feature in the landscape, and the eye of the commander was no doubt anxiously directed towards it, when it was suddenly found that the water was gaining on the pumps, after the ship had floated off the reef. To our left was Weary Bay, the scene of incessant labour in efforts to save that ship; and far a-head appeared the narrow opening of the Endeavour River in which she was repaired and once more rendered fit for sea. It is singular that throughout this thousand miles of coast, more recent surveys have not brought to light a single port that would have answered the navigator's purpose one half part so well as this.

The mountain range, which had been seen extending along the coast for more than six hundred miles, was suddenly lost near Cape Tribulation. It may continue running to the north-west towards Cape York, further in the interior; but, if this be the case, its height must be diminished, since no mountains were seen in this direction by Flinders, when he traced the eastern shore of the Gulf of Carpentaria; and to the north of Cape Melville the land, from sea to sea, contracts to the width of little more than a hundred miles. The sudden disappearance of these

> mountains is rather singular, for at the point at which we lost them, they appeared to be considerably higher than in any part of the range we had previously seen. I find noted in my journal that we estimated the height of this extreme group at 10,000 feet; and a statement to this effect, with a reservation in favour of the over-estimation that travellers are liable to fall into under these circumstances, was made by me in some evidence upon points connected with Australian geography, given before a committee of the Legislative Council of New South Wales. Captain King, however, whose experience upon these coasts gives his opinions very great weight, considers this to be considerably above their actual height.

The reason why these mountains were 'lost near Cape Tribulation' was because they never existed. North of Cape Tribulation the land slowly flattens out as Cape York is approached and there is nothing over an elevation of 2000 feet. After days of fine weather and fair winds they arrived at Cape York, the northernmost point of Australia on the 20th of October 1838. A good anchorage was found and Captain Sir Gordon Bremer, as instructed, landed with a party of officers and Royal Marines in order to carry out a most important duty. They ascended a hill at the Cape, the boats' crews carrying a spar that was to be erected as a flagstaff. Accompanying them was a crowd of native people waving branches and mother-of-pearl shells, otherwise not showing much interest in what was going on.

At the summit of the hill, a hole was dug for the flagpole and George wrote: 'soon a union jack of very considerable dimensions was waving over our heads. Sir Gordon Bremer now proceeded to take formal possession of the entire north-east coast of Australia and, if I mistake not, of the north coast too, in the name of Her Majesty the Queen; after which the Marines fired a volley, all hands gave three cheers, and as we descended the hill, the ship's guns were making the woods echo with a royal salute. The flag and its staff were left for the admiration of the natives who had thus suddenly become British subjects.'

The two ships pressed on to cover the remaining 600 miles of open sea to Port Essington where they arrived on the morning of the 27th of October, almost six weeks after leaving Sydney. George wrote of their arrival:

> In the grey of the morning the tops of the trees on Cape Croker were visible from the deck. We now hauled up for Port Essington, and all hands were anxiously looking out to catch a glimpse of the spot which would probably be our head-quarters for some time to come. ...The

scene was a perfectly quiet one. There appeared to be nothing stirring, with the exception of a few birds which were running along the beach, and occasionally wading into the water as it washed up, to seize upon any little denizen of the sea that might come within their reach. Nor was there much noise on board, for everyone appeared to be occupied with his own thoughts, and the general silence was only occasionally disturbed by a remark from some keen observer, who supposed that he had been the first to discover some striking novelty. It was indeed an absorbing moment to the whole of us, for probably no expedition ever sailed upon a similar service in which both officers and men took a more general interest than in this.

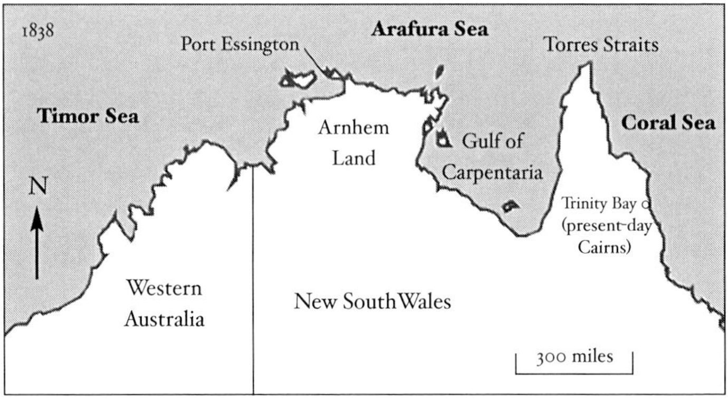

Captain Stirling's exploration party, fifty miles up the Swan River, March 1827.
Engraving dated 1830 based on an 1827 painting of the same subject.

Captain Percy Earl, father of George, Percy and Elizabeth Earl. Noel-Paton

The view from Mount Eliza (Kings Park) looking eastward towards the South Perth peninsula up the Canning River (1827). Museum of Perth

A syndicate of investors headed by Thomas Peel, a cousin of Secretary of State Robert Peel, was to be granted 250,000 acres of prime land around the Swan River. Their party arrived in the area six weeks after the Government's stipulated deadline and received poorer land, leading to the failure of the scheme.The text reads: *Cousin Bob's letter did the job. I shall feather my nest however. The best parts of the Swan River Settlement only to be got at the hands of Mr. The P–L.* 1829 cartoon.

View of Singapore River and Chinatown from Government Hill,
Print attributed to Isidore Laurent, 1824.

Singapore River, Presentment Hill and Government Hill,
print attributed to Francois-Edmond Paris, circa 1830
(*Overleaf spread*): Map (colourized) from *The Eastern Seas*, 1837.

Geo. Windsor Earl.

London. Wm. [illegible]

Allen & Co. 1837. John Arrowsmith.

Aborigines, engraving from *Narrative of the Surveying Voyage of HMS* Fly, 1847.

1801 map by John Cary with topographical features of the East Indies and Southeast Asia.

Port Essington. View from Barrow Bay towards Point Record, (middle right-hand side). Watercolour by Captain Phillip Parker King., 1818. NLA

Cape Upstart on the East coast of Australia of which Captain Cook wrote: *...in the clear moonlight, with its rugged outlines softened by distance, its appearance was truly beautiful.* Watercolour by Edwin Augustus Porcher, 1843. NLA

Engraving of Victoria, Port Essington by L. LeBreton from Jules Dumont d'Urville's, *Journey to the South Pole and Oceania on the Corvettes L'Astrolabe and La Zélée to Execute the Order of the King during the Years 1837–1838–1839–1840 under the Command of Dumont d'Urville. Pictorial Atlas.* Published 1846.

Settlement at Port Essington. Watercolour of June 1845 by Edwin Augustus Porcher, the scientific observer and unofficial artist aboard the Royal Navy's corvette *Fly* which carried out the first hydrographic survey of the north-eastern Australian coast in 1842-45. NLA

Aboriginal Australians at Port Essington. Watercolour by Herman E. Melville who was attached to the surveying expedition of HMS *Fly*. Late 1840s. NLA

HMS *Pelorus* (at low water), Victoria. Wrecked in the hurricane of November 1839, she was refloated, after being buried in 9 feet of mud for 86 days, and repaired by February of the following year. Watercolour by Captain Owen Stanley, 1840. NLA

1839 view of Victoria, Port Essington by M. Goupil, the official artist with Jules Dumont d'Urville's expedition of 1837-1840. Engraving published 1846.

– Chapter Nine –

First Steps

1838

...Our curiosity to see these denizens of the forest did not long remain ungratified, for shortly after anchoring, a small canoe, containing two men, was seen approaching the ship...

•

The *Alligator* had a gentle sail down the great inlet of Port Essington. The schooner *Essington* had arrived ten days beforehand and was riding at anchor at the mouth of the inner harbour by Point Record. The new arrivals dropped anchor nearby. Captains Bremer and McArthur, the two senior officers, immediately set out to identify the precise location for the new settlement. The four main requirements were: military security; the availability of plentiful water; fertile ground; easy accessibility to the ships. The whole of the inner harbour, the area south of Point Record, was carefully examined. The site was chosen on 3rd of November 1838 and named Victoria, in honour of the new Queen.

The site was about halfway down the inner harbour opposite Middle Head. The fleet moved down to the new anchorage and the large task began of off loading supplies and material. Immediately, the ground plan of the new settlement had to be prepared, an undertaking with which George was familiar after his experiences ten years beforehand at Augusta. The prime consideration was that the site needed to fulfil the requirements for a secure garrison and port. Civilian and settler concerns were secondary. Initially, as at Swan River, all accommodation was in tents and, in spite of the great heat to which people were unaccustomed, foundation work continued vigorously day after day. The ground was cleared and enclosures for livestock set out; rough tracks made and a pier built; barracks and simple housing erected including a slightly less simple construction grandly named Government House. Church, hospital, workshops, kitchens and storerooms were all prepared and water wells bored. It was not long before the new little town of Victoria began to look the part. The gardener, John Armstrong, assisted by some of the marines, laid out and enclosed some land for the temporary lodging of plants brought from Rio de Janeiro and Sydney. The surrounding woods abounded with game: pigeons, partridge, quail and kangaroo – the latter not being accustomed to the sound of gunfire, made for an easy kill. Seine net fishing off the beach provided a plentiful catch. George recalled his first meeting with some of the natives:

> ...Our curiosity to see these denizens of the forest did not long remain ungratified, for shortly after anchoring, a small canoe, containing two men, was seen approaching the ship... both the men stood up, and the elder made a short speech, the purport of which, as may be imagined, was perfectly unintelligible to us. They seemed very reluctant to come close, and it was not until after repeated invitations, that they at length came alongside. The elder, whose name was Langari, singled out Sir Gordon Bremer the moment he came on board, and delivered a long address, shedding many tears, and frequently touching his shoulders with both hands in a sort of half embrace. From his repeatedly pointing towards Raffles Bay [the settlement abandoned ten years previously] and making use of the term 'commandant' in a tone of endearment, it appeared that Langari, who, although belonging to the Port Essington tribe, had been a frequent visitor at our settlement at Raffles' Bay, had mistaken Sir Gordon Bremer for Captain Barker, the last commandant there, to whom the natives had been very much attached.
>
> The younger man, Wanji-wanji, who must have been under twenty years of age, was in a state of the most intense fright from the very commencement of the interview... his teeth chattered, and his eyes rolled about in an agony of alarm and apprehension which had not completely subsided when he returned to the shore, after a visit of upwards of an hour, loaded with presents, and possessed of a greater amount of wealth than he had ever before even contemplated. This youth ... soon after became an almost constant resident among us, and proved highly intelligent and useful.

Wearing his ethnologist's hat, George noted carefully the appearance of these new friends with a view to comparing them with their brethren on the other coasts of Australia:

> Both visitors had the skin embossed with raised cicatrices, the septum of the nosed bored, and each had lost a front tooth. Nor did their hair differ greatly in its texture from that of the southern natives. Wanji-wanji however, who was a small but exceedingly well-made young man, displayed a skin, when the dirt was washed off, much fairer than is generally met with among Australian aborigines, and scarcely a shade darker

> than that of the Polynesian tribes of the Indian Archipelago. With this single exception, I saw nothing about them which would have led me to single them out, had I met them among the tribes of the southern part of the continent.

So started what was to prove a long and harmonious relationship with the native people that was to endure through the next decade. Immediately after the arrival, a large group of natives established themselves just to the south of Victoria. Their main occupation was fishing for crab, oysters, fish and other edibles. These were then exchanged with the settlers for old clothes, biscuit and articles that took their fancy. Several of them proved to be adept at pilfering, an art which they had learned to practice on their annual visitors, the trepang fishermen from Macassar. George further observed:

> Knives, clothes which had been hung out to dry, and, occasionally some of the carpenters' tools were found missing from time to time, and at length Mallamaya, a brother of Wanji-wanji, was caught one evening after dark in the very act of stealing a shirt from a clothes line within the men's encampment. Notwithstanding an immense deal of struggling and noise upon his part, he was dragged by his captors to the tent, where we were sitting after tea, chatting upon the topics of the day, and presented before Sir Gordon Bremer for judgment. The native, who afterwards proved to be a very Mercury, or prince of thieves, was evidently in a great state of alarm; for I suspect that the Macassers had been in the habit of dealing very summarily with plunderers; but he had his wits about him and his eyes were constantly wandering in search of some mode of escape. He was, however, in the hands of men to whom his strength was but that of a child; two stout marines, each of whom grasped a wrist of the offender. I must confess that they presented a rather ludicrous appearance as they stood 'attention' before the door of the tent, with the native between them, while the sergeant of the guard came forward and made his report. The prisoner spoke very energetically in his own defence, making a most elaborate use of the few English words that he had picked up; and Sir Gordon Bremer, thinking the fright he had endured would be sufficient punishment, and in consideration of this being the first offence, allowed him to depart, no doubt to his great joy, for I really think he expected to have been put to death. On being released, he walked away for a few yards in as composed a manner as he could assume, and then bounded off through the dark forest like a deer.

In addition to the day-to-day physical work in the settlement, George assembled his plans for the first voyage of exploration by the *Essington*. Fresh from his translation of Kolff's narrative of the journey through the islands to the north and east of Port Essington, George knew that they were likely to be a rich source of needed supplies. On Sir Gordon Bremer's instructions, George was to establish relations with these islands, and fly the flag on behalf of the new settlement. The *Essington* had on-board a cargo of British goods to exchange for island produce and thus initiate a pattern for future trade.

She sailed on the 1st of December, only a month after their arrival on the coast. Her destination was the island of Kissa, about 300 miles north-west of Port Essington and just off the north coast of Timor. The *Essington* was not the first English vessel to visit Kissa, as whaling ships had been calling there over many years. Kissa had the reputation of being the most civilised of the Serwatty group of islands, probably because of a population of around 8000, about a quarter Christians of the Dutch Reformed Church. Included in this number were a considerable number of descendants of the Dutch who had lived there under the Dutch East India Company. George busied himself by talking to the resident missionary from the Netherlands Missionary Society, the local chiefs and trades people from whom he derived a fund of information including that the population of Kissa (and surrounding islands) were of the greater Polynesian race and similar in customs, personal appearance and language to the people of the Society and Sandwich islands.

The *Essington* then called at a number of closely neighbouring islands including Moa and Leti, with George assessing them for future supplies of food and livestock. He also discovered the fate of two English ships, the *Stedcombe* and the Government brig *Lady Nelson*. The vessels had been

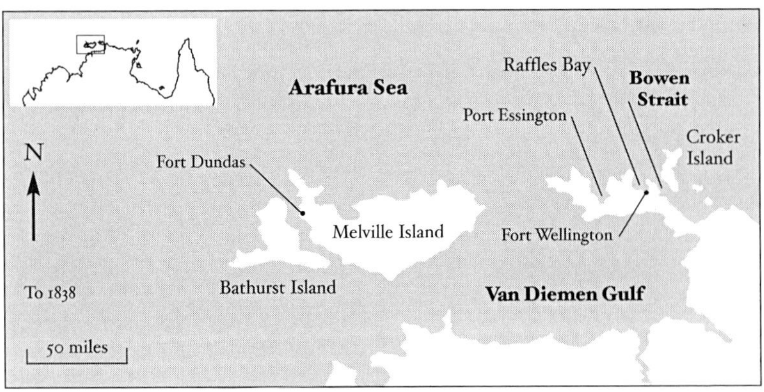

entrapped and seized by pirates from the island of Baba and the crews, except for two boys, murdered. The *Essington* herself had to make a quick escape and return to Kissa after an incident with several prahus from Baba, whose crews were intent on piracy and murder.

It was on this voyage that George met and employed on the island of Kissa a young man by the name of Shadrach Philippus who was to become an invaluable assistant and friend. George was later to write of Shadrach: 'he was one of many young men who offered their services to me on my expressing a wish to take one with me and I have never had cause to regret bringing him away'.

At Kissa, a full cargo for the new settlement was negotiated for which comprised nineteen buffaloes, 60 pigs, more than a hundred sheep, several tons of yam, a quantity of poultry and a number of banana stems, cocoa-nuts and planting seeds. George reported that only one of the buffaloes died on the voyage back to Port Essington, along with two or three pigs 'which were too fat to stand on their legs and fretted themselves to death' along with almost half of the sheep, 'these being wretched long-legged things not at all fitted for a sea voyage'. The voyage had been reasonably successful and, of particular satisfaction to George, most of the banana stems began to shoot soon after being transplanted at the settlement.

The *Essington* returned to Port Essington on December 15th 1838, and two days afterwards a major disaster occurred. The *Orontes*, the big merchant ship which had sailed from Sydney to Port Essington in the first fleet the previous September, embarked for India. While standing out to sea, well outside the main harbour, she struck an uncharted reef of rocks (thereafter known as Orontes Reef) and was so badly damaged that she only just made it to the nearest landfall at Vashon Head, about five miles away. Found to be too badly damaged to be repaired, she had to be abandoned. The whole crew and such cargo and stores as could be saved were brought back to the settlement, the population of which once again expanded considerably. This necessitated an immediate voyage by the *Essington*, this time without George on-board, for supplies. Since there was also a requirement for ponies, she sailed for Dili, about 400 miles away at the northeast end of Timor.

Work on the pier and houses continued apace so as to beat the arrival of the monsoon. The health and morale of the settlers were good, although there were signs of scurvy beginning to appear among the crew of the *Alligator*, and a few days before the sinking of the *Orontes* the first child to be born in Victoria arrived. George commented that New Year

1839 commenced with 'the usual festivities and...an abundance of good cheer'. The *Essington* returned from Dili in the latter half of January with supplies and an unusual luxury: English newspapers, albeit dated many months beforehand.

Dili was the nearest European (Portuguese) settlement from Port Essington and regular communication was an important objective, so much so that Sir Gordon Bremer, content with the situation at Victoria, decided to go there himself in the *Britomart*. The brig sailed in mid-February 1839 into the teeth of the westerly monsoon, which made for a slow and tedious journey of a fortnight, twice the normal time. This was mainly a flag-waving exercise for Bremer in which he as the Commander sought to establish first-hand relationships and spread the news of the development of the new settlement at Port Essington. George accompanied him; his knowledge of languages and local people made him a key adviser although, in his eyes, Dili was a 'miserable slave station'. Nevertheless, the *Britomart* fired a Royal Salute of 21 guns in honour of the Portuguese flag and Sir Gordon was received with full honours. The visit was a success and plans were agreed for regular trade and exchange. Bremer took the opportunity whilst there to write to the East India Company's Resident Councillor in Singapore, confirming developments at Port Essington and asking him to disseminate as widely as possible this news for potential trade.

After five days the *Britomart* sailed from Dili to Kissa and Moa with the same objective. Bremer also made contact with the Dutch Governor at Coepang on the southern point of Timor to convey the same information and received, under the circumstances, positive and friendly replies. Almost exactly a month later, Bremer arrived back at Victoria to find the settlement in good order, although no ships had visited. How-

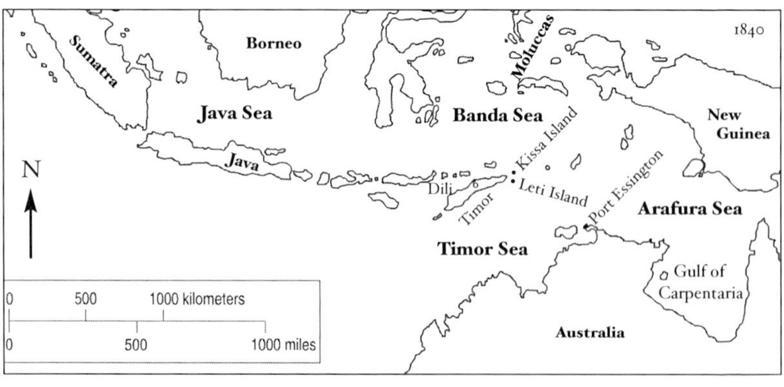

ever, at the end of the month two Aborigines arrived from the eastern side of the peninsula with news that several Macassar prahus were anchored in the Bowen Strait and, having heard of the new settlement, were planning to visit. They also brought news that two large ships with all-European crews were in Raffles Bay and that houses were being built on the shore. This was both mystifying and slightly alarming, so Sir Gordon Bremer dispatched Lieutenant Stewart of the *Alligator* in the ship's cutter to pay a visit to Raffles Bay. On arrival he saw the two ships at anchor near the abandoned settlement and the French Tricolour flying over a few tents on the shore.

The vessels were the corvettes *Astrolabe* and *Zélée* of France under the command of Commodore d'Urville on a research and exploration mission. These two ships had left Toulon about six months before Bremer and his expedition sailed from England at the beginning of 1838. Their voyage had taken them west around Cape Horn, visiting various Pacific islands and, latterly, Dutch possessions. They were in the course of surveying the Bowen Strait which separates Croker Island from the mainland, and they reported that some 30 Macassar prahus had passed through the Strait during the ten days that they had been at anchor. This would have been encouraging to George to whom the development of the trepang fisheries business at Port Essington was crucial.

Lieutenant Stewart returned to base and en route investigated what proved to be a fine harbour, some seven miles in length and two miles wide which he named (to general approval) Port Bremer after his Commanding Officer. He had also inspected the ruins of Fort Wellington in Raffles Bay, abandoned ten years beforehand, which had reverted to bush. Having been briefed, Bremer sent the lieutenant back to Commodore D'Urville requesting him to visit Victoria before he left the coast. After a few days the two corvettes sailed into Port Essington and anchored off Point Record. At about the same time, five Macassan prahus also arrived and commenced trepang fishing. Each prahu had four or five canoes attached to it, the crews of which would gather shoals of these sea slugs. George gives a vivid description of the activities:

> In point of size and appearance it resembles a prickly cucumber, except that the colour is a whitish brown. I here allude to the most common description, for there are several varieties, one of which is perfectly black. The trepang is found in all the sheltered harbours, where it gropes about the bottom, and feeds upon weeds and Mollusca. It is taken at low water, upon the shoals or mud-banks, over which the fishermen wade

> knee-deep in water, dragging their boats after them, and when the feet come in contact with a slug, it is picked up and thrown into the boat. They occasionally search in deeper water, when the fishermen avail themselves of the services of the natives, who are expert divers, or if they cannot obtain such assistance, they prick for them with barbed iron darts, provided with long bamboo handles. The process of curing is very simple. The slug, on being taken from the boat, is simmered over a fire in an iron cauldron for about half-an-hour, after which it is thrown out upon the ground, and the operation of opening commences, this being effected by a longitudinal cut along the back with a sharp knife. It is then again placed in the cauldron and boiled in salt water, with which a quantity of the bark of the mangrove has been mixed for about three hours, when the outer skin will begin to peel off. It is now sufficiently boiled, and after the water has been drained off, the slugs are arranged in the drying-houses (small huts covered with mats), upon frames of split bamboo spread out immediately under the roof. Each slug is carefully placed with the part that has been cut open facing downwards, and a fire is made underneath, the smoke of which soon dries the trepang sufficiently to permit its being packed in bags or baskets for exportation...

At the end of this process they became a valuable commodity, 'articles of commerce' as George put it. He was delighted to see this activity at last taking place. The Macassans welcomed the security from pirates and Aborigines which the settlement provided, while he saw this as the start of the trading patterns he had forecasted.

Commodore d'Urville and his officers were richly entertained at Government House and Sir Gordon and his senior men visited the two ships. In this friendly atmosphere there was much talk of the scientific research in which the French were engaged and the wide range of features relating to those Eastern seas and islands. Captain d'Urville was charmed by Bremer: 'I admired this white-haired man, who had left his country, his family, to come to this inhospitable land to undertake such a laborious and difficult task. He seemed happy, surrounded by his little colony, of which he was the founder and father. One single thought seemed to animate his mind: that of seeing Victoria flourish; and although we did not entirely share the ideas for the future which he entertained for his settlement, not one of us had the heart to destroy the illusions which this happy father had nurtured round the cradle of this child.'

There must have been relief to learn that the intentions of the French were confined to those of a scientific nature. On the 9th of April, farewells were said and the *Astrolabe* and the *Zélée* weighed anchors and sailed off on the next stage of their long journey, ultimately unsuccessful, to find the South Pole.

A letter from George Earl to Captain Francis Beaufort at the Hydrographic Office in London gives a good account of contemporary events:

Victoria
Port Essington
4 April 1839

My Dear Sir

The arrival of Dumont D'Urville's ships, L'Astrolabe and La Zélée in Raffles Bay, affords me an opportunity of communicating with England by way of Hobart Town, a much more direct mode than any that has presented itself to us for a considerable time.

My last letter to you went by way of Coepang six weeks since. Since then several events of some importance have taken place in our little colony. ...The *Britomart* has made a visit to the islands, and three Macassan prahus are at anchor off the town, the crews being busily employed in collecting trepan and tortoise shell, in the search for which they have been very successful.

I accompanied Sir Gordon Bremer on his recent visit to the islands in the *Britomart*. We first proceeded to Dilli, the capital of the Portuguese settlements in Timor, which has been so much abused by Kolff..... Dilli stands in the same relation to the Portuguese colonies in India that Norfolk Island does to Sydney: – it is their penal colony. The convicts of European extraction are transformed, on their arrival, into soldiers. You can readily imagine how oppressed the natives of the country must be when power is put into the hands of characters of that description. In fact the town is in a continual state of siege, the inhabitants of the interior frequently making inroads to the very walls of the forts.

On our return to Port Essington, we stayed a few hours at Kissa and Moa. The *Britomart* was the first British man-of-war that had been seen by the natives, and the urbanity of Sir Gordon made a most favourable impression on them. A whaler (English) had touched there a few days before us. Now that this island is known, it is likely to be a great resort for whalers, for I never saw a place where the wants of a passing vessel could be supplied with more readiness, or on more moderate terms. I found, on this my second visit, that nearly all the natives who crowded the beach, could speak a few words of English, which they must have learned since my first visit a few months ago. In fact they are perfectly aware of the great benefit they are likely to derive from communication with us. A young man, a dependent and distant relative of the raja, came with me to Port Essington in the capacity of domestic [Shadrach Philippus]. He is a Protestant, writes a good letter in the Malayan language with English characters, and is by no means deficient in general knowledge, which of course, he has obtained through the Missionary established at Kissa. In common with most of his countrymen, he rejoices in a most amiable and docile disposition, and has proved of great service to us in giving us hints in tropical agriculture. I purpose letting him visit Sydney, which he much wishes to see. Wherever we shall want them (and they are the best of agricultural labourers) there will be a perfect rush of islanders into our colony. All the young men are anxious to come with us, the most intelligent appearing the most enterprising.

...This part of the world is interesting in the extreme, particularly as far as the native inhabitants are concerned.

I will conclude, my dear Captain Beaufort, by thanking you once more for having permitted me to converse with you thus, for sometimes, while writing I fancy that I am addressing you in proper persona, and you will naturally suppose it brings forward many pleasing associations.

With the highest respect I remain
My dear Sir
Yours very sincerely
Geo Windsor Earl

Work continued on the completion of the infrastructure in Victoria. Under the supervision of Lieutenant Stewart, the pier was completed to the low-water mark. It was an excellent piece of engineering, almost 50 yards in length, the outline of which can still be seen today. Final touches were made to the main buildings: the hospital; the storehouse; the blacksmith's smithy; the victualling store. Victoria Square, around which many of the houses were built, looked, after a fashion, rather like an English village. The gun batteries were under construction and the guns themselves, five 18-pounders and four 6-pounders, had been hauled up and were ready to be installed at Adam Head overlooking the harbour. Nevertheless, it must be remembered that Victoria was a rough-and-ready place, isolated and some fifteen miles inland from the open sea. The conditions were testing for the 60 or so garrison and settlers.

The settlers had been encouraged to grow vegetables such as cabbages and pumpkins, and the rains had provided good conditions for the gardens to flourish. The soil was reasonably rich, and bananas, oranges and lemons were growing well, while the sugar cane and cotton were looking stronger. In May, the rainy season ceased, the south-east wind blew steadily, and the weather became cool and agreeable. With the settlement reasonably established, expeditions took place around the Cobourg Peninsula and into the country beyond it. Lieutenant Stewart returned with favourable reports. George did not go on any of these expeditions, preferring to stay in and around the settlement and at his cottage where he had all his books, his papers and his writing. He was recording anything and everything of note, exemplified in the letters, papers and reports he sent back to the Royal Geographical Society and the Royal Asiatic Society, among others. At the same time he would not shirk a duty or an opportunity to help or be involved in activity at the settlement. He was popular, if opinionated and irrepressible.

By the end of May 1839, Sir Gordon Bremer felt satisfied that Victoria was well established. In addition to the village and its battery, imposing with its guns on top of the white cliff commanding the entrance to the harbour and giving the settlement quite a warlike appearance, an excellent survey of the great Port Essington and the coast to the east had been carried out by the crew of the *Alligator*. He decided that the time had come to travel back to Sydney and report on all matters directly and personally with Governor Sir George Gipps. George Earl, who had prepared a comprehensive report to enable Sir Gordon to give a detailed, positive account to the Governor, would also make the voyage accompanied by his manservant, Shadrach Philippus. Gipps would not yet have had any authoritative news on the progress of the settlement and eight months had elapsed since that founding fleet set sail from Sydney bound for the North.

Taking over the command of the settlement was Captain John McArthur, Royal Marines. Aged 47, a man of great experience from 30 years of soldiering in many parts of the world: an artilleryman, engineer and administrator, artist and draughtsman, he was well qualified. About 40 marines and nine civilians remained at Victoria, along with the sturdy *Britomart*.

On the 3rd of June, the *Alligator* set sail, taking with her the crew who had laboured hard in the building of Victoria, as well as the survivors of the *Orontes* whose hulk lay on its side at the north-west end of the port.

Scurvy, the ever-present danger for seafarers, broke out on the *Alligator* as she made her way to Sydney, and it was feared that the inhabitants of

Port Essington had also been affected. Soon after the *Alligator*'s arrival in Sydney after a 36-day voyage, the sixteen-gun sloop, HMS *Pelorus*, left without delay for Victoria laden with stores for the settlement and some supplies for the *Britomart*. (These fears were unfounded because Victoria had supplies of vegetables from the gardens as well as cabbage palm from the interior of the peninsula.) In addition to the *Pelorus*, a 500-ton former convict ship, the *Gilmore*, was hired to proceed to Victoria with cattle and working oxen.

It had been hoped that orders throwing open Port Essington for settlers would be received at Sydney before Bremer and the *Alligator* arrived. Bremer was greatly disappointed to find that this was not the case and that, in fact, Sir George Gipps, the Governor, had received instructions from the Secretary of State in London that he was not to encourage permanent settlement at Victoria, nor to grant permanent title to any adjacent land. This was an obvious impediment to development for who would provide the investment for the establishment of the merchant houses necessary for trading, as well as that needed for the growth of the settlement? Bremer brought every pressure open to him to bear on the Governor. He worked hard to find a compromise as otherwise Victoria was doomed to the long-term status of a garrison and no more. In all these discussions, George acted as adviser to his Commander. The Governor had his orders but was finally persuaded to compromise and to agree that 'permissive occupancy' could be given to those seeking land within the township of Victoria. More in hope than conviction, Bremer was able to issue the following notice:

PORT ESSINGTON.

> Notice is hereby given that persons of respectability resorting to Port Essington for purposes of trade, will be permitted to occupy, for a period not exceeding seven years, town allotments, containing each about half-an-acre of land, within one mile of the pier at 'Victoria', and suburban allotments of five acres each, within five miles of the same, on the conditions undermentioned.
>
> Parties desirous of availing themselves of this permission are requested to transmit written applications to that effect, addressed to me, at the Harbour Master's Office, in Her Majesty's Dock-yard, Sydney, specifying the allotments they wish to obtain, and the time within which they will be prepared bona fide to enter upon the land, if approved.
>
> The conditions are the following; viz. the lease to continue for a period

not exceeding seven years, but renewable or not at the discretion of the commandant, or of Her Majesty's Government.

The payment of an annual rent, at the rate of five shillings per half acre; the lease to be determinable at any time by the commandant, on giving a twelve month's notice.

All improvements to be effected at the expense and risk of the lessee.

The lessee not to destroy or injure timber, &c., without previous permission.

(Signed) J.J. GORDON BREMER,
Commandant of Her Majesty's Settlement of Port Essington. Sydney, Sept. 1839.

Not one person in Sydney or elsewhere took up the opportunity presented. There were too many other options for investment, and freehold land was easily available around Sydney and in New South Wales. In addition, there were rumours that the settlement was not to be permanent and would soon be abandoned, as others had been in the North. Bremer and Earl were sharply disappointed.

The *Alligator* was due to return to Port Essington but was diverted because of disturbances by convicts on Norfolk Island. About 800 miles to the east of Sydney, Norfolk Island had been discovered by Captain Cook some 70 years before and was now a small penal colony. Sir Gordon Bremer and his man-o'-war were the only present source of hard power and discipline available. It is possible that George was on this expedition to restore order. The mission was successful and the ship returned to Sydney.

The *Alligator* prepared to return to Port Essington at the beginning of November. Due to the unfavourable monsoon winds, it was the wrong season to sail westwards through the Torres Strait. They took the southern passage around Cape Leeuwin and up the west coast of Australia. The *Alligator* did not proceed directly to Port Essington as Bremer sailed to Penang, Madras and finally to Trincomalee, where he received news that would change the direction of his life. Admiral Sir Frederick Maitland had died and Bremer was appointed Commander-in-Chief of the Indian Station and took his command in the 74-gun HMS *Wellesley*. This was to be a parting of the ways for George Earl and Sir Gordon. They had shared a vision and ardently believed that Port Essington would prosper given the proper support, funds and management. With Bremer's departure the settlement had lost a great champion.

George stayed with the *Alligator* for the return in due course to Victoria where life went on as before with the building of roads and clearing of scrub. The gardens were tended and building completed. The livestock landed from the *Gilmore* had to be looked after and throughout there was an air of peaceful industry. As November 1839 passed, it grew hotter and more humid; the regularity of rain showers accompanied by thunder and lightning increased. George, still stranded a great distance away on the *Alligator*, was not in Victoria to witness the catastrophe.

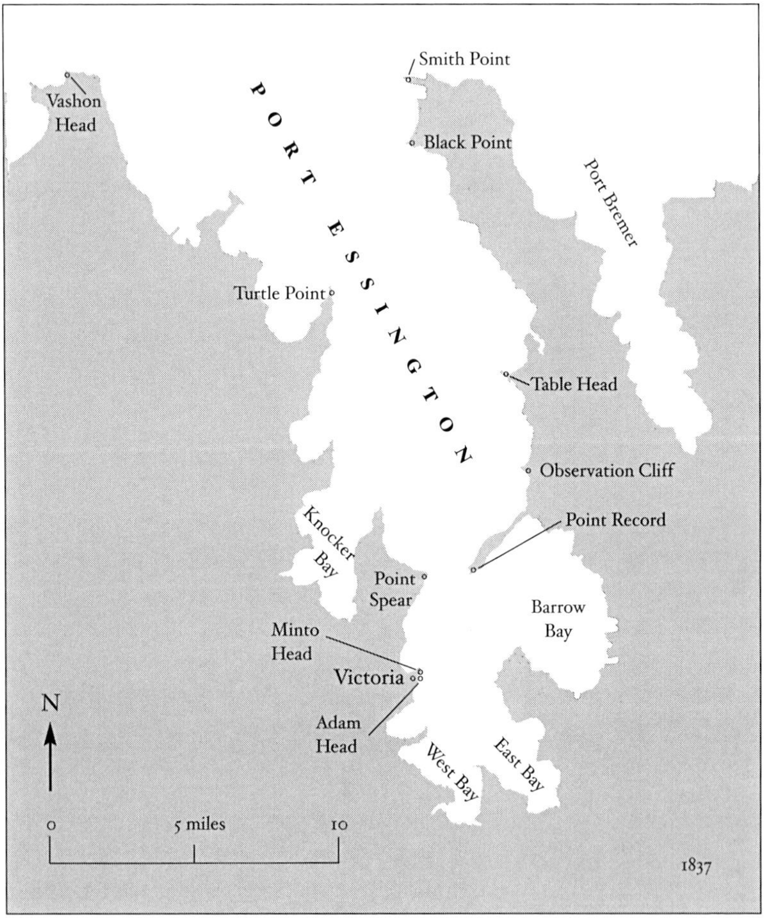

– Chapter Ten –

Winds of Change

1839-1842

With respect to the settlement, everything is going on most favourably. No sickness, and there has not yet been a single death in the garrison. We have done all we can do until this place is open to settlers.

•

During the evening of the 24th of November 1839, a very heavy thunderstorm accompanied by forked lightning hit the Cobourg Peninsula and Port Essington. This continued for about three hours, then the sky gradually cleared. On the 25th, the atmosphere grew ever more ominous during the day and by 8.00 p.m. it was blowing a heavy gale and the barometer continued to fall until 10.00 p.m., when a great hurricane struck Port Essington. Roofs were blown off, houses were demolished, the partially completed church (for which £300 had been donated by the Bishop of Australia) was destroyed. Government House, unceremoniously lifted off its stone base and dumped a few yards away, was one of the few structures to escape destruction. Many parts of the village were flooded by raging seas. Small boats were lost, the pier washed away and storehouses flooded.

The *Britomart*, which had been preparing to sail for Sydney the next day, was held to her mooring by her short anchors. She would require repairs before being seaworthy again. But the *Pelorus*, which had recently arrived from Sydney to relieve the settlement, rolled and shipped water so badly that she became unstable, dragging her anchor as she was swept towards the shore which she struck with great force. The terrifying power of the wind and tides ten feet higher than normal put the vessel onto her side and with the seas breaking over her, the masts were smashed and her superstructure obliterated. Twelve members of her crew were lost, but the rest were rescued by a wheeler under Captain Owen Stanley from the *Britomart*. On land, crops were destroyed and many of the trees broken or uprooted, with the leaves stripped from those that remained. The hurricane had raged unabated until the dawn of the 26th. It was four days before relative calm returned. Little escaped this catastrophe. Captain Stanley wrote: '...what has been done during the last eighteen months by a hundred men is entirely destroyed'.

The settlement was not only shattered, it was profoundly isolated. The nearest European colony was in Dili (in present-day East Timor), some 400 miles away across the Timor Sea. To reach Sydney and return would take more than ten weeks by ship. Work had to begin anew, with the rebuilding of the settlers' morale an early task. Spirits may have been down and tempers frayed, but determination was paramount. Rations were tight, materials limited and so the best that could be achieved was essential patchwork. With the *Pelorus* a wreck, work to make good the *Britomart* proceeded apace, and by the beginning of February 1840, she was ready to sail to Sydney. Fortuitously, within a few weeks of the disaster and during the next three months a few commercial ships arrived at Victoria, bringing vital supplies.

Early in March 1840, the faithful *Alligator*, under new command, returned from Singapore with food and medical supplies on her way from India to China. On-board were George and Shadrach, back after an absence of nine months. George was in despair at what he found, but immediately threw himself into the reconstruction. Then, to his joy, at the end of that month the first of the hoped-for Macassar prahus arrived. This was a trade that he had predicted and knew to be vital as it could underpin a successful commercial future for the settlement. The major interest for the prahus was the trepang fishing, but all the vessels brought needed supplies of rice, sugar, poultry, cloths of various manufacture, artefacts and general goods.

During 1840, Victoria was largely rebuilt and restored, as supplies and materials arrived from Sydney and elsewhere. The *Pelorus*, initially written off as a wreck, was painstakingly refloated and repaired, a work of extraordinary brilliance under the circumstances. A year after coming to grief she was considered seaworthy (only just), and sailed from Port Essington never to return. She limped into Singapore in July 1841 where Sir Gordon Bremer, who was there at the time in his capacity as Commander-in-Chief of the Indian Station, decided that she was of no further use to the Navy and was sold.

Throughout the year, the morale of the inhabitants of Port Essington had been fragile. In spite of the preoccupation of the existential need to rebuild the settlement, the shock of the hurricane and its destructiveness had taken its toll on residents and trade alike. The situation was exacerbated by a schism between the crew of the wrecked *Pelorus*, who felt marooned and frustrated, and the pioneering settlers. Victoria was not able to offer much in the way of traditional divertissements for sailors on shore leave and George's diplomatic skills were called upon on many an occasion. This was particularly so in the strained relationship between Captain McArthur, the wise and steady, if sometime crusty, Commandant of the settlement, and the perverse and unpredictable Captain Chambers of the stranded *Pelorus*, who considered himself to be the senior officer. Peace broke out every now and again but, until Chambers finally left for Singapore with the *Pelorus*, the atmosphere was bitter and the community suffered. There was a conspicuous sense of relief for all parties after she sailed away.

The *Lulworth*, one of the ships that had visited in the aftermath of the hurricane, again sailed in from Coepang with a cargo of buffalo. On her departure she carried away John Armstrong from Victoria. He had fulfilled his role as appointed botanist to the original party that had sailed from England and had worked diligently both as botanical collector for the Royal Gardens at Kew, as well as gardener to the new settlement. Personally, he considered that he was overqualified for the latter role and felt that it was time to move on. He had, in fact, dispatched 597 specimens from the Cobourg Peninsula on the *Britomart* when she had sailed in February 1840 – no mean achievement. George keenly felt the loss of an educated and informative companion.

Nevertheless, George thought that McArthur was 'in excellent health, notwithstanding annoyances, and is the same good-hearted, upright old man [he was 49!] as ever.'

Life now unfolded with monotonous routine. George wrote many reports and letters to the like of Captains Washington and Beaufort. He had described his main responsibility at Port Essington to be the collection of information 'which might prove useful to the colonists in the event of the settlement being thrown open to private enterprise by the sale of Crown Lands', and stuck assiduously to this task.

Early in 1841, the good ship *Heroine* made her first visit to Port Essington. This was of particular satisfaction to George as the vessel was owned by his old friend in Singapore, Dr José d'Almeida. She was a Colonial brig of 130 tons and ideally suited for trading among the islands from her base in Singapore. She would work as far south as Sydney and become, virtually, the mothership for Port Essington, bringing livestock and refreshments, along with those little articles of luxury manufactured in the home country which become almost necessary to Europeans in tropical climates. It is fair to say that the regular presence of the *Heroine* was largely due to George's personal relationship with the d'Almeidas. The Macassar prahus arrived for their season, loaded with welcome supplies of rice, fish and turtle. The visitors sometimes outnumbered the garrison sevenfold, but as George observed, '... their conduct was invariably ordered in the extreme'. The pattern of life in Victoria was further enhanced early that June by the arrival of the merchant vessel *Sesostris* and the *Britomart* under Captain Stanley, both from Sydney and carrying provisions. These two ships were greeted with intense excitement and pleasure, as they brought not only stores but also news of the outside world, fresh faces and mail. Captain Stanley had resisted the assignment from Beaufort to visit Port Essington, believing it to be a colony doomed to failure, and noted the sharp deterioration of Victoria since his previous visit. He wrote that George Earl looked 'wretchedly ill'. Earl complained to Stanley that Commandant McArthur's authority was being undermined by visiting naval officers who considered themselves superior in rank to McArthur who technically was still Acting-Commandant. An (anonymous) observer wrote of McArthur: 'Interfered with, and opposed, as he had hitherto been, by the commanding officers of men-of-war touching at this post, I can only wonder that he has had the temper to persevere in such uphill work.'

The *Sesostris*, after replenishing her water tanks and stocks of fresh vegetables, continued her voyage a few days later to India, while the *Britomart*, old friend of Port Essington that she was, stayed for a few days longer. There was always some pressure not to overstay a welcome as the settlement's own supplies were always somewhat restricted. The *Sesostris* carried on her departure the following letter from George to his 24-year-old sister, Elizabeth ('Libya'), in England:

Port Essington
June 10th 1841

My dear Libya,

The Britomart with a store-ship arrived a few days ago, and brought me a letter from you dated March 23rd last year ... and is the only one I have received from you since July last year. I know you have sent many, but suspect that Captain Beaufort enclosed them as usual with Sir Gordon's packet and that they went on to China from Sydney instead of coming here. I am just recovering from an attack of inflammation in the eyes in consequence of a boat excursion along the coast, so do not be surprised if my pen spells badly.

The arrival of the Britomart has altered my plans a little. I accompany Captain Stanley to Amboyna, Banda and the other islands in the neighbourhood, returning to this place in about five months. After that I shall proceed in her to Singapore and I trust from that to England but of this I am uncertain for Captain McArthur our Commandant does not like the idea of my leaving although no one would more readily forward my views. The fact is we are unfortunately situated with respect to Colonial officers. I hear that an officer of engineers is coming here. In that case, as he will be sure to be a man of ability I shall be able to go home without leaving Captain McArthur unsupported. Tell our dear Mother that I am quite well and as happy as I can be when absent from you both. My position is in fact as favourable as can be conceived.

Colonel Breton takes this letter to Madras and forwards it overland so that you will receive it before one that I wrote to our dear Mother nearly a month ago. God Bless her and give her a hundred kisses for me. Your letter is full of marriages and deaths. I am so glad that you have given that Captain something, with the mustachioes and flummery I think his *congé* [undoing/unceremonious dismissal].

The 27-year-old George then dispenses, with some lightness, his worldly wisdom as the paterfamilias, albeit at a great distance, of the Earl clan.

I did not like him [probably a reference to Libya's future husband, John Loftus Hartwell] much from the two lines in your letter I received last year. So the 'Newfound Hero' is plausible is he? I am afraid Miss Libya that you have too many strings to your bow. Take care they don't slip through your fingers. You are right however not to take so serious a step without looking well before you leap and rather than choose badly, choose not at all. Do not be in a hurry as you have plenty of time before you. Poor Mi! So she really is not married yet. I think I must take compassion on her when I go home. I am glad to hear that Belle Bremer is married for it would have been a pity that a girl of so fine a disposition and so well calculated for a married life should have remained single. I don't half like Captain Browne [Belle's husband?] though, a tinge of jealousy perhaps. If you show Belle this letter, I will give you a trouncing, mind. I am glad you are intimate with her and thought you would be from the first. There are so many points of similarity in your characters. So poor Sarah is still single.

The *Britomart* has been at Pt. Nicholson, or Nick as it is called, and some of the officers saw Dan and Mrs Riddeford. The Doctor and his squaw were at Sydney. Dan was flourishing about with an old fisherman's hat on his head and a 'they-know-there-is-no-pride-about-me' sort of an air. Miss had sole possession of the Doctor's house. The doctor has got into a scrape from which he can never recover. He first lost the confidence of the Company [the East India Company] by tampering with government for a situation, and then offending government by signing a violent paper against the governor and the best of the joke is that, in repentance coming, he said that he signed the paper while laboring under an opiate administered by his wife. That woman has mined an excellent man.

Do you know that I anticipate not a little credit my dear Libya for my labours in this part of the world. I shall be able to produce on my return, in conjunction with Stanley [Captain Owen Stanley] who will contribute charts and drawings, one of the most interesting works that has appeared for some time. The present voyage is to extend our observations to every island of the group. You know I am not vain, so will give me credit for what I say upon this point.

Shadrach sends his humble respects. He returns to Kissa with us after having been in my service for two years and a half. Parting with him will be losing my right hand, but I want him to see his friends. I shall take him again into my service if I come out again after my return to England. He takes with him a pig and a ram to improve the island breed and I have given him my dog Smike who will be a sort of canine missionary to the uncivilized dogs of Kissa. Kindest remembrances to Major and Mrs Sweetman and love to Percy [his brother whom he thought to be in England]. A thousand good wishes to our dearest Mother and believe me my dear Libya yours ever most affectionately

Geo. Windsor Earl

There were a few afterthoughts scribbled on the outside of the envelope, including:

Remember me to William James and tell him we will have a long talk when I return about matters familiar to us both. At Amboyna I hope to hear something of Captn. Gardner and his wife (late Miss March) who went as missionaries to New Guinea. You have heard that my poor friend Williams the missionary has been killed at Errolmango [sic].

I have plenty of dogs but no cat. I had a Malay one with a crooked tail but he ate my chickens so I gave him to the natives who ate him. Shakaloo and Juno [family pets] must be getting up in years. You have told me nothing of the Douglases which is wrong. Sir Bentinck is my well-wisher so you must be certain I should like to hear of him. Adieu.

A short while before the *Sesostris* and the *Britomart* had arrived, a report was received from local Aborigines that a large ship had been stranded in Van Diemen Gulf and that small boats containing men had been seen sailing away. George, consummate sailor that he was, had set off on the voyage of some 50-60 miles in the settlement's decked boat to investigate, but had to return because of a sudden illness. We do not know precisely what the affliction was, although he had referred to 'inflammation of the eyes' in his letters. Shortly afterwards, two small boats containing the captain and crew of the English ship *Montreal*, which had been wrecked after striking a reef in the Torres Strait, sailed into the harbour. Although they were warmly welcomed, it was immediately recognised they would be a further drain on the settlement's supplies. Nevertheless, an incident such as this was one of the justifications for Port Essington's existence.

The *Sesostris* had also carried away a letter from Earl to Captain Washington, Secretary of the RGS, giving an upbeat account of the settlement:

9 June 1841

My dear Washington
The *Britomart*, with a store ship, arrived here four days ago, and has put us all in high spirits, for she had been absent so long that we scarcely expected to see her again. You will be glad to hear that Stanley has determined to sail for the islands in a few days, going first to Dobbo, on the Arru [sic] Islands then to the Ki Islands, and after gathering all the information possible at these places, proceeding to Banda and Amboyna, and returning by way of Kissa. I accompany him this time, of course, and am delighted at thus having an opportunity of seeing the islands of this group that I have not yet visited.

I am suffering from inflammation of the eyes, resulting from exposure to sun and night air during a recent boat excursion along the coast to Cape Don, but I hope you will be able to read my writing.

The prahus came in earlier than usual this year, and, I am sorry to say, brought more goods than we had money to purchase. They did very well however, and their supplies were most seasonable. The men indeed are almost entirely clothed in the cotton goods they brought – the slops in the store having been expended long before. Among the nakodahs [Malay chiefs] was one whose prahu had been driven past the Wellesley Islands (the usual limit of their voyages) by a strong NW wind, into the bottom of the Gulph [sic] of Carpenteria, where she anchored in 1½ fathoms on the mud bank, the low land barely visible to the southward. He found the water so fresh he filled up his water-casks along-side the prahu. On making enquiries of the old nakodahs, I found they have nearly all, at different times, experienced the same thing. In fact, from this circumstance they call the sea to the east of Wellesley Island the 'Eyer taman' or fresh water. There must be a considerable body of water formed out here during the rainy season to render the sea fresh as far out...

With respect to the settlement, everything is going on most favourably. No sickness, and there has not yet been a single death in the garrison. We have done all we can do until this place is open to settlers. We have a nice little town, tolerable fortifications, and gardens which supply us abundantly with vegetables, while the ships which call occasionally to see what is to be done here, furnish us with all the luxuries we may wish for. The rains last season were rather more abundant than usual. We had showers nearly every day for five months, while in former seasons we used to have intervals of sometimes of a week of clear weather. The consequence was that the gardens situated in the settlement, where the soil is poorer than elsewhere, produced better than the others, as in the latter the yams, sweet-potatoes, and other roots, vegetated too luxuriantly to produce good crops.

I shall endeavor to get home to England after my return from the islands, but fear that I shall not be able. Captain McArthur does not like the idea of my leaving, nor should I wish to leave were I not certain that a viva voce statement of what we have been doing here is very much wanted at home. I shall only say that every doubt I had concerning the probability of success to the colony has been cleared up, and many advantageous points have come to view that I never before anticipated.

God bless you, my dear friend. My last letter from you was dated 2 years ago; but I suspect that many of my letters have been sent to India under cover to Sir Gordon Bremer.

Believe me ever yours sincerely
Geo Windsor Earl

PS Captain McArthur is well and desires to be remembered to you. We have not yet had the slightest difference with the natives, and owing to the extremely judicious conduct of Captain M. they are more orderly and under better control than I think were ever Australian natives before. Not even a petty theft has occurred for nearly six months. We have discovered a large Banian tree near Knocker's Bay, which the natives

> hold in high veneration, and call it the tree of the Spirit by whom they suppose it to be inhabited.

Earl's reference to the fresh water found at the southern part of the Gulf of Carpentaria alludes to the contemporary belief that the enormous mass of Northern Australia contained a vast inland sea that drained into the Gulf. In *The Eastern Seas* he had written: 'The shores of this sea, from the smoothness of the water and the consequent accessibility of all parts of the coast, would present a field for European colonisation unequalled in any known part of the world, and it should be an object of the British to take possession of them, were it merely to prevent any foreign nation from posting themselves at the back of the settlements which we already possess in Australia.'

Later that month, George set off for a two-month voyage on the *Britomart*, now commanded by Captain Owen Stanley. This was to be both a flag-waving exercise, and a charting expedition to the Arafura Islands. After their return in mid-August, George filed a detailed report containing an overview of the native peoples, including their agriculture, trade, religions, resources, governments, history and economics to Captain John McArthur. However, Captain Owen Stanley of the *Britomart* did not see much merit in George's endeavours. Stanley wrote to Captain Washington: 'To Mr Earl I must refer you for all minute details about these people as he has been longer about them, and has never had anything else to do than to make himself acquainted with their manners and customs.' Perhaps this observation could be interpreted in the spirit of the Duke of Gloucester's comment to an author upon seeing yet another large volume of his work, 'Always scribble, scribble, scribble! Eh, Mr Gibbon.'

In July 1841, Earl presented a bill for payment with regard to his salary of £50 for the period April 5th to the 5th of July. Normally, such bills would be payable 30 days after presentation, but George drew it for payment at three days. This matter (deemed an 'irregularity') would ultimately come to the attention of Sir John Barrow and the Lords Commissioners of the Admiralty. George Windsor Earl would (in 1842) receive a minor wrist slap from London (to be administered by McArthur) but this incident was serious enough to be taken up at the very highest levels of the Navy and indicates, perhaps, George's sometimes cavalier attitude at times toward authority.

Just after the *Britomart*'s return to Port Essington in the middle of August 1841, the *Beagle*, which had been surveying in the Gulf of Carpentaria, arrived. She was now under the command of Captain John Lort

Stokes, a well-known figure in the early days of North Australian exploration. Anxious not to stay unnecessarily long in the harbour, both vessels prepared for their next voyages. The *Beagle* set sail for Sydney via the Swan River, carrying with her lists of stores required back at Victoria. It was George's familiarity with the *Beagle* which is partly responsible for the belief among his descendants that he sailed 'with Darwin on the *Beagle*'. He never did so; Darwin's friend, Augustus Earle, sailed with Darwin on the *Beagle* as the appointed artist, hence the confusion.

The *Britomart* sailed for Singapore mid-September 1841, Captain Stanley having decided to transport the stranded crew of the *Montreal* so that they could arrange their return to England. He also wanted to pick up orders from his Commander-in-Chief, Gordon Bremer, as to his further duties. George accompanied him, under orders from Captain McArthur, to obtain in Singapore cattle, medicines and other supplies needed at Port Essington. When the *Britomart* arrived in Singapore, leaking badly, the duty senior officer there decided that her condition required a full survey. She was ordered to sail with Stanley to Moulmein (a port in southern Burma famed for its shipbuilding and repairs) where she was again surveyed, and condemned. It was the end of her naval service and her long association with Port Essington, begun nearly five years beforehand when she had sailed from Plymouth with the first party.

George was now marooned in Singapore, a prospect which probably did not overly disturb him. Not for the first time he based himself with his friends, the d'Almeidas. He spent about four months there as it was not necessarily an easy task to obtain passage to Port Essington. He was able to do so in February 1842, when he sailed on the *Heroine* bound for Victoria with a cargo of buffalo, pigs, medicines and other supplies for the settlement. Also on-board was the owner Antonio d'Almeida, son of George's mentor in Singapore, Dr José d'Almeida. The d'Almeidas were to be a source of much support in the anticipated development of Victoria as a thriving entrepôt between Singapore and Sydney, and for the islands to the north.

From March to August 1842, George was on base in Victoria and commanded the team that '[a]fter six days' unceasing exertion', according to Captain McArthur, refloated the merchant ship *Lord Auckland* that had foundered on a reef while leaving the settlement. The gardens and plantings had suffered badly from the poor weather earlier in the year and there was little real progress to report. In August, Earl sailed on the brig *Camelian* to Sandalwood Island and Macassar, locales previously unfamiliar to him, with the intention of furthering his trade enquiries.

When he returned to Port Essington, Earl prepared a comprehensive report detailing many aspects of Timor, the Celebes, Bali, Lombok and Sumbawa. Addressed to Captain McArthur and dated 20th of September 1842, of particular note is its ethnological study of the interconnecting relationships of the different races among the islands with particular focus on the Aborigines of the greater Cobourg Peninsula. He also had collected artefacts (including skulls) which were sent back to England (although what became of them is not known).

His general reports were forwarded by McArthur to Sydney and then onward to the Colonial Secretary in London. In these reports, and certainly as we see in his letters to Washington and Beaufort, George continues to describe conditions at Port Essington in the most optimistic language. Residents, crops, health, climate, animals, morale, prospects, are all referred to glowingly. Was he deceiving himself as well as others? Perhaps; but they certainly demonstrated his optimistic spirit and unceasing efforts to promote the settlement.

The Reverend John Williams, Earl's friend who perished at the hands of cannibals on Eromango in the New Hebrides.

Macassans curing Trepang at Victoria, Port Essington.
Drawing by H. S. Melville, 1845.

– Chapter Eleven –

Storm Clouds Gather

1843-1845

...a more zealous, acute, or intelligent gentleman I have scarcely ever met...

•

A year and a half had now passed since George had written in high spirits to his sister, 'Libya', but there were no signs of fulfilling his plan to return to England. As the wet season passed into 1843, a few vessels came and went including, again, the *Heroine* with Antonio d'Almeida, this time on-board with a cargo of buffaloes, pigs, general items and equipment. The wet season, usually from late November to early March, had begun in October and was to last, with unceasing damp, into April 1843. In the middle of February, there was the first sign of coming troubles. A Royal Marine, a man of great strength and fitness, caught a fever and, after a few days, died.

To the surprise and delight of the settlement, two large vessels appeared in the dawn of an early March day, both men-o'-war. One ship was immediately recognisable as the *Alligator* which had brought the founding settlers four years beforehand; the other was the 28-gun warship, HMS *North Star*. Both had sailed from China in the aftermath of the August 1842 signing of the Treaty of Nanking that ended the First Opium War between Britain and China. The *Alligator* had been converted into a trooper and carried a cargo of surplus material left over from the conflict which was to prove very useful to the settlement's stores. The *North Star* carried as commander, Captain (Sir) Everard Home, who had been ordered to visit Port Essington and to report back to headquarters on the progress made there and to assess the very viability of the settlement. He and his party were royally welcomed by Captain McArthur who proceeded to give a thorough and detailed update on every aspect of the life and business of the settlement, all parts of which were visited and examined by Captain Home. In Home's report of April 1843 to his Commander-in-Chief, Vice-Admiral Sir William Parker, after describing the buildings, gardens and livestock holdings, he noted the following:

> Although the present state of Port Essington is by no means inviting to a casual visitor, it holds out, in my opinion, great hopes of success to the

> permanent settler; its geographical position is admirable, more particularly since the fortunate results of the war with China, which will in all probability bring the subjects of that empire into close contact...

In the same report, Captain Home also described the 31-year-old George Earl, '...a more zealous, acute, or intelligent gentleman I have scarcely ever met, and to whom I am indebted for a great deal of useful information...' Earl is further cited a number of times in the report:

> ...In the opinion of Mr. Earl, settlers from Timor, and the islands northward would be best. ...I have consulted Mr. Earl, and his opinion is, that one of the objects in forming this settlement was, that it might become a port of refuge for vessels that had received damage in the adjacent seas, and for crews of such as might be lost, it has certainly proved beneficial.

In conclusion, Home wrote:

> Among the probable advantages to be derived, were this place permanently established, would be the increase of coasting vessels, commanded by Europeans and manned by natives, which would be likely to engross the trade of the islands northwards, as far west as Celebes, which is at present carried on by means of prohus [sic], an inferior description of vessels which can only make one voyage to and from in the course of a year. As the coasting vessels above alluded to would make several voyages in the same period, they would supply European goods, almost the sole article of trade at these islands, and which are now only attainable at Singapore at a much cheaper rate.

However, incidences of sickness and fever in Victoria now became a major concern. Men who had been hale and hearty, now in addition to those who had not been so, succumbed to fever and malaria. Deaths occurred regularly, while many suffered intermittent fevers of varying seriousness. Activity in the settlement ground to a standstill. Building work ceased and little or no attention was paid to the gardens, the animals or general maintenance. An outbreak of scurvy added to the problems. Peter Spillett in *Forsaken Settlement* writes: 'Out of the total number of forty-six people in the settlement, including the women and children, only two people escaped the epidemic'. George was not one of the lucky ones, he wrote of 'a severe attack of rheumatic fever, caught while exploring the Lumpo Batang Mountain of Celebes'. The local fever was impartial: even natives living near Victoria caught the illness. George's servant, Shadrach, drew attention to a crucial fact; the Macassar trepang fishermen found the inner harbour (south of Point Record) the best water to crop the trepang, but would never stay or camp there. They knew they would sicken. The shores of the outer harbour seemed to be a much healthier spot.

The chosen site at Port Essington had not been favoured by George, amongst other sceptical voices. He had felt that Victoria, some 21 miles down the inlet, was too far from the open sea and too far from the shipping lanes. Large vessels would find it hard to enter and leave because of the prevailing winds and physical hazards. At some 600 miles from the dangerous Torres Strait, it could not provide immediate aid to distressed ships from that area. Earl's choice would have been to the east at Barkers Bay, some 80 miles away near to the Bowen Strait and between Croker Island and the Cobourg Peninsula. In this he was influenced by the advice of Captain Laws who had then recently surveyed that area. However, the Admiralty, fully supported by Bremer, had opted for Port Essington because it fulfilled the requirements for a naval station. The voices of those who envisaged a commercial emporium in the area of Barkers Bay were not heeded. Later, George Earl was often credited, or for that matter criticised, as having been the main advocate for the Port Essington site, but this is not so. However, his official position on the viability of Port Essington was another matter, as evidenced by his comments to Captain Home.

Governor Gipps in Sydney wrote to Lord Stanley, the Secretary of State for the Colonies on the 13th of April 1843 and enclosed reports he had received from Captain McArthur and George Earl, dated the 20th of September 1842. McArthur had written:

> ...[R]especting the settlement Port Essington [and the correspondence from Lord Stanley] I have perused with intense interest. ...Mr Earl has been constantly urged to collect and embody information that might tend to dispel the doubts which seem to influence the public mind respecting the internal capabilities and external connexions of this portion of North Australia. ... Mr. Earl has this moment presented to me his Report. It is rather voluminous; nevertheless concise and perspicuous [sic] in style, much more interesting than the last, and opening out sources of trade, in a manner, to my apprehension, so decided, that I shall wonder indeed if it has not some effect.

The *Alligator* set sail for England, taking with her some of the sick, and at the end of April 1843, Sir Everard Home departed for Sydney in the

North Star, arriving there after the 2,000-mile journey on the 16th of July. On-board were George Earl and Shadrach Philippus with a letter dated the 26th of April 1843, from Captain McArthur to the Colonial Secretary in Sydney, Deas Thomson, explained the reasons for George's journey:

> Mr. Earl proceeds to Sydney by this opportunity. I beg to submit to his Excellency [Governor Gipps], that he is a gentleman eligible to the appointment of magistrate, and to add that his health has suffered severely, but I trust, only temporarily, and that the voyage may restore him to his usual activity and strength.

Governor Gipps concurred with McArthur's recommendation and on the 17th and 22nd of August, George Samuel Windsor Earl was, appointed, respectively, 'a Magistrate of the Territory [Port Essington] and its Dependencies', and 'Commissioner of Crown Lands at Port Essington', as noted in *The New South Wales Government Gazette*, of August 29th 1843.

It was possibly a mercy that George was able to escape Port Essington, as the epidemic there continued and the death toll mounted. Governor Gipps had recommended to Lord Stanley in his letter of March 1844 that the garrison be relieved, but that this would have to be done by the Navy as were he to do so it would, 'in no way accord with the views of Her Majesty's Government were I to send troops from this colony to Port Essington'. In the same letter Gipps wrote:*

> Mr. Earl, who arrived in Sydney by the "North Star" will return to Port Essington by the first opportunity, after having been made a magistrate and a commissioner of Crown Lands. I shall avail myself of the opportunity of his return to send two or three cows to the settlement.

Amongst the ships that came and went occasionally from Victoria over the subsequent months was the HMS *Royalist*, sent for the regular protection and support of the settlement. She had arrived in July and by

* That Sir George Gipps, Captain-General and Governor of New South Wales, should concern himself with the cows at Port Essington is indicative of the care he took as an administrator. His governorship (until 1846) was marred by unceasing invective from the locals over land, education and Aborigine issues. Today he is considered to have been one of the finest of the Colonial Governors in Australia.

mid-September 1843, four crew members had died including her captain, Philip Chetwode. Even that iron-man, Captain McArthur, was afflicted. When the *Royalist* sailed for Singapore in early October, Port Essington had again lost its protection.

While George was recovering his health in Sydney, he could have not but been aware that the future prospects for the settlement were very much in the balance. The long-held official position from London was that Port Essington was primarily a naval station, and not necessarily a permanent one. Much as in the case of the Swan River development, the government in London was ambivalent about the settlement's commercial development as this would require further state expenditure. The powers in London were obliged, and probably predisposed, to look more closely at existing facts than to imagine what might be. That London had blocked the sale of land in Port Essington on terms that matched sales elsewhere in Australia continued to be an impediment to development there. In Australia herself, although Sydney had not been particularly concerned in general with Port Essington, the Legislative Council of New South Wales was to determine what benefits might accrue from the establishment of an overland route to the settlement. On October 9th 1843, a committee met and George Earl was one of the principal witnesses. The line of questioning directed at him primarily dealt with Port Essington's ability to attract native labour and of the religious persuasions of those who might come.

Earl was, of course, very positive about the prospects for new labour, especially from the Serwatty Islands, Timor Laut and Kissa. Surprisingly, the Committee also questioned Shadrach Philippus, and one can imagine that this was at George's urging. Shadrach outlined his education, Christian upbringing and belief that the port would attract native labour. John Dunmore Lane, DD, was a spectator at the hearing and wrote that 'Shadrach Phillippus [sic] was remarkably interesting and intelligent young man, somewhat intermediate in physiognomy between a South Sea Islander and a Malay'. Shadrach's testimony appeared in Sydney's *The Australian* on November 2nd. The Committee forwarded their recommendations to Governor Gipps along with the desire that £1000 be set aside to cover the expenses of an exploration party. Gipps demurred and forwarded the report to London.

* * *

In a letter from Lord Stanley to Governor Gipps of the 14th of March 1844, Stanley wrote:

> I have received and had under my consideration your dispatches... together with the enclosures it contains from Captain M'Arthur and Sir E. Home.
>
> I regret to say that the result of the perusal of this correspondence is not such as to show the settlement of Victoria at Port Essington to have advanced so rapidly towards becoming a commercial entrepôt...
>
> Under these circumstances Her Majesty's Government have felt that they would not be warranted at present in incurring any larger expense than is already allowed for the maintenance of the settlement, nor in placing it upon any more permanent or regular footing...

In the same letter, Lord Stanley recommended that McArthur be allowed to lease land in the settlement under the Australian Land Sales Act but that: 'It will, I am afraid, be impossible to give these persons a certain or permanent tenure...' Land matters at Port Essington remained as per the 14th November 1843 statement from the Colonial and Land Emigration Commissioners: 'the commandant not to sell any lands, but only grant leases for periods not exceeding one year at a time...'

The letters and reports sent by Captain McArthur to the Governor and the Colonial Secretary in Sydney during 1844 were to become increasingly discouraging. Sickness among the inhabitants continued to cause distress and alarm, and supplies of medicines were in short supply. McArthur sent the settlement's decked boat, the *Lady Jane*, to Cape Croker to beg medicines from passing ships, but without success.

The *Bintang*, a merchant ship, arrived from Sydney in May 1844 carrying supplies and medicines as well as George Earl, returning reasonably fit after an absence of just more than a year. After recovering from the serious effects of malaria, he had managed to spend the rest of his recuperation in Australia with friends. He was also able to do some travelling around New South Wales. This was of particular relevance to his later interest and involvement in the discovery of Australian gold. He had stayed with his old friend, Edward Cox, at Mulgoa, some 40 miles west of Sydney, and Cox had told him that a shepherd in the nearby Wellington Valley had found gold nuggets. In the course of his travels over the previous years, George, wearing his geological hat, had developed a theory that the mountain ranges of Australia were a continuation of the Asian ranges which extended south-easterly from the Urals through the Cambodian and Malayan ranges. With his guide and companion, Thomas Hood, he traversed the Blue Mountain range and the Wellington Valley and became certain that minerals, including gold, were there to be discovered.

Captain McArthur remarked in a letter to the Colonial Secretary's Office after George had arrived back: 'I was truly happy at Mr Earl's return and hope he will have escaped all the evils of our unwholesome seasons'. But George had not escaped altogether. On his return to Victoria in May 1844, he wrote to Captain Beaufort at the Hydrographic Office in London, recording the details of his journey back from Sydney. For the first time, one of his letters sounded less than optimistic.

> I am sorry to say that on my arrival at Port Essington I found the garrison suffering very much from ague. During the first three years scarcely a case of this occurred, but the men have now been so long in a tropical climate, living upon provisions not affording sufficient nourishment to sustain men working under a tropical sun, that they have not now, as formerly, stamina to resist its attacks.

Earl concluded with:

> I trust, my dear Sir, to have the pleasure of seeing you soon in England. I have enjoyed tolerable health for the last three months, my stay in Sydney having done me so much good, but I suffered so acutely during the previous twelve months that I cannot hope to have my health fully reinstated until after some months' stay in the old country. I am also anxious to go home from my having now visited every place of importance in these seas.

Two months later, in July 1844, Captain McArthur wrote to Captain Home who had visited Port Essington a few months previously. The letter contains nothing of encouragement. 'I cannot report favourably on our condition and state in any point of view.' Then, in November 1844, McArthur sent a letter to G.W. Hope at the Colonial Office in London that fully captures the existential issues concerning the settlement at Port Essington.

> Victoria
> North Australia
> 28 November 1844
>
> Sir
> I am honoured by the command of Lord Stanley, as communicated in your letter, dated 15th March last, with its various documents for my

information. I have perused them with all possible attention, and can only avail myself of this opportunity so far as respectfully to submit such immediate impressions as some passages make on my mind...

I respectfully submit that we have been established here six years under Her Majesty's Commission forbidding any encouragement whatever to occupation of the lands, and afterwards terms were offered which no man felt would secure him such a tenure as could remunerate for any outlay.

I did receive some enquiries and overtures notwithstanding, so that this incipient attempt evidently created attention and is satisfactory in proof that there are parties willing to speculate, but the terms once named, and they directly or very soon withdrew. Thus it appears to me that no sufficient encouragement to erect a commercial entrepôt here has been proposed. I beg leave to say, I confine myself entirely to what has come to my knowledge.

I believe His Lordship is right in concluding that these regions are inimical to European labor, but it is only necessary to exercise a circumspect regard to the public interests with the busy pushing capitalists, who are searching every quarter of the globe, whilst a population fitted for the labour is quietly introduced. These, once naturalized and satisfied by a judicious treatment, then the capitalist generally will perceive that he has encouragement and can speculate with a degree of security. Then land ought to have a respectable and permanent value.

I hope I am not delivering my crude sentiments in a manner that will excite the most distant suspicions of an intrusive disposition.

...You will further please to inform his Lordship that the settlement has suffered much dilapidation from the want of labourers. I have had about me most willing minds, but I regret to say prostrated powers; and free of all venal and every predilection, never could a small body of men have exerted themselves with more constant fortitude, amidst great suffering.

...As a military post, strictly considered, we are too far up in the port. Spear Point would be more suitable in every respect. In fact, it is the key to the harbour. Hence, I have abandoned all thoughts of executing the fortifications in stone on Minto Head which were formerly projected. It would be an error. Still, great advantages have derived from our present position, procuring more communication with, and better command over, the natives of distant tribes south east of us who are the most troublesome of them all. I believe they have learnt to respect us more than formerly they did.

...We must not expect the influx of capital and property, which the more genial climes of the south have received, but the position will be analogous to that of the first settlers of Botany Bay until motives shall arise to induce shipping to visit the infant colony. I say the position will be analogous because I can conceive it can avail nothing that the extension of commerce since the olden times has produced such prodigious traffic to and fro, we shall be passed by as though we were not, cut off by position from participating in the benefits of a stream of commerce which is silently but certainly gliding past our very door. I cannot view this fact without pain, and I am sure it will instantly occur to His Lordship's mind that if we had the power of opening this facile communication ourselves we could do more towards encouraging commercial intercourse in one year than we shall now by hard labour in six. I believe I am not mistaken.

...I hear reasons expressed that there is no reason why this port should not present the scenes of another Singapore. Let this be supposed, then ask what is the character of its population? When did Europeans settle there, and to what extent? It must, I think, be replied: for a long period, as far as Europeans are concerned, it had only a solitary adventurer or two, but respecting its inhabitants generally it cannot even now be viewed as a European population, but as a mimic Babel of the extreme East, and owes its best attractions not to a fine, deep, land locked harbor, but to its simple position standing immediately in communication with a great thoroughfare, the highway of Indian commerce, and as that source of wealth extended itself, so did Singapore, under the auspices of an enlightened government benefit, spring up and at a few bounds became what it is. In this respect, and this only, do I perceive any reason for turning our eyes upon Singapore as an example of encouragement. If the first settlers here are introduced from the Islands, or whatever other place, there will be formed a good basis, if put in judicious position at first; but if it be where they must be isolated will, I conceive, mar the very object to be obtained – poor they come, they will see no hope of improving their condition, and poor they will gladly return from whence they came. But upon the coast they will, during the East monsoon, have frequent opportunities for bartering the little fruits of their industry. The masters of vessels will soon become acquainted with the fact and perceive the advantage they presented to them. Trepang, tortoise shell, fish and garden produce, I expect, will be immediately available. For other more valuable commodities we can only speculate.

If among the settlers there be Indians or Chinese possessing a little property, it may be supposed they will employ small craft to navigate amongst the Islands which are not exposed to interdict of Dutch Treaties and laws. The passage is short and easy. They will procure and bring here in safety the first fruits of their voyage and by gradations commerce ought to be better understood, and shipping will be bought to this place.

I have hastily thrown these observations together, at a moment when application to other affairs is demanded. I must beg to claim His Lordship's indulgence, and his pardon if aught herein should bear the semblance of impropriety. I feel sensible I need his consideration.

I have the honour to be, Sir,
Your most obedient servant
Jno McArthur
Captain Royal Marines, Commandant

This letter is a true *cri de coeur* and skates the boundaries of the time in addressing one's superior officers. McArthur was a man of staunchness and loyalty, not given to exaggeration, and is here fighting as best he can for the continued life of the settlement and for it to be given an opportunity to flourish.

While George's health had been greatly improved, he was still clearly not fully recovered, and conditions in Victoria reactivated the distressing symptoms of malaria. Returning to England, about which he had thought and written for three years, became a necessity rather than the wish expressed in his letter of May 1844 to Captain Beaufort. Captain McArthur, in a letter to the Colonial Secretary's Office in Sydney, added a postscript: '14th September – Mr Earl has been recommended by the Medical Officer here to invalid and was brought forward for that purpose. I regret to say there was too sufficient cause. He, with three men of the detachment, are to take passage on the Royalist.'

Captain McArthur, was to miss George's presence – for his company, intellect, energy, experience and support. In addition, his departure would be keenly felt because of his facility with the Malay languages spoken by visiting fishermen and traders. Fortunately, McArthur was soon able to employ George's former servant, Shadrach Philippus, as linguist and general assistant.

With his normal energy and *joie de vivre* somewhat dimmed by illness, George carried out the duties of his new appointment as Magistrate and Commissioner for Crown Lands. Meanwhile, he assembled and packed his belongings: the most important were his papers, notes and research documents. HMS *Royalist*, on which he was due to sail, arrived in Victoria in July and anchored there for six weeks. George had ample time to compose his mind and make all his farewells, the most difficult being those to his close friend and servant, Shadrach Philippus, and to Captain John McArthur.

Victoria, Port Essington, had been his home and lodestar for six years, although he had been absent on his various travels for circa two-and-a-half years during that time. That a short period in England would be beneficial to his health was the official position, but deep down he must have wondered when, or if, he would return, given the precarious existence of Victoria. On the 14th of September 1844 the *Royalist* weighed anchor and set sail for Singapore on the first leg of its journey back to England.

Chinese Junk in Singapore harbour, engraving from Jules Dumont d'Urville's, *Journey to the South Pole and Oceania...* Scene from the late-1830s.

Back view of Wildwood House, family home of the Earls,
Hampstead, 19th century drawing

– Chapter Twelve –

A Change of Circumstances

1845

...an affair of the heart...

•

Bound for home, George travelled first on the brig *Royalist* to Singapore. There, after a reunion with the d'Almeida family and seeing other friends including the Logan brothers (of whom we will hear more), he took ship for England, arriving in April 1845, after an absence of seven years. It was the third time he had made the long, East-to-West voyage, but on this journey he was unwell: malaria and dysentery had seriously debilitated him, and whilst his intellectual powers remained unaffected, his energy was greatly reduced. Wildwood and Hampstead could not have been bettered for sorely needed rest and recuperation.

His mother, now 60, was as welcoming and vigorous as ever and the household provided such nursing needs as he required. In order to regain his strength, he had to rest and learn to pace himself, two traits that did not come naturally. He also had to reckon with the news that his brother Percy, who had left his wife and three children and sailed from England three years previously, had also just returned to England (from New Zealand), and that his sister Elizabeth had married, perhaps unwisely.

The England to which they had returned was in a dynamic phase of expansion and development. The 1840s was a period of great national macroeconomic transformation from mercantilism to free trade. During this decade the population of England and Wales would grow from sixteen to eighteen million. The Industrial Revolution was progressing strongly and the country's mills and factories began to earn the appellation 'workshops of the world'. The railways were spanning across the country; journeys that once took seven days were now taking twelve hours. Parliament had recently passed the Reform Bill, which was to create a vastly improved people's representation, while the Chartists continued to upset the ruling classes with their demands for better and fairer treatment. The controversial and protectionist Corn Laws were finally abolished by Peel in 1846, too late to prevent the misery of Ireland's Potato Famine, but relieving the growing pressure of feeding the people of Britain. Free trade and the growth of Empire were very much the mood of the nation, and very much in George Earl's mind as a leading expert in an area that would largely contain the new Empire in the East.

Accompanying George on his return to England were his notebooks and papers and he set about consolidating and organising the wealth of information he had gathered. He focused on two subjects – anthropology and economic development, and began to produce a series of articles on racial types for *The Journal of the Indian Archipelago and Eastern Asia* which were to be published in Singapore. He also was preparing a paper (which was to prove of future controversy and significance), 'The physical structure and arrangement of the islands in the Indian Archipelago', for the Royal Geographical Society for publication in their *Journal* later in that year. However, his major task was now to complete, and arrange for publication, his new book, *Enterprise in Tropical Australia*.

The book is both a brief historical account of the Port Essington venture and a wide-ranging commentary on tropical Australia with its 'capabilities for producing articles of commerce'. With his usual eclecticism, he covers the geographical features of the Cobourg Peninsula, its soil, seasons and climate, and sources of labour, then considers the progress in general of other tropical and subtropical areas to the south in Australia. His purview had expanded from the trading role of a settlement such as Port Essington, to the wide-ranging trading potential of the other newly established colonial areas on the continent, based on what he saw as a plenitude of cheap Asian labour. In the writing of it, he was very mindful of his position as Commissioner of Crown Lands for Port Essington; and the book is warmly dedicated to Sir Gordon Bremer.

As George Earl saw to his need for physical recovery and to the task of preparing his forthcoming publications, in the family sphere his sister's husband, John Loftus Hartwell, was to play an important, if brief, role in George's life. Hartwell was born in 1801, but there is no account of him until Army records show that he was enrolled as a military hospital assistant in 1828, and then placed on half pay in September 1829. Recalled as an assistant surgeon at the beginning of 1831, he was employed for some years in various military capacities, latterly in Kent. In 1839 or 1840, he had met George Earl's sister, Elizabeth, when she was 22 or 23. Their relationship began and it was probably a cautious affair. Elizabeth, as we know, had some sort of physical deformity; she was well-educated, extremely close to her arguably indomitable mother whom she had chosen to look after, and had not been given to gadding about. It is fair to say that she was unlikely to have been well-versed in the niceties, or otherwise, of amorous or romantic matters.

Mr Hartwell, on the other hand, had had an adventurous life. He was twice shipwrecked; first in 1829 off the coast of Newfoundland when he and the captain were the only survivors, rescued after 'frost-bite and starvation'; and second in 1836, when he was rescued after clinging to the mast of the wreck and injuring his head whilst firing a distress signal when the gun burst. He seems to have been a rather elusive character of the 'charming rogue' type. Nevertheless, their relationship blossomed and Elizabeth accepted his proposal of marriage.

They were married in the parish Church of St John's Hampstead (where she and her brothers had been christened) on the 22nd of February 1841, their witnesses included Elizabeth's mother and her brother, Percy William Earl. In a family memoir written some 75 years later it was recorded that: '[Elizabeth] had vowed she would never marry an Irishman, a soldier or a doctor. She married the three in one!'

George was in Port Essington at the time and in his letter to Elizabeth (Libya) of June 1841, he presumed that she was still unmarried. John Hartwell's residence was given as Canterbury in Kent; he was about 40, at least sixteen years older than his wife. There is no reason to suppose they were not happy, although there were some unusual aspects to their union. For instance, later in that year of 1841, the first Census in England took place and it lists Elizabeth Hartwell as living at Wildwood, but not John Loftus Hartwell, as if he had not moved in with Elizabeth or she with him. There is also the suspicion that he might have married her for her 'expectations', but had failed to charm the Trustees of the Earl family. Perhaps it was after discovering that Elizabeth's financial assets, while undoubtedly considerable, were of a long-term nature and legally tied-up; and that after a respectable period of time he decided to accept a posting with the Army Medical Service in Sydney, and left for Australia in 1846, where he was to die in 1849. The family view today is that he abandoned her, but it is perfectly possible that he had left to make his mark, and perhaps his fortune, and had every intention of returning to England or bringing her out to the East.

At the time of his marriage to Elizabeth, Hartwell was Staff Surgeon at the Royal Military Asylum in Chelsea where he remained until 1846. From 1844, he was a colleague there of a Captain William Siborne. Sometime soon after George Earl's return to England, Hartwell had introduced George to Captain Siborne, and this in turn led to George's introduction to Siborne's sixteen-year-old daughter, Clara. Up to this point, there is no record, of any sort, of George's interest in or experience with the female sex. There had been no real opportunity in his life, except perhaps when he was in London between 1835 and 1837, to develop friendships with girls of his own ilk, or pursue serious relationships with women. The nature of his life simply had ruled out anything of the sort, although in the letter he wrote to his sister from Port Essington in 1841, he was very much alive to questions of marriage, the suitability of young ladies, and so forth. In his written work there are many references to the female sex, but they are always detached, intellectualised, clinical – observations rather than experiences. And yet it is improbable that as a healthy, adventurous, good-looking man he had not been led astray on any number of occasions between the ages of sixteen and thirty-two. It is not overromantic to suggest that on meeting this lovely young girl he became smitten. Neither of them had much romantic experience or emotional baggage from previous relationships to complicate matters. If the nature of their relationship during the ensuing years is indicative, they approached each other in an open-hearted way.

She was attracted to this fine man with his handsome, sensitive face and blue eyes, his skin tanned by sea air and Eastern sun. She was impressed, too, by his talk, his laughter, and stories of the experiences he had had in the wide world. She must have been somewhat in awe of him, unusual as he was; known to Ministers of the Crown, Governors, Admirals, senior people in all walks of life as well as Malay seamen and Chinese traders; a man whose book *The Eastern Seas* was read far and wide; whose views were listened to and debated by the Royal Geographical Society and the Royal Asiatic Society; and who, above all, she found personable and amiable.

There was of course a difference in age and situation. At sixteen, Clara was little more than a schoolgirl, bright and intelligent, and from a good family with a strong tradition of military service. Apart from England and Ireland, she had not travelled. Although her brother Herbert had left home to join the Army, she and her sister were living in the shelter and comfort of a close family life, still very much in the care of their mother and father. They lived while in Chelsea in a respectable, middle-class Victorian London home, although in somewhat straitened circumstances. Until she was about thirteen, home had been in Dublin, but this would have made little difference to her development and education. Generally, girls were not properly educated in Victorian England and Clara and her sister were no exception. But they will have absorbed the culture of a professional military family and have been very aware of the high moral standards and the expectations which society demanded from them.

George and Clara will have had what can only be described as a whirlwind romance. Clara's mother and father clearly approved of him and, one suspects, more than just encouraged the match. Helen, Clara's mother, must have played a pivotal role in this romance which without her support and approval, would not have prospered. She herself was only thirteen years older than George and they, too, may have been fond of one another. Indeed, he signed the name Helen twice on the marriage licence application, crossing it out to write 'Clara'! A case of nerves, no doubt. He also entered Clara's age (incorrectly) as seventeen.

They were married by the Rev. George Clark, Chaplain of the Royal Military Asylum, at Trinity Church, the parish church of Upper Chelsea, on the 4th of April 1846, a year after his arrival back in London from the Far East.* The marriage was organised by Captain Siborne as befitted the occasion of his first daughter's wedding, and the witnesses included William Siborne himself and his friend Hayes Marriott (later General Sir).

Clara was born in Dublin in 1829, the third child of William Siborne and his Scottish wife Helen Aitken. Helen was the daughter of George Aitken of Todhall, Cupar, Fife and his wife Janet Ponson of Edinburgh. The Aitkens were a distinguished and long-standing Fife family; George Aitken was a banker, landowner and colonel of the Militia.

George's father-in-law, William Siborne, was an only child whose father and grandfather, both also only children, had been Army officers. William's father, Benjamin Siborne, had seen service in many places, not least in the Peninsular War where his regiment, the 9th or East Norfolk Regiment of Foot, took part in more than ten battles. In November 1813, he was severely wounded at the Battle of Nivelle in France and, after further postings, died on service at St Vincent in the West Indies in July 1819, aged 47, due to the after-effects of wounds received at Nivelle. Benjamin had married a Scottish girl, Charlotte MacCulloch, who accompanied him whenever possible during the six years of the Peninsular War. Her maternal grandmother, Mrs Janet Forbes of Peterhead near Aberdeen, is said to have helped the Old Pretender (father of Bonnie Prince Charlie) when he landed in 1715 at Peterhead. In return, he presented her with a silver quaich that is still owned by the family.

* Holy Trinity Church, also known as New Church, Sloane Street, had been built early in the 19th century, but was demolished and replaced in 1888. It is a wonderful building, designed by the architect John Dando Sedding. Although badly damaged by incendiary bombs during World War II, the great east window, the work of Burne-Jones and William Morris, survived.

Charlotte Siborne had given birth to Clara's father, William, on the 15th of October 1797. As his mother accompanied his father while on active service, William probably stayed with his godfather, Captain Douglas RN, in Greenwich until at the age of fourteen in 1811, when he joined the Royal Military College at Great Marlow and where he was commissioned as an ensign in 1813. After service in England he was transferred to his father's regiment and marched with it to Paris, remaining in France during the occupation by the allied armies. At the end of 1815, he was promoted to lieutenant but, when the regiment left for the West Indies, it had been reduced in strength to one battalion and he did not accompany it. He was placed on half pay in 1817 and remained in this state of limbo until 1824 when he was commissioned in the 47th or Lancashire Regiment of Foot.

The half-pay gap of seven years was disastrous for his career. We do not know how he kept himself busy, except that he published in 1822 'Instructions for Civil and Military Surveyors in Topographical Plan Drawing' and when in Scotland during 1824, he met and married Helen Aitken. In March 1826, William was appointed Assistant Military Secretary to Lieutenant General Sir George Murray, Commander of the Forces in Ireland. He held this appointment for seventeen years, serving three subsequent Generals: Sir J Byng, Sir R Hussey Vivian and Sir E Blakeney. During his time in Ireland, his four children, two daughters and two sons, were born. His eldest son, George, did not live long, while his younger daughter later married an Irishman. His younger son became Major General Herbert Taylor Siborne (1826-1902). Clara was his third child.

William Siborne was never able to resurrect his career but, although touched by melancholy as a result, this never crushed his spirit. He followed up his 1822 work on topographical plan drawing with a further book on the same subject in 1827. In 1830, General Sir William Hill, then Commander-in-Chief of the British Army, asked him to supervise the construction of a model of the field of Waterloo. He was given long leave from Ireland and lived for eight months at the farm of La Haye Sainte on the battlefield, where he made an accurate survey of the ground. The model was to show the positions of the troops battling at La Haye Sainte at 7.00 p.m., June 18th 1815. About 20ft by 20ft, and on a scale of 1 inch to 6 feet, it is truly a remarkable construction containing some 70,000 figures, each about an inch high and all with moveable arms and incredibly detailed uniforms. Trees, hedgerows, buildings, even the crops which covered the battlefield, are all precisely rendered. By way of further research, William corresponded with every surviving British officer of the battle as well as with military representatives in the Netherlands and Prussia. He received more than 700 replies. In 1833, the Ministry reneged on a promise to allot funds for the work, the completion of which he then undertook at his own expense, though ill able to afford it. The model was completed in 1838, at a cost of £3000 (approximately £200,000 today), and is now on permanent display at the National Army Museum in Chelsea.

William also comprehensively researched the history of the engagement at Waterloo and, after completion of the model, wrote his renowned book, *History of the War in France and Belgium, in 1815*. Published in 1844, it is still a standard work on the subject and a basis of all subsequent accounts. Unfortunately, both the model and the subsequent success of the book earned him the undying enmity of the Duke of Wellington, as both called into question the Duke's version of events at the battle, particularly with regard to the importance of Prussia's role in the victory.

Siborne had returned to Ireland while preparing his book and in 1840 purchased an unattached captaincy which was on half pay. In November 1843, his Irish sojourn came to an end when Army friends obtained a sinecure for him as Adjutant and Secretary of the Royal Military Asylum Chelsea (actually an orphanage) which position he held until his death at 62 in January 1849, not three years after his daughter's marriage to George Earl. He is buried in Brompton Cemetery. A sort of epitaph may be found in Fitzpatrick's *Life of Charles Lever*:

> I have endeavoured to give a sketch of the two principal figures who sat at Lever's dinner table as they were; of Captain Siborne, it will suffice to say that he was a perfect gentleman and a most accomplished officer, a man of fine intellect and judgment, thoroughly scientific, most unpretending in his manner and very well informed. Pity that the British Army was so constituted as to condemn a man like Siborne to an utterly subordinate and inadequate sphere of duty.

* * *

In addition his marriage to Clara, George had achieved much during his year back in England. He had attended numerous meetings at the Colonial Office concerning the future of Port Essington and saw through to publication (coinciding with his wedding) of his *Enterprise in Tropical Australia*. He also addressed the RGS with the paper, 'On the Aboriginal Tribes of the Northern Coast of Australia', which was to be published in

1846 in the Society's *Journal*. Captain Owen Stanley, well-known for his volcanic temper and his often unsuccessful attempts to control it, attended the reading and remarked, 'Master Earl always settles his theory first, and then observes facts in such a way as to make them subservient to his theory.' Stanley disliked Earl, finding him superficial and largely (but unfairly) responsible for the selection of Port Essington as the site for the naval station in Northern Australia. George, in common with others such as T.H. Huxley, had initially enjoyed pleasant relations with Stanley but these had soon soured. Earl also addressed the RGS with his paper, 'The physical structure and arrangement of the islands in the Indian Archipelago', and, as we shall see, there were to be long-running controversies arising from the material.

Not long after his return to England, Earl had also been in discussion with groups of entrepreneurs and investors looking for commercial opportunities in the East. However, his recurring malaria was a worry, causing him to pen a note to the Secretary of the Royal Geographical Society, dated February 6th 1846:

> My Dear Sir,
> I have received your note of yesterday and have to apologise to you for not having yet sent you anything, but I have been a great sufferer from rheumatic head-ache for some time past and the few moments I could devote to business have been occupied with the little affairs of our settlement at Port Essington.

Other concerns and pressing issues now confronted him. He was officially in London on sick leave but was expected to return to the settlement as he was still its Commissioner for Crown Lands and still receiving an income, albeit at half-pay. Pressure from the Colonial Office was growing for him to return to his post, malarial attacks or not. He wrote to his friend, Colonel Jackson, at the Royal Geographical Society:

> My dear Colonel Jackson
> I fear I cannot give you a continuation of the paper before the end of the week. I am going to be married in a day or two and I cannot bring my mind to bear on anything else, as you will very readily imagine. You should have it completed however before I leave England.
> Believe me,
> Ever yours truly
> George Windsor Earl

Clearly, the decision had been made to leave England. Earl was probably referring to the paper he presented to the Society which was to have been extended to cover the Aborigines of the neighbouring islands, but Colonel Jackson was never to receive this continuation.

George settled his other business affairs and arranged with the Trustees to sell the balance of his remaining inheritance for £958 14s (approximately £160,000 today). With this sum, his income such as it was from his books, lectures, papers, and his continuing salary as Commissioner for Crown Lands, he was for the present adequately funded. Moreover, discussions in the previous year with investors interested in developing railways in New South Wales had borne some fruit.

England in the mid-1840s was in the throes of a railway-building boom. In 1844, British investors saw the colony of New South Wales as a potential opportunity for railway development. They had sounded out various leading colonists there but found no immediate support, the latter believing that the colony would be unable to pay a sufficient return on the required capital outlay. Nevertheless, in 1845, three companies were formed in London to back construction of railways in NSW, and it was one of these companies that approached George Earl. He quickly recognised that the development of the colony would be considerably spurred by the availability of rail transport and advised them that, under the right circumstances, there was potential for a profitable venture. He was engaged to take the matter further on their behalf and commissioned, perhaps surprisingly, his brother, Percy, to prepare the ground in Sydney for the venture before George's own eventual return to the area. Percy had sailed for Sydney in October 1845.

The 33-year-old George and his 16-year-old bride now bade farewell to their families. For Clara, leaving her friends and close family at such a young age to journey halfway around the world to a relative wilderness and an uncertain future with a newly minted husband must have been daunting. It was an undoubted mercy that she did not know that she would never see her father again. For George, although he no doubt worried for his aged mother, the state of his sister's marriage to John Hartwell and brother Percy's wife and three children left in England (not to mention Percy himself), he was now returning to an area where he had already spent fifteen years of his life, and where he saw his and Clara's future.

The farewells over, they set off for Australia on the *Berkshire*, a 529-ton barque, on the 3rd of May 1846, exactly one month after their wedding. George and Clara Earl so began their new life together.

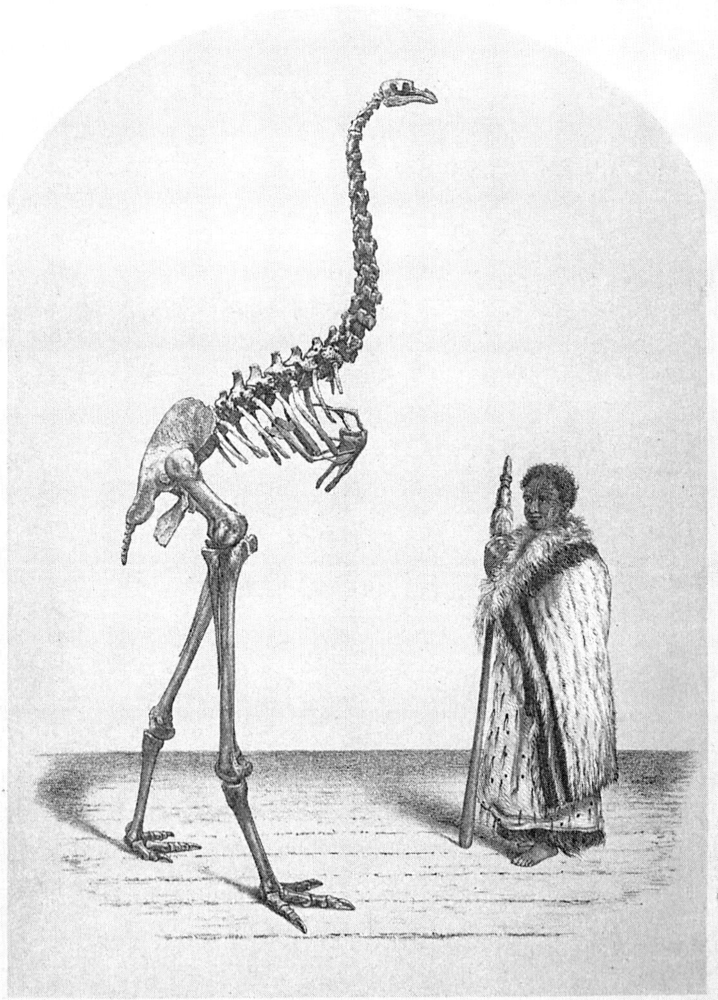

THE MOA OF NEW ZEALAND.
(DINORNIS GIGANTEUS)

– Chapter Thirteen –

Percy William Earl

1846

...Mr. Percy Earl, the enterprising naturalist...

•

George's brother, Percy, had arrived in Sydney on the 24th of January 1846 on the *General Hewitt* which, coincidentally, was once commanded by his father, old Captain Percy Earl, 30 years beforehand when she had sailed as a prison ship to the same destination. Percy immediately saw to representations on behalf of railroad investors in England by contacting one of the leading colonists in Sydney, Dr Charles Nicholson. At Percy's urging, Nicholson convened a meeting of local worthies on 29th of January, five days after Percy's arrival. *The Sydney Morning Herald* later reported:

> On the 29th January last, a public meeting was held in Sydney, for the purpose of taking the subject into consideration. This meeting was called at the instance, we believe, of Dr NICHOLSON, who had just received communications from England, which he thought it was desirable should be made known to the public. The correspondent to whose letters the Doctor attached the chief importance was Mr GEORGE WINDSOR EARL. This gentleman left the colony only two or three years ago; and from his local knowledge, combined with his high character as a man of scientific attainments and sound judgment, and with the circumstances of his being now resident in the British metropolis and moving in well-informed and influential circles, his opinions on this question were entitled to more than ordinary respect: and those opinions were decidedly in favour of the immediate introduction of railways into the colony. There was present at the meeting a brother of Mr EARL, who had lately arrived from England by the General Hewitt; and who stated that there was a strong impression at home, amongst the friends of these colonies, as to the desirableness and practicability of extending to Australia the great benefits of railway communication, and a disposition to invest capital in such undertakings. Indeed, Mr EARL assured the meeting, that if the colonists could make out a feasible case, could show that Australian railways would yield a moderate profit on the investment, they might calculate upon obtaining money in England to any amount; and that,

> notwithstanding the panic which was then anticipated from the crisis of the railway mania.
> At this meeting, which comprised many of the most wealthy, respectable, and intelligent of the colonists, a committee was appointed to collect information on the subject, and to report to a future public meeting.

Dr Nicholson, confessing to having become only recently a supporter of railway development, indicated that the route would be from Sydney to Goulburn, about 120 miles south-west of Sydney. The *South Australian Register* also reported on the meeting:

> The meeting was ably addressed, and at considerable length by the Chairman: by Dr Nicholson, MLC: Mr Earl (brother of the celebrated Mr George Windsor Earl); Mr W C Wentworth MLC; Captain MC O'-Connell, MC; Mr McDonald, of Pitt Town; Mr GC Turner: Mr HG Smith; Mr Campbell Brown; and Mr Raymond, Postmaster-General of the colony; and although there was much unanimity as to the general principle, the differences in the (mentally) proposed modes of carrying it out may be inferred from the various shades of avowed opinions as to cost per mile, which varied from £6000 (as broached by Mr Earl) down to £600, which Mr McDonald, who had lately inspected several railroads in the mother-country, declared to be sufficient for the Hunter River district, the claims of which he advocated.

No clear consensus was reached (there were a number of voices urging 'circumspection' and 'restraint'), but it was agreed that committees should be appointed to explore all aspects of the proposed enterprise. Percy was to spend a further eight months in Sydney and then, possibly because of plans made with his brother whilst they were in London, prepared to sail to the northern coast of Australia.

Percy had pursued an unusual path in gaining some worldly note as a naturalist. By accounts he was a chip off his father's block – energetic, fractious, volatile, charming and erratic. He had married without his mother's approval and support, and effectively was estranged. However, whilst he may have had many failings, he was creative and clever. After the disastrous Australian venture with George at the Swan River settlement, he returned to London in 1831. He married, had a child, and soon emerged, with the support and influence of his new wife's family, as a naturalist. He quarrelled with his mother over financial matters and we have seen how critical his Trustees were in 1835: 'I cannot think that you will attempt to deprive your mother to relieve yourself'. George had earlier written: 'Percy is doing no good for himself' and 'however, he is old enough to care of himself though I assure you it gives me great uneasiness'. Then, at the end of April 1836, he sailed to America from Liverpool on the ship *Florida*, along with his wife and small son (also a Percy William). His movements and activities over the following eighteen months are obscure, although we do know that his second son, Alfred Huntley Earl, was born in America on the 19th of August 1836. It is likely that during his time there he was involved with various American naturalist organisations.

He was back in London early in 1838, where his daughter, Elizabeth Rosa, was born on the 9th of April. Her birth certificate states place of birth as No.83 Quadrant, Regent St, while her mother's residence is given as No. 82 Quadrant. These properties were almost certainly owned by Percy's wife's family, specifically by her Uncle William, a relatively prosperous naturalist and mentor to Percy. Both Rosa and the second son, Alfred, were baptized at St James Westminster on the 31st of January 1839.

Between 1838 and 1842 it is probable that he was based in England; there was not the time available for him to have been far removed, and he was a witness at his sister's wedding in February 1841. He attended his children's christening, and the Census of 1841 lists him as being with his mother in Highgate, while Ann is given in the Census as being at the Quadrant. There is no mention of the children, but this is not wholly surprising as that Census was notoriously inaccurate. At the end of this period he seems to have abandoned his wife and three children who continued to live in the Quadrant, supported by her family and, perhaps in some way, by his mother in Highgate.

Percy had left London on the brig *Nelson* on 15th of May 1842 bound for Port Nicholson in New Zealand, where she arrived on the 24th of September. He had travelled under the auspices of the Royal Medico-Botanical and other learned societies for the purpose of collecting specimens of natural history and to help set up the Society of Natural History there. His arrival was noted in *The New Zealand Gazette and Wellington Spectator*:

> This gentleman is a Naturalist of the very first order, in the prime of life, and possesses all the requisite qualifications suiting him for the important commission which we were aware... had been entrusted to him.

> Mr Earl will immediately commence his labours by giving the Natural History of the Mollusca in the harbour of Port Nicholson.

Percy received a warm reception and while in Wellington he mixed with the good and the great, and was a prominent member of the Horticultural and Botanical Society, and sat on their committee. After a few months, he left Wellington for Akaroa, close to Christchurch in the South Island, at one time the proposed site for a French colony that never materialised. Nestled in the crater of an ancient volcano, it possessed a superb deep-water, sheltered anchorage. He sailed on 26th of March 1843 aboard the schooner *Shepherdess* and made Akaroa his base before slowly working his way southwards down the coast to Otago while undertaking his research.

Otago is the large territory of approximately 12,000 square miles, roughly south and west from Christchurch. Percy arrived at the whaling station, Waikouaiti, about 400 miles from Akaroa, in early November 1843. During the next seven months or so, he carried out his investigations and explorations in the area. As *The New Zealand Gazette and Wellington Spectator* was to report later:

> ...Mr Earl, who, it will be remembered, left this place for Otago about fifteen months since, for the purpose of collecting specimens of natural history in that vicinity. We visited him a few days ago, and were much gratified in viewing his specimens of birds, shells, insects etc. but especially so at the sight of part of the skeleton of the gigantic Moa. These are the first specimens which have been discovered in the Middle Island and are intended we believe for Museums on the Continent.

It was Percy's retrieval of the skeletons of the extinct giant-Moa, a flightless, ostrich-like bird that had stood some twelve feet tall, which would earn him contemporary note as a naturalist. The private secretary to the Governor of New Zealand and ethnologist, Edward Shortland, was accompanied by Percy, and Shortland gave this account:

> 4 Nov [1843]...On my return to Waikouaiti, I was shown some large bones, which had been discovered accidentally by a whaler, who, as he was walking along the neighbouring beach, struck his foot against one of them which projected above the surface. This he naturally enough mistook for a human bone; but on bringing it to the village, it was recognized by the natives as that of a bird now extinct, called by them a

> 'Moa,' and a search was at once made for more, with the idea that they would be saleable at Sydney or Wellington. Unfortunately, a pick-axe was used for this purpose, which, although very few were obtained, produced sad havoc among those left behind; as I discovered, a few days after, nearly the whole of a large number which I then collected, on the same beach, being more or less mutilated. These had been washed ashore during the night by a gale, the sea having, no doubt, stirred up the soil loosened by the former digging; and, as I was the first to visit the place, they fell into my hands.
>
> On examination, this part of the beach was observed to be composed of sand nearly as far as low water mark: then came a stratum somewhat resembling peat, being a mixture of fine sand and earth, with a large proportion of vegetable matter. In this the bones were embedded, as far as could be judged, in great numbers; but as they were always partially under water, it was not easy to get at them.

George French Angas, the English-Australian naturalist, explorer and painter (later Director of the Australian Museum) visited Port Nicholson in August and September 1844 and wrote:

> My friend, Mr. Percy Earl, the enterprising naturalist, was, happily for me, at Wellington during the period of my visit: and we spent many pleasant hours together, talking over the natural history of New Zealand. Mr. Earl had recently been travelling and exploring in the Middle Island, where there are but few inhabitants; and he intended shortly to return to Europe with the collections that were the result of his researches. Amongst other most remarkable specimens, he had obtained some recently fossilized bones of the gigantic moa, a struthious bird, formerly inhabiting New Zealand: this creature, according to the measurement of the bones, could not have been less than seventeen feet in height! Mr. Earl found his specimens at the mouth of a river on the East coast, buried in an alluvial deposit; this had been carried down by the stream from the mountains of the interior, and the bones were partly exposed by the receding tide. The natives have strange tales and legends respecting this bird; and some of the inhabitants about Otago affirm that it still exists in the extensive and unknown plains of the Middle Island.

Percy Earl and '6 cases Natural History' listed as cargo (and presumably Percy's) left New Zealand on the 15th of October 1844 on the *Bella Marina* bound for London. The ship came up the Channel in the February/March winds and landed a few weeks before George Earl's arrival from Singapore. While George Earl was in Hampstead and beginning his recovery from ill health, Percy began negotiating the disposal of his very considerable collection which included, in addition to the Moa skeleton bones, specimens of birds, bird's nests, molluscs, crustaceans and insects. There was much interest. Richard Owen, who was to become a driving force behind the establishment of what is today the Natural History Museum in London, organised the purchase of the majority of the collection for £130 (approximately £13,000 today) for the Palaeontology Department of the British Museum. There were 55 specimens with 32 collection numbers, many of which contain the name 'Earl' in the Latin designations.

The August 1845 sale of the collection was a considerable achievement. Percy remained in London for a further two months before his sailing for Sydney on the 20th of October 1845 to take up his career again.

After making representations in Sydney on behalf of his brother George and the railroad promoters, Percy left on his journey north on April 8th 1846 on the schooner *Heroine*. The *New Zealand Spectator and Cook's Strait Guardian* later reported that he '... intended to prosecute his researches as a Naturalist on the north coast of New Holland' (New Holland being the old, colloquial name for Australia). To travel to the north shore of Australia was not an everyday undertaking. Perhaps he and George and arranged earlier to meet at Port Essington whereupon Percy would journey on to New Zealand. The newspaper report quoted above mentioned his researches to be on the 'North Coast of New Holland', but *The New Zealand Spectator and Cook's Strait Guardian* one month later referred to 'researches as a Naturalist on the North coast of New Zealand'.

The *Heroine*, as noted before, was the regular supply ship for Port Essington on her voyages between Singapore and Sydney and was owned by George's Singaporean friends, the d'Almeidas. She was under the usual command of Captain McKenzie who, because of his knowledge of the route and experience in navigating the reefs, had agreed to act as commodore for two other ships sailing in company, the *Enchantress* and the *Sapphire*. Just over two weeks into an unremarkable voyage, the group reached the Torres Strait and on the 24th of April 1846 at about 1.00 a.m. the lookout spotted a reef ahead. Before any lifeboats could be lowered, the *Heroine* struck the reef at a speed of eight or nine knots and sank within six minutes. Captain McKenzie attempted to retrieve papers and 300 gold sovereigns meant for Victoria from his cabin, but it was already inundated.

Peter Spillett, in *Forsaken Settlement*, takes up the story:

> As the ship sank he [Captain McKenzie] took his infant daughter on his back and swam for their lives. He failed to see the reef and swam further away from the wreck. He was a strong swimmer, but with the weight of his child on his back and the long hours in the water, he nearly despaired of being picked up when, as the sun rose, he could see the *Sapphire* about a mile away. He gained further strength from the sight of her and again struck out, swimming with all his diminishing power. He managed to get within a quarter of a mile of her but no one appeared to notice them in the water. He called out at the top of his voice but there was no response. He saw the ship turn away from him and in his despair he turned his head to look at his child and found that she was dead. His mind was in a torment as he released his precious burden to the sea, and again swam frenziedly after the ship, shouting for all he was worth. The mate of the ship was up aloft taking a last look around for any survivors when he could just make out the figure of McKenzie in the water and immediately sent one of the boats to pick him up. He was lifted aboard in a naked and exhausted state after six hours exposure in the sea. After a few days spent in the vicinity of the wreck McKenzie transferred to the *Enchantress* and with the other survivors eventually arrived at Port Essington.

Eight people drowned including two young Irish-Catholic catechist missionaries who were accompanying the 33-year-old Capuchin, Father Angelo Bartolomeo Confalonieri, an Italian from the South Tyrol region. He had journeyed to Australia with a mission to seek converts in the north among the settlers and the Aborigines. Despite being unable to swim, Father Angelo survived the sinking. He later wrote:

> I had just been speaking with my dear companions James Fagen and Nicholas Hogan, when we struck on a reef... The sea has swallowed up everything. I saved only one shirt, the one I have to wear and a little crucifix about my neck, which, being tossed here and there by the violence of the waves and every moment being on the point of being carried before the inescapable tribunal of Divine Justice, I pressed fervently in my hands, recommending myself to the all merciful God. ...At daybreak, I found the Captain [McKenzie] clinging to some part of the wreck, I think it was the mast which I too providentially lay hold of. The Captain helped me as much as he could for I was both wounded and exhausted... This disaster has deprived me even of the letter of introduction to the Governor and with it hopes of succour in these regions! What will be my destiny for the future I do not know.

Percy Earl was not amongst the survivors. He was reported to have tied himself to 'his wife' with a rope that in the panic and confusion he believed to be loose. It, however, was part of the rigging and when the ship sank, it tugged the couple to their graves below. The 'wife' in question was a Miss Potts about whom nothing is known. Perhaps she was one of those adventurous, intrepid Victorian lady travellers, bound for Singapore or one of the East Indian islands at which the *Heroine* would call, and perhaps she was also a girlfriend of Percy's; the latter most likely.

Percy's life ended two months short of his 35th birthday. The wreck of the *Heroine* was not generally noted other than in Singapore, Australia and New Zealand as such sinkings were not unusual. However, news of the disaster reached Colonel Jackson, the Secretary of the Royal Geographical Society, who had last heard from George Earl in that letter written a few days before his wedding. As Jackson was putting through the press the Society's 1846 *Journal* that contained George's paper 'On the Aboriginal tribes of the northern coast of Australia', he appended the following note to the article:

> It was the intention of Mr Earl to have added to this paper his observations on the aborigines of the neighbouring islands of the Eastern Archipelago; but indisposition for some time prevented him from accomplishing the task, and when scarcely recovered, he re-embarked for Australia. We had hopes that Mr Earl would at some future period continue these interesting ethnological notices; but grieved are we to state that these hopes have been frustrated by his death. He was drowned, by the wreck of the vessel in which he had taken his passage to Port Essington.

This news must have had a terrible effect on both the Earl and Siborne families. William and Charlotte Siborne, receiving the news that husband and wife had drowned, would have faced the loss of their beloved teenaged daughter, only recently married and just beginning her adult life. George's mother, Elizabeth, would have had to absorb the shock of losing her favourite son and effective head of the family. For the Sibornes, there must have been a providential relief when they heard of the misapprehension. For Elizabeth, it could have been only a bittersweet outcome.

– Chapter Fourteen –

New Horizons

1846-1848

Not a place in the world like this can be found...

•

George and Clara Earl sailed, safe and sound, into Sydney Harbour on the 28th of September 1846. The *Berkshire* was the 'Post Office Packet' for the month of May 1846. She carried 3,624 letters and 11,700 newspapers for the colony and her late arrival caused much consternation. Shortly after her departure from England, in the Bay of Biscay, she 'sprang' her foremast which severely restricted the amount of canvas which could be set. The 147-day journey, a month more than usual, was often a misery for Clara who, as George noted, suffered dreadfully from seasickness. Unless George had received the news of his brother's death when they docked at the Cape of Good Hope, he will have arrived to hear for the first time of Percy's and the *Heroine*'s fate.

The couple found accommodation in Woolloomooloo, also known as Farm Cove, a pleasant and fashionable area on the southern shore of Sydney Harbour, about a mile from the business and government districts.

More than two and a half years had passed since George was last in Sydney and his immediate obligation was to present himself to the new Governor of New South Wales, Sir Charles FitzRoy, and to the Colonial Secretary. He needed to learn the latest news of Port Essington and, as Commissioner for Crown Lands, to discuss future plans for the settlement as well as scheduling his return to Victoria. Also high on his agenda was liaising with his dear friend from earlier days in Sydney, Edward Cox, and the investigation of future railway development in New South Wales.

George soon met with principal members of the group from the meeting addressed by his brother at the beginning of the year. As had been proposed, the project entailed the use primarily of English capital and this had resulted in a counterproposal for the establishment of a local company, the New South Wales Southern and Western Railways. While enjoying the interest of reputable local backers, it, too, had been unable to generate sufficient financial support. Other groups joined the bandwagon, but none developed a realistic prospectus that made plausible the necessary return on the required capital investment. It was generally thought that the attempt to form a railway company was premature: more accurate surveys (especially in the Blue Mountains) and viable traffic-revenue forecasts were required. George soon grasped that the project was nowhere near to inception, and although success was to come with the first public line opening in 1854, he was not to be involved.

George's future prospects must have caused him concern. He had not set foot in Port Essington for two years and his official positions required his presence there. Although during this period he had written and had published *Enterprise in Tropical Australia* – a work which in addition to its ethnological merits promoted Port Essington and the cause for development in Northern Australia in general – questions continued to be asked both of George Earl and of the settlement itself. In the near to eight years that had elapsed since the settlers first set foot there, no great progress had been made. True, the fear of foreign intervention on the Australian north coast had diminished, the safety of the seas in that area from piracy greatly enhanced, and a facility for damaged vessels and shipwrecked crews established. But the scale of the anticipated trade developments had not been fulfilled, further settlers had neither desired nor been encouraged to come, and little success had been achieved in growing crops or rearing and maintaining livestock. Morale had not been sustained and the climate was now discovered to be life-threatening. The record was not exactly one to earn the undivided support of the Colonial Office, given their cautious attitude to the site that had been apparent throughout.

The settlement's Marine detachment had finally been relieved in December 1844, with Captain John McArthur alone from the original garrison remaining behind, still in command. With the 56 marines on-board was First-Lieutenant George Lambrick RM, who had commanded the *Cadet* on the voyage to Port Essington from Dublin. The 30-year-old Lambrick would be second in command of the garrison at Victoria and be in charge of Pay and Quartermaster duties. He was accompanied by his wife, Emma, their eighteen-month-old daughter (also named Emma) and an infant son born during the voyage.

Peter Spillett in *Forsaken Settlement* captures the moment of the *Cadet*'s arrival:

> The pier drew closer and they could see the women and children and the marines clustered around the flag flapping a welcome to the vessel of mercy. Their faces were alight with excitement at the realisation that the long-awaited relief had arrived, but a closer look revealed the drawn,

> yellow faces of ones who had been long deprived of proper diet and medical care and the aftermath of long illness.

Captain McArthur's son, John, the settlement's quartermaster who was to be relieved in that post by Lambrick, had penned some doggerel verse of life in that remote spot:

> Not a place in the world like this can be found,
> If you search from the Poles the whole earth around,
> If to grumble and growl forever's your wish,
> Why, come and reside in a place just like this.
> If living you'd call't, from the world quite shut out
> Why then you'd do well, there's not the least doubt,
> And should you not know, how the time you should spend,
> I'll soon tell you how if attention you'll lend.
> You'd get up at six, walk and breakfast at nine,
> And then you might write, read, or sleep till you dine,
> That is if a few thousand flies, and the heat
> Would allow your poor body, or mind, such a treat.
> At three you'd perhaps dine off (such exquisite stuff)
> A slice of Queen's Own (which she's not known to touch).
> After which, if digestion to help was your plan,
> You'd go shooting or riding (that is if you can)
> Or if liking it better, you'd sail on the sea,
> You might spend your time thus till you came home to tea.
> The tea being over it brings on the night,
> The flies go to rest, the mosquitoes they bite.
> Then three or four hours, spent as you'd best like,
> Brings time for your bed, whence you'd rise with the light...

Another pest, far more dangerous, that plagued the settlement was the white ant (termite). They could, with the help of the damp, structurally destroy a building within a period of a couple of years. Preventative measures were only partially successful and, eventually, even the blockhouse and fort came under attack.

The rainy season of 1844-45 had passed with some serious illness and a few deaths, but with coming of better weather, morale improved somewhat. During the next few months, McArthur spoke to a couple of Malay *Nakodas* (Chiefs) and was encouraged about the prospects of a number of Malays coming to settle, as they felt restricted and exploited by the policies of the Dutch. Port Essington was widely, and officially, deemed unsuitable for European labourers due to the climate, so McArthur had had a notice (dated the 9th of June 1845) published in Singapore inviting Chinese settlers to rent land in the hope that they would, by their industry, stimulate the growth of a trading entrepôt.

Concurrently, there was discontent in the settlement, especially in the new garrison, as many of the men had not expected their military duties to include labouring, building and farming. In a letter of the 1st of September 1845 from Governor Gipps to Lord Stanley, he noted that Captain McArthur considered that the relieving party of Royal Marines, '... composed in great part of young recruits... less fit for the service than those who accompanied him to the settlement in 1838'. In the same letter, Gipps wrote:

> The accounts [from Port Essington] which I now transmit are, I think are satisfactory, though I am still impressed with the opinion that a further British Settlement is much required at or near the entrance of Torres Strait, and in the neighbourhood of Cape York, on which subject I shall, most probably, again address Your Lordship on the arrival of Captain Blackwood of Her Majesty's Ship "Fly," now daily expected at Sydney.

HMS *Fly*, on a surveying voyage, had visited Port Essington some four times from August 1843 to June 1845. A narrative published by J Beete Jukes, the ship's naturalist, noted:

> There is some talk of throwing open Port Essington as a colony, and selling land to anyone willing to purchase at the common Australian rate of £1 per acre. I'm at a loss to conceive what any one could do with land here, if he even had the whole peninsula given him...
>
> I believe it to be utterly worthless as a colony, or as an agricultural or commercial possession, and conceive the only argument for our continuing to hold it must be a political one.

Jukes probably had little or no idea of the political storm brewing behind the scene. In February 1846, three months before George and Clara had sailed from London, Queen Victoria had signed letters patent granting a charter for the creation of a new colony of North Australia to comprise all the territory north of latitude 26°, approximately what is now the border between New South Wales and Queensland. Then, six weeks after George's arrival in Sydney, the *Government Gazette* announced the imminent establishment of this new colony. Its main purpose was to provide a place of exile for transported, expiree and reformed convicts from British and Australian jails. The general mood in New South Wales was one of bitter opposition to the *raison d'être* of the new colony, and indeed to any further importation of criminals to Australia herself. From 1846 to 1853, transportation was one of the main political issues in Sydney and elsewhere. Although what was to be the last convict ship (with 269 male passengers) for settlement in New South Wales had arrived in November 1840, further attempts during the decade to land transportees had led to noisy demonstrations in Sydney and Melbourne. The perennial drollery that Australia was marked for glory, for its people had been chosen by the finest judges in England, was wearing thin.

Nevertheless, Port Essington was initially considered as a potential location for convicts from Britain and then for those who had gone through 'probation' and would be awarded land – until reports deemed it unsuitable for those purposes, which did little to recommend its suitability for those who were not convicts. George's long-held opposition to the use of convict settlers there was now largely irrelevant, but left hanging was the settlement's future status. In England, the new Secretary of State for War and the Colonies, William Gladstone, had been asked by the First Lord of the Admiralty, the Earl of Ellenborough, to sanction the withdrawal of the Royal Marines garrison from the settlement. Gladstone recognised that such would almost certainly lead to its abandonment, so he called for a report on this question and an exploration into the possibility of new settlements elsewhere in the Cape York Peninsula area. Uncertainty was to rumble on through 1846 and 1847.

* * *

Port Essington was in the limelight when news arrived in Sydney that Ludwig Leichhardt and his exploration party had stumbled out of the undergrowth at Victoria after a trek of nearly 3,000 miles. Leichhardt was a Prussian explorer and naturalist who had arrived in Sydney in 1842. He unsuccessfully tried to get government financial support for an overland trek but was able to raise funds from the private sector. The party of ten had left Jimbour, near Brisbane, on October 1st 1844 to attempt the first crossing of the land route to the north coast. Two of the party had soon turned back and one, the botanist, John Gilbert, had been killed by Aborigines during an attack on the explorers' camp on June 28th 1845. The remaining seven arrived in Victoria on the 17th of December after a

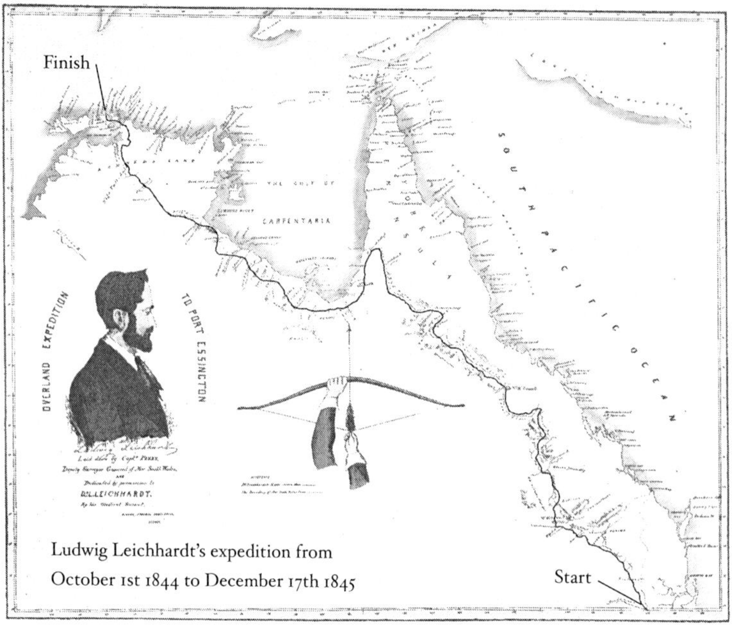

Ludwig Leichhardt's expedition from October 1st 1844 to December 17th 1845

gruelling journey of nearly 15 months. As the months had rolled on from their departure, their fate had become a national obsession, and the general assumption was that they had perished, probably at the hands of hostile natives. When they surprisingly arrived back in Sydney on March 24th 1846, they were hailed as national heroes: £1000 was donated by the government and £1500 raised from the public. Leichhardt wrote of his arrival in Victoria:

> We were most kindly received by Captain McArthur, the Commandant of Port Essington and by the other officers, who, with the greatest kindness and attention, supplied us with every thing we wanted. I was deeply affected in finding myself again in civilized society, and could scarcely speak...*

The success of Leichhardt's journey had raised the profile of Port Essington, and *The Sydney Morning Herald* was to report on May 10th 1847:

* McArthur was less taken with Leichhardt. His verdict: 'Bitter, virulent, malicious, dishonest and mean.' Leichhardt was to lead further expeditions and in 1848, he and his party vanished on an east-west journey to the Swan River. Their disappearance was to become an enduring popular mystery in Australia.

> Port Essington has given rise at various times to much speculation as to whether the Government intend eventually to colonise it; the successful overland route of Dr. Leichhardt will probably be more conducive to such an end than all that has been said and sung on the subject.

Nevertheless, the controversy over the future of the settlement was to continue with supporters and detractors equally adamant about their respective positions. That the issue – the existence of a tiny settlement of fewer than 100 souls 2,000 miles from Sydney – should give rise to such public passions is in itself perplexingly noteworthy.

* * *

Soon after his arrival in Sydney at the end of September 1846, George was in touch with Edward Cox and his wife, Jane Maria, of Fernhill, their estate in Mulgoa, some 40 miles west of Sydney. Clara will have heard much about the couple as George had visited Fernhill many times when previously in New South Wales, and he and Cox had ridden together on various expeditions into the nearby Blue Mountains. Three years earlier, Edward had told him that gold nuggets had been picked up by a shepherd in the Wellington Valley, just over the Blue Mountains, and George had travelled there on horseback and found 'eruptive' rocks associated with the presence of gold. Cox warned his friend of the dangers of a gold rush and cautioned circumspection. They agreed that George should advise the colonial authorities to carry out a full geological and mineralogical assessment. This was the basis for George's (not unrealistic) claim to have been the first person to anticipate the discovery of large amounts of gold in New South Wales and Victoria, but later on, considerable controversy was to erupt between Earl and the Royal Geographical Society over the matter.

The Coxes were then one of the premier families in New South Wales, if not in all of Australia. The founder and patriarch, William Cox, was born in 1764 in Wimborne, Dorset. He entered the Army and as paymaster joined the New South Wales Corporation. With his wife, Rebecca, and four sons, he sailed on the Minerva, a convict ship that arrived in Botany Bay in 1800. She carried 160 convicts, mostly Irish. William Cox grew to know them well during the voyage and came to see that they were mostly political prisoners, sentenced in the wake of the Irish Rebellion of 1798, rather than criminals. Cox was held in high regard amongst them and he was eventually to hire the Irishman, 'General' Joseph Holt, as foreman when Cox bought his first property, a 100-acre farm just outside Sydney. A long and close relationship ensued. Cox was to gain a reputation as having real ability and genius for managing men.

This 100-acre farm was the start of a property empire that encompassed sheep and cattle stations, and the creation of important, award-winning herds. Shortly after acquiring the farm he purchased much more land, but also managed to overstretch himself financially. The result was that in 1803, his liabilities were such that his assets were placed in the hands of trustees. He was still a serving military officer and, so meteoric had his short career in Australia been, suspicions were aroused that Regimental funds had been misused. He returned to England in 1807 to answer these charges, was cleared in 1808, and returned to Australia two years later.

William Cox also became a celebrated builder of roads, bridges and buildings. Famously, he was asked by Governor Macquarie of New South Wales to build a road through the Blue Mountains to the Bathurst Plains beyond. The route had already been charted and its purpose was to open up for settlement the lands beyond the mountains. Cox was determined

Detail of a watercolour by John Rae entitled *Woolloomooloo Bay and New South Head Road*. Dated 1842, it may have been executed later in the decade.
NATIONAL LIBRARY OF AUSTRALIA

to deliver an outstanding performance. With 30 convicts (whose reward was to be their freedom), five freemen and a guard of eight soldiers, he took six months (July 1814 to January 1815) to build embankments, cuttings, more than a dozen bridges, and 101 miles of 4-metre-wide road for wheeled vehicles. It was the stuff of legend and is still regarded so today. Governor Macquarie is reported to have said that, under a government contract, the building of the road would have taken three years. As a result, Cox was awarded two thousand acres of good, pastoral land near Bathurst.

After his wife Rebecca died, William married again and had more children. He set up all his children in various careers and businesses. His son Edward was born in 1805 and thus was eight years older than his friend George. Edward Cox had been given sheep stations as well as the Fernhill property, where in the early 1840s he built the mansion house, steadings and stud for his thoroughbred horses. When Edward and his wife learned that Clara was pregnant, Jane Maria appointed herself depute mother to Clara, and dearly wanted George and Clara to come and stay at Fernhill. George declined because he had to be within easy access of Sydney's business and government offices; and because Clara was going to have her first-born, he wanted her to be close to the best available medical facilities. Also, George's brother-in-law, John Loftus Hartwell, now an Army surgeon, would be close at hand. Hartwell had left London six months after the Earls when his contract with the Royal Military Asylum ended and was now at his posting in Sydney.

George and Clara gladly accepted the invitation to go and stay with Edward and Jane Maria after the baby was born. *The Sydney Morning Herald* of the 18th of June 1847 announced the birth: 'At Woolloomooloo, on the 17th instant, the lady of George Windsor Earl, Esquire, of a daughter'. This was, short of a few days, nine months after they had arrived in Sydney. They left their residence in Woolloomooloo and went to the luxury of Fernhill, with its servants and beautiful location, and where, on the 29th of August, Elizabeth Christiana Fernhill Earl was baptized by the Rev. Thomas MacKinson at the Mulgoa parish church. It was recorded by Elizabeth (much later in her 'Memoirs') that the name Fernhill 'was given me unexpectedly at the font by my Godfather, Edward Cox'.*

* Elizabeth Christiana was known to the family as 'Annie' and will be referred to as so in this book. Her unpublished 'Memoirs' are entitled *Some Memories of Elizabeth Christiana Fernhill Alt (née Earl)*, and were compiled in the years leading up to World War I.

There followed an idyllic six months at Fernhill with the Cox family. George had been able to persuade the Colonial Office in Sydney to delay his departure from New South Wales because of the birth. By December 1847, however, matters could be postponed no further. As no sailing to Port Essington was available in the near future, passage was booked to Hong Kong for the end of that month. They would stay there only a few days, just long enough to arrange onward travel to Singapore whence, arguably, it would be relatively easy to travel to Port Essington.

The little family, with their portmanteaux, trunks, and cases containing most of their worldly possessions, boarded the British ship *Hashemy* in Hong Kong on the 2nd of February 1848. From there, the ship's Captain Ross had a fine, twelve-day run down the China Sea and arrived in Singapore on 14th of February 1848. The family repaired immediately to stay with George's old friend, Dr José d'Almeida. It was the first time George had seen him since the loss of the d'Almeida-owned ship, *Heroine*, on which Percy had drowned.

George had now been away from Port Essington for three-and-a-half years and it was time for him to make arrangements for his return.

View of Port Essington, drawing by William Nicholas, 1839.

– Chapter Fifteen –

Singapore and Port Essington
1848-1849

I have no hesitation in saying that half of this was the result of ill-management.

•

George and Clara had been married for nearly two years and this had been an eventful period with the long voyage out from England, a year in Sydney filled by Clara's pregnancy and the birth of their daughter, the stay at Fernhill, the voyage from Sydney to Hong Kong, then on to Singapore. The young family initially stayed as Dr José d'Almeida's guests.

However, it was only a matter of weeks from their arrival in February 1848 that it was decided that they would stay in Singapore for the time being. It is probable that George was unwilling to expose Clara and, especially, Annie, to the rigours of the climate and life in Victoria, and that he was also unwilling to leave them in Singapore or send them elsewhere whilst he returned alone. He did not resign from his official offices at Port Essington (thus continuing to present bills of exchange for his half-pay) and his attempts, or lack thereof, to square the circle between duties there and his absence would later be the cause of official criticism.

Within seven weeks of arrival, George Earl was serving as a member of the Singapore grand jury. His name was listed in the 5th of April 1848 edition of *The Straits Times* as one of 23 jurors (including the foreman). The grand jury was as near to a parliament as could be found there. Community and business matters were raised, discussed and acted upon, and as a debating chamber, it provided an important link between citizen and administration. It was also an ideal forum for raising a public profile amongst the 350 or so European residents of Singapore.

The Earl family soon moved from Dr d'Almeidas' to a rented house in Kampong Glam, near to the d'Almeidas' mansion, an increasingly desirable rural area overlooking the harbour just east of the city centre with a mixed population that included Malays, Arabs, Javanese and Chinese.

George rekindled his acquaintance with the Logan brothers and this marked the beginning of what was to prove a long-standing and fruitful collaboration. Abraham Logan and his younger brother James Richardson Logan were born in Scotland in 1816 and 1819, respectively. They attended the University of Edinburgh where both read Law. Suitably educated, they decided to go East and arrived in Penang in February 1839. There they were admitted as Law agents, subsequently leaving for Singapore in 1842 where they set up in practice under their own name.

The two brothers and George had much in common. The younger brother, James Richardson Logan, was the founder and editor (1847-1863) of *The Journal of the Indian Archipelago and Eastern Asia*, to which George would contribute a number of important articles during the next years. (As would J.R. Logan, himself a scholar of no mean achievement.) While in Penang, James had edited the *Pinang Gazette*, and after moving to Singapore he edited the *Singapore Free Press and Mercantile Advertiser* from 1843 to 1845, when he was succeeded as editor by his brother, Abraham. Abraham, in turn, bought the paper in 1848 and functioned as owner/editor, a position of great influence, until his retirement in 1865. All this was in addition to their busy law practice. The 1847 prospectus for *The Journal...* stated, *inter alia*:

> The bulk of the Journal will consist of articles...relating to Sumatra, Java, Borneo, Celebes, the Philippines and the Moluccas, Bali and other islands of the Archipelago. These will be very varied in their nature, embracing as they will the history, language, literature and ethnography of the various races who inhabit this great region, and contributions to every department of natural history and physical science, as well as topographical agricultural, economical and miscellaneous subjects.

Moreover, *The Journal...* would aim (and prove to be successful, especially with Dutch scholars) to include works from contributors outside of the British academic mainstream. J.R. Logan wrote:

> It will not be the least beneficial effect of our Journal that we shall be able to introduce our neighbours to our English readers in a character in which they have not been accustomed to view them, and thereby, we trust, help to soften those asperities of feeling that are apt to be occasionally engendered when Dutch policy seems to conflict with British interest.

Earl's first article to be published in the *Journal*, 'Specimens of the dialects of Timor & of the chain of Islands extending thence to New Guinea', would appear in the volume for 1848. He was also to frequently write for Abraham Logan's weekly *Singapore Free Press*, but since it was the custom that few articles were signed, it is not possible to identify Earl's contributions or know the extent to which he was responsible for its editorial views. But George Earl was beginning to make his way in the Singapore of 1848.

* * *

The settlement at Port Essington had continued in its struggles. The loss of the *Heroine* (on which Percy Earl had drowned) in April 1846 was to cause serious long-term consequences because the vessel was Victoria's regular supply ship. Captain McArthur had done what he could for the survivors of the sinking, including Father Angelo Confalonieri who arrived bereft of all possessions, including the all-important letter of introduction from The Reverend Doctor Georgy, Vice-General of Sydney. Given clothes, food and supplies by McArthur, Father Confalonieri was to busy himself through joining the Aborigines in their peripatetic ways, learning their languages, caring for them, and by bringing them the Gospel. In June, Captain McArthur, himself now unwell and battling failing eyesight, had the Royal Marines construct a stone cottage for the Father on the eastern side of the harbour at Black Point, just south of Smith Point, some 18 miles from Victoria. John Sweatman, the clerk of HMS *Bramble* that had arrived in June 1846 and would remain in the area until September, was to write of Father Confalonieri:

> He was exceedingly industrious and zealous too in his endeavours to convert the natives. He had already in a great degree mastered their language, a thing no other European had even succeeded in doing and he was constantly in the bush amongst them notebook in hand.

The settlement's chronic shortage of medicine and food was compounded by the voracious appetite of the local cockroaches (of the flying variety, with claws). Stores could be depleted by them (with aid from the termites) by as much as a half within a month. By August, HMS *Bramble* (and her tender, *Castlereagh*) were so infested that conditions on-board became intolerable. It was decided to scuttle the ships temporarily to remove the infestations. This was done at Point Record to prevent the insects from overwhelming Victoria, and it was estimated that roughly 1,000 gallons of them were drowned on the ships or washed up on the beach, the latter to the delight of the Aborigines, who considered them a delicacy.

In October 1846, a month after both ships had departed, the settlement was deeply shocked when Lieutenant Lambrick's wife, Emma, grew progressively unwell and died. As one of the few women in Victoria, her loss was keenly felt. She was buried beside an infant son who had predeceased her by eighteen months. The next month her recent infant son died and was buried with them. Lieutenant Lambrick's grief was deep and perhaps made greater with the knowledge that McArthur's previous pleas for an experienced permanent medical officer had, due to bureaucratic muddle, gone unanswered.

Although there was ongoing uncertainty in the background concerning the proposed new colony of Northern Australia for transported, expiree and reformed convicts, Victoria prospered somewhat in 1847. In a mercifully mild dry season with its cold nights and pleasantly cool days, fruit and vegetable crops were abundant. The clement weather also made repairs to the dilapidated buildings a much easier task. Only the Aborigines were affected by this unusual weather: an epidemic of influenza broke out and Father Confalonieri, assisted by the settlement's surgeon, Richard Tilston, was credited with saving many lives. Indeed, for such efforts, Father Confalonieri was given, in an extremely rare if not unique occurrence during that period, a tribal name, *Na-Wuyuk*.

Relations between the settlement and the Aborigines had been relatively good since Victoria's founding a decade before. The absence of settlers no doubt played a part in keeping tensions down. Then, a couple of incidents changed the entire tenor of the relationship. A few of the older Aborigines resented Father Confalonieri. In October 1847, he was robbed and, after reporting the theft to McArthur, was threatened and told he would now be regarded as an enemy. Earlier, the settlement's sergeant, William Masland, shot and killed an Aboriginal who was attempting to escape custody after being arrested for theft from the settlement. It was an unfortunate incident: Masland had warned the culprits that he would shoot if escape was attempted and when two of them dived off the boat in the night, he fired. McArthur was shocked (it was the first death by violence in the settlement's history) and ordered the arrest and bailing of Masland. Ultimately it was decided by the Attorney-General in Sydney in February of 1848 (around the time the Earls arrived in Singapore) that the circumstances did not warrant prosecution.

There were to be further repercussions. The Aboriginal killed by Masland was a man of the Manobo tribe and they, not daring to seek revenge on one of the Europeans, killed Neimal of the Binanolombos. Neimal was a friend of the settlement and highly thought of. He spoke English well, was learning to read and write it, and had earlier accompanied the naturalist, John MacGillivray, of HMS *Fly* on a trip throughout the greater area. Neimal was avenged by the Binanolombos when they killed a member of the Manobos. Captain McArthur no longer had much control over the deteriorating situation.

On the evening of the 20th of November 1847, an earthquake hit Victoria and greatly weakened the buildings. Torrential rains soaked everything and when these persisted they made living conditions miserable for the following months, during which on December 28th 1847, Queen Victoria had revoked the Charter for the proposed colony of North Australia. Earlier that year, the report that William Gladstone had commissioned as Secretary of State for War and the Colonies, and a further examination by the Colonial Land and Emigration Board, concluded that there were but two reasons for the continuation of the settlement, as a possible coaling station for ships between Singapore and Sydney, and to preclude a foreign power from claiming the territory. All the other main arguments which had been made for the existence of Port Essington were disregarded.

The dry season of 1848 slowly made its way in. Repairs, needed especially to the pier, were now possible. Sickness abated, but McArthur struggled with turmoil from the natives as they made vociferous complaints. In their desire for revenge in tribal animosities, they sought his sanction to commit murder in satisfaction. McArthur's refusal exacerbated the situation. Then, in June, Father Confalonieri contracted a serious fever and was found prostrate in his hut at Black Point. He was taken to the hospital at Victoria, but died a few days later in his 35th year on June 9th. McArthur oversaw the burial in the little cemetery by the shore. All of the officers and soldiers of the settlement, in an unusual show of unity at that time between Catholic and Protestant, escorted the coffin through the still bush to the grave.

There was the usual problem of supplies, some of them arriving close to spoilage from the calling ships, but the harvest had been good and meat supplies acceptable from local livestock. In November, a schooner arrived with needed supplies, including medicines, shoes, boots and material for uniforms, as well as 264 gallons of no doubt much appreciated rum.

Later that month, HMS *Rattlesnake* on a surveying mission came into view. She was captained by Earl's old antagonist, Owen Stanley. In addition to John MacGillivray, formerly of the *Fly*, a 24-year-old serving as assistant surgeon by the name of Thomas Henry Huxley was on-board. He recorded his youthful impressions of the port in a letter written from Sydney to his mother on the 1st of February 1849:

> The only place we have visited since my last budget was Port Essington, a military post which has been an object of much attention for some time past in connection with the steam navigation between Sydney and India. It is about the most useless, miserable, ill-managed hole in Her Majesty's dominions. Placed fifteen miles inland on the swampy banks of an estuary out of reach of the sea breezes, it is the most hot and enervating place imaginable. The temperature of the water alongside the ship was 88 to 90, i.e. about that of a moderately warm bath, so that you may fancy what it is on land. Added to this, the commandant [McArthur] is a litigious old fool, always at war with his officers, and endeavouring to make the place as much of a hell hole morally as it is physically. Little more than two years ago a detachment of sixty men came out to the settlement. At the parade on the Sunday I was there, there were just ten men present. The rest were invalided, dead, or sick. I have no hesitation in saying that half of this was the result of ill-management. The climate in itself is not particularly unhealthy. We were all glad to get away from the place.*

It is to be wondered if Huxley would have had 'no hesitation' in condemning McArthur had Huxley spent more than a decade of struggle in Port Essington facing not only the hostile elements, disease, lack of supplies, the need to keep military discipline and uncertainty over the future, but also the denigration and snooty interference too often dished out by visiting officers of the Royal Navy.

The *Rattlesnake* soon departed as the wet season of 1848-9 came in with a vengeance, first bringing soaking rain and then, in February, another outbreak of fever. The first death in that month was of one of the strongest young men of the garrison, who died only a few days after contracting the fever. One by one, people fell ill; even the two doctors were stricken. The Surgeon-in-Charge, Doctor Crawford, became delirious (he would recover) and his assistant, Richard Tilston (who had aided Father Confalonieri during the influenza outbreak among the natives) succumbed and, to the shock of the settlement, died on the 4th of March. McArthur went down with the fever and George Lambrick, who was but one of three who would escape illness, became the *de facto* head of the station. Most duties ceased, with those who were not ill tending to

* Huxley wrote elsewhere of Port Essington: 'the most wretched, the climate the most unhealthy, the human beings the most uncomfortable and houses in a condition most decayed and rotten'.

those who were. 26 were in need of constant care and attention. Half of the garrison was incapacitated and the remainder so weak as to be incapable of anything but the lightest duties.

* * *

The Earl family was well out of the troubles in Port Essington, and George continued to make career progress in Singapore. The Court of Judicature of Prince of Wales' Island, Singapore and Malacca enrolled him as a Law agent on the 28th of April 1849. No specific professional qualifications were necessary at the time to practise, but candidates had to possess desirable levels of education, experience, character and probity.*

A Law agent's work embraced many aspects of business and community life in the Straits Settlements. An advertisement for a fellow Law agent, a Mr R. C. Woods, in the *Singapore Directory* proclaimed: 'Debts recovered, Rents collected, Bills and Loans of money negotiated, and every branch of Legal Agency conducted.'

It would have been around this time that the family learned of the death of Clara's father, William Siborne, who had unexpectedly passed away the previous January, aged 51. This must have come as a great shock to Clara, just under 19 years old and so far away from her remaining family.

In September 1849, Earl joined the firm of Abraham and James Richardson Logan and began to practice as a Law agent and advocate from their office in Commercial Square, (renamed Raffles Place a few years later). At about the same time the family moved to Spottiswoode Park, overlooking the new harbour. He had also been working on a number of papers, three of which appeared in 1849 in *The Journal of the Indian Archipelago and Eastern Asia*. Two of these were translations: 'The Island of Mindoro', from Dutch and 'The Molucca Islands' from the French of Count van Hogendorp's Coup d'Oeil sur L'isle de Java etc., but the beginnings of what would become a major work, 'On the Leading Characteristics of the Papuan, Australian & Malayu-Polynesian Nations (Chapter One)' appeared as the lead paper in that year's *Journal*.

In London, the much-debated future of the settlement at Port Essington had been resolved. An enquiry had been made by the Colonial Office to the India and Australia Mail Steam Packet Company in early 1849

* As the importance of the Law agent grew, so did the need for qualifications. In 1852 it became necessary to pass an exam in order to qualify. The first trained lawyer to be admitted would be in 1859.

to the India and Australia Mail Steam Packet Company in early 1849 as to whether they intended to use Victoria as a port of call or coaling station. They reply was negative. Also, the view was now taken that the withdrawal of the marines would not affect British sovereignty in the area. The Home Secretary, Sir George Grey, perhaps with some reluctance, ordered the station to be abandoned and this instruction was issued by the Admiralty on June 6th 1849. It is a consideration that this decision might not have been taken at the time but for Sir John Barrow's death the previous November. Although Barrow had retired from the Admiralty in 1845, he had remained influential and the station at Port Essington was a necessary link in his vision of a ring of military establishments around Australia to establish and defend Britain's stake to the entire continent.

On August 28th 1849, *The Straits Times* carried the following brief notice:

> H.M.S. Mæander as soon as refitted, will proceed to Port Essington and break up the Establishment there. Captain Keppel, we hear, has received orders to form a station at Cape York, or other coaling depot for the Steamers which will, shortly, take up the line from Singapore to Sydney. Having completed these arrangements, Mæander will cruize [sic] in the Pacific.

George Earl now knew that his tenure of offices in Port Essington (and half-pay) were to cease. What he probably didn't know at that time was that in the months before the June 6th decision he had been the subject of some debate in the Colonial Office as to whether the bills he had presented for his half-pay should be honoured. During the course of the discussions, a Mr. Elliot wrote in a March 1849 CO memo of Earl, 'I do not know that a clearer condemnation could be pronounced on Port Essington that one of its warmest Advocates, would have consumed more than two years in a fruitless attempt to find an opportunity of reaching the place.' However, the Colonial Office clerks may have not had a full picture of the situation. Earl's duties at Victoria were of a great variety insofar as regular travel to Sydney and to the islands to the north of the continent was required. In addition to his nominal posts, he effectively acted as a intelligence gatherer throughout the greater area, especially for the Admiralty. Whether or not these activities were sanctioned unofficially or were taken on at Earl's initiative is not known. When the question of the bills reached the higher levels of the government, it was decided that the pay he had received would be final compensation for the loss of his offices. As we shall later see, Earl had foreknowledge of the decision to abandon Port Essington. No doubt off the back of these developments that had clarified his position, George made the decision to stay in Singapore and join the Law agent firm of Abraham and James Richardson Logan.

He also began studying the plants and crops of economic importance growing in Singapore and the Malay Peninsula which might in turn prove profitable in tropical Australia. Looking at the methods employed in growing these crops, he hoped to find ways of improving cultivation and reducing costs. A trip to Province Wellesley (the stretch of land opposite Penang on the Malaysian coast, some 375 miles from Singapore) was made, and he examined the methods of growing of sugar cane by Chinese smallholders. Of particular interest to him was the cultivation of cotton in the Straits and he gathered material for an article, 'On the culture of cotton in the Straits Settlements' which would be published in J.R. Logan's *The Journal...* the following year.

* * *

When the dry season arrived in Port Essington in April 1849, the fever abated and the men started to recover. In spite of the valiant efforts of Captain McArthur, forever working though wasted, ill and covered with ulcers, there was an all-pervading sense of futility and despondency during the next eight months. Needless to say, the wet season had again seriously dilapidated the buildings and the termites were back in force. The common hope was that the garrison would be relieved as Captain McArthur had been requesting this for more than a year. Relief of a sort came on the 13th of November 1849, when a man-o'-war approached the inner harbour. She was the HMS *Meander* under the command of Captain Keppel. Peter Spillett in *Forsaken Settlement* captures the moment of her arrival:

> The whole settlement turned out to welcome the ship as she came to anchor at the end of the pier, waving and shouting and full of excitement and expectation of the good news they were sure the ship had brought.

Captain Keppel and his officers were rowed ashore and heartily greeted by Captain McArthur and the officers and men of the garrison. The party made their way to the Commandant's house where, after suitable refreshment, Keppel delivered the orders to the station. McArthur read to his astonishment that not only was the present garrison to be withdrawn, but the entire settlement at Victoria was to be abandoned. The news of the decision published in Singapore in August had only reached them now. Adding to the shock was the realisation that the entire north shore of Australia would now be abandoned for the foreseeable future as well.*

There was little time for reflection. The north-west monsoon was arriving and Captain Keppel made it clear that he was in a hurry to leave. The extraordinary Captain McArthur, who ten years earlier had overseen the very beginnings of the settlement, now took charge of the ending of it. Orders were given to transfer all the viable stores and provisions to the *Meander*. Everything which could not be transferred to the ship was left to the Aborigines, including horses and cattle and any other livestock that remained. The Aborigines joined in and helped with the operation, both mystified and exhilarated at the largesse they were about to receive.

The task was completed in about two weeks, during which the storms increased and the almost unbearable humidity made life miserable. Two members of *Meander*'s crew, the surgeon and an ordinary seaman, died before the ship sailed. The job done, farewells were made to the Aborigines and to the distressed and damaged buildings which had been home for so many for so long. On the final day, the *Mæander* prepared for sea. Peter Spillett offers a moving account of their 1849 final departure:

> At 9am on the morning of 30th November, Captain John McArthur, Captain George Lambrick, Lieutenant George Shedden Dunbar, the Surgeon John Irwin Crawford and thirty-three NCOs and men of the Royal Marines, led by the lively band of the *Meander*, marched down from the deserted town to the pier and came to a halt as the flag was hauled down for the last time. A salute of twenty-one guns was fired from the *Meander* in final farewell. Then the men were ferried out to the warship and embarked. Only a few of the natives came to watch the final enactment for, apart from some of the women, the rest were busy salvaging what they could find in the deserted town. At sunset, parties were sent ashore to destroy what remained of the unserviceable stores and, on their re-embarking, the decked boat which had served the settlement so faithfully, was blown to pieces.
>
> Daylight brought the last glimpse of the little town of Victoria, spread out on the cliff top, and the settlers crowded to the rails as the *Meander*

* The British Government would decide in 1851 to abandon the establishment of the colony of North Australia.

weighed anchor and made all plain sail, gradually drifting away from the pier into deep water on the ebb. A quiet fell over the watchers as their thoughts ranged over the good and bad days of their long exile and they considered the probable future of the little town which had been their whole world for so long. They could just make out the little buildings above the white of Adam Head as the rising sun came over the cliffs to the east and they passed the beacon on Spear Point. At eleven am, after passing Coral Bay, the ship hove to off Point Smith and remained there until four pm when, after setting her Royals and Flying Jib, she sailed past the beacon and out into the open sea.

It was a cancellation of the great hope of a flourishing Port Essington, and Victoria, capital of the Australian northern shore, and a setback for the vision George Windsor Earl had outlined some 13 years before in the Preface to his translation of Kolff's *Voyages of the Dutch brig-of-War Dourga, through the southern and little-known ports of the Moluccan Archipelago...*

...now that we are about to found another settlement in that part of the world; H.M. ships *Alligator* and *Britomart*, again under the command of Sir Gordon Bremer, being on their voyage to the northern coast of Australia for that purpose. The arrangement of the work for publication has afforded the Translator occupation and amusement during a long voyage, and he trusts it may be by the means of conveying useful information concerning a simple and industrious people, occupying a number of richly productive islands, in the immediate vicinity of a continent which may be considered a vast British colony, and with whom his countrymen may open an intercourse likely to prove advantageous to both parties.

HMS Mæander

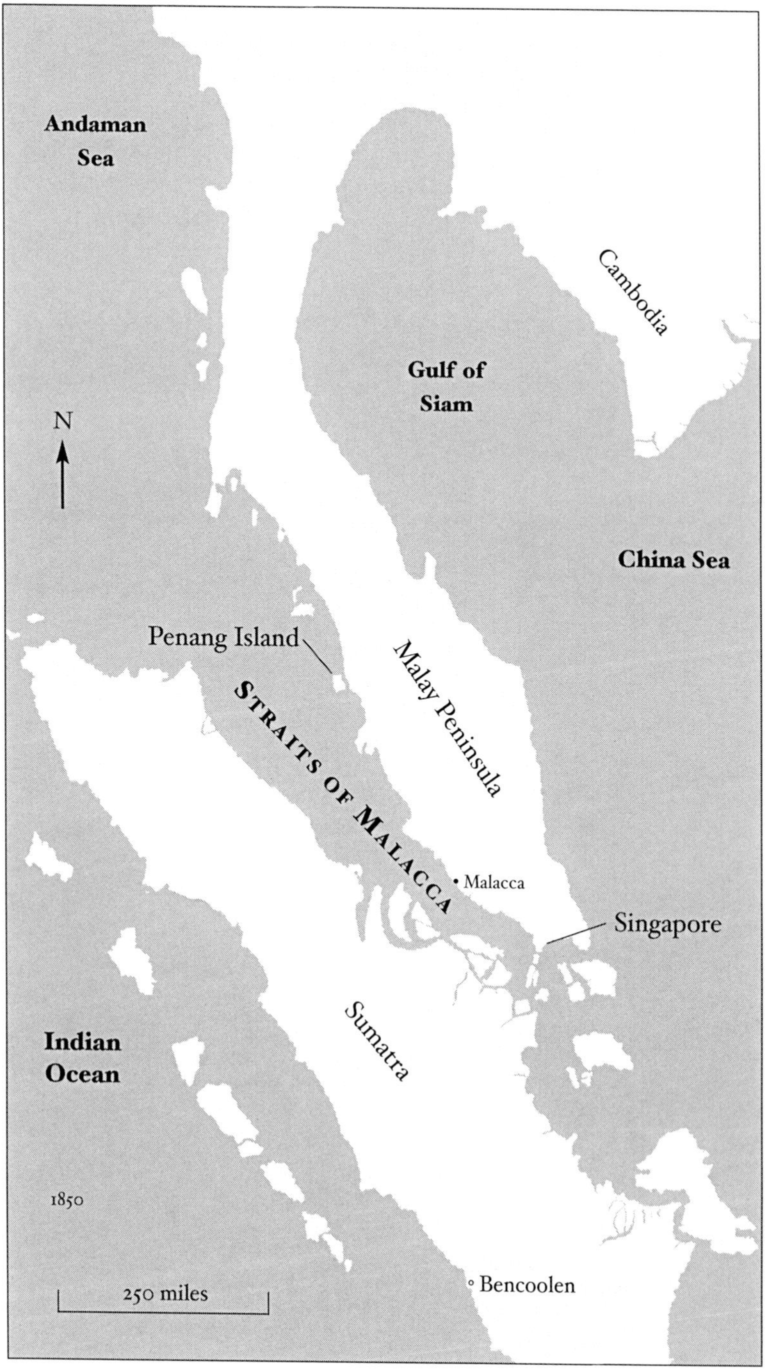
Andaman
Sea
Cambodia
Gulf of
Siam
N
China Sea
Penang Island
Malay Peninsula
Straits of Malacca
Malacca
Singapore
Sumatra
Indian
Ocean
1850
Bencoolen
250 miles

– Chapter Sixteen –

SINGAPORE

1850-1852

Let all men be considered equal in the eye of the Law

•

As the settlement at Port Essington lay abandoned, controversy concerning its fate and that of the future of Northern Australia continued. In Adelaide, the *South Australian Register* of November 21st 1849 carried the following:

ABANDONMENT OF PORT ESSINGTON

> It would seem to be understood that the British Government has decided on withdrawing the Captain and party of Royal Marines stationed at Port Essington, for many years past; and this withdrawal is said to be intended as expressive of a resolve to abandon the establishment altogether.
>
> We can easily believe that the climate is not a delectable one for Europeans; but the proposed abandonment of Port Essington, just now, is a blot upon our national character. Has it never occurred to our rulers that they might colonise Tropical Australia from British India? If the attempt were made, or authoritatively suggested, we venture to augur the most happy and prosperous results.

The end of British presence at Port Essington perhaps did not come as a shock to George Earl. Although he had been one of the settlement's most vocal supporters and a bulwark against its critics for more than a decade, he also knew that the vision he had helped create for a great trading entrepôt in Northern Australia to rival Singapore remained unfulfilled. What no doubt disturbed him was the all but total abandonment by the British authorities of the vast territory in the north of the continent. Earl's deep conviction that this area could and should become a cornucopia through intensive cultivation manned by a multi-ethnic Asian workforce – a sort of agrarian Singapore – was to never be abandoned by him, even in a continued absence of tangible progress.

With all pressure off to return to Port Essington, Earl was now in the position of being able (and perhaps having) to reconsider the family's future course. For the time being, it was decided that they would move to a house in Armenian Street, at the foot of the Singapore Hill.

In *The Eastern Seas*, Earl had devoted 75 pages to the city and noted that Singapore was 'considered to be more agreeable as a residence than any other town in India, for the daily arrival of ships from various parts of the world creates constant excitement, while in point of climate it is certainly not inferior to any intertropical sea-port town in the world'.

Now, that settlement of 21,000 or so people that he had then visited had grown during the ensuing 16 years to 1849 to more than 59,000. By 1850, it can be estimated that there were 350-400 permanent European residents among some 39,000 Chinese, 9,000 Malays, 8,250 Indians and 4,000 of mixed/other native races. The total population including Malacca, Penang and Province Wellesley exceeded 100,000.

The lifeblood of Singapore was the sea-trading business, and this was largely controlled by the great merchant houses. The historian CM (Constance Mary) Turnbull detailed them:

> ...twenty were British, six Jewish, five Chinese, five Arab, two Armenian, two German, one Portuguese, one American and one Parsi. Singapore's commercial system depended mainly on a combination of European capital and Chinese enterprise. Most European merchants imported goods on consignment, which they sold on commission, and they relied on Chinese middlemen to handle dealings with their own countrymen and with other Asian traders.

The value of imports and exports in the Straits Settlements in 1850 exceeded £8,000,000 (approximately £1 billion today), making it one of the busiest shipping areas in the world at that time. But there were external and internal threats: some were geopolitical (mostly with the Dutch) and others included serious attempts by rival ports in the region to compete commercially. Endemic piracy in the area was a grave threat to the shipping on which Singapore's trade depended, but there had been little done to tackle this scourge until the late-1840s when the Royal Navy, on the instruction of the Government in India, undertook a major campaign to diminish, if not eradicate, it in the South China Sea. During the ensuing 20 years this campaign was to prove largely ineffective as piracy, whilst certainly not considered an honourable pursuit by the indigenous societies, was an understandable and, to an extent, a tolerated one that also frequently proved useful as a power in its own right to squabbling rulers in the region.

Of course, a great advantage of the Straits entrepôt was its status as a free-trade area; but concomitantly interwoven were political, economic and social challenges. In 1833, the East India Company had lost its monopoly of the China trade, which the Straits Settlements largely had been established to facilitate and protect. Too valuable, if only for its strategic location on the Straits of Malacca, to be allowed to fall into other hands, the EIC reluctantly carried the ultimate responsibility for governing and financing costs. In the absence of custom duties or tonnage and harbour dues (the major methods of raising revenues during that era), local tax revenues perennially fell short of total running costs and this gap required funding from EIC's Governor-General in Calcutta. The relationship between these two areas that had little in common was ever contentious. CM Turnbull wrote:

> Despite her lovely setting and orderly planning, many parts of Singapore in the mid-nineteenth century were unsightly. The main streets frequently flooded at high tide and were lit by feeble coconut-oil lamps. The town was plagued by stray dogs, and dead ponies were left to rot on the beach. The city's refuse was thrown into the swamps, the roads were littered with garbage, and the Singapore grand jury complained at almost every session about pollution and stench. The problem was lack of money. Residents demanded more amenities but refused to pay higher property assessments while Calcutta did not consider that lightly-taxed Singapore deserved further government subsidies. The Company [East India Company] refused to build a new bridge near the river mouth or to mend the two existing bridges, which could not cope with the increased traffic and fell into a dangerous state of disrepair.

A relatively small civil service oversaw this substantial multi-ethnic group of settlements, and it is a testament to the perceived fairness of and respect for the system by all parties that the greater civil order was maintained. While immigration contributed to the city's growth and success, an ever-present transitory population, overwhelmingly male and on the make, created the air of a 'Wild West' town – bustling, virile and active, but given to crime and disorderliness.

The greatest threat to overall public order was the clash of vying Chinese secret societies in their struggles to control the illegal gambling and legal opium markets. In 1854, there were to be widespread riots in Singapore arising out of a quarrel between the Hokkien-dominated Ghee Hock against the Teochew-backed Ghee Hin. In what descended into an eight-day running battle with roughly 5,000 belligerents, more than 400 Chinese were killed, many shops looted and property destroyed. In these internecine conflicts amongst the ethnic majority population, the Government could do relatively little beyond attempts at containment once trouble broke out.

Although the suppression of gambling by the government had been vigorous and successful (at least with regard to its practice in the open) during the 1840s, the circumstances of the open opium market presented much greater difficulties. The government licenced for a fee opium 'farms' for the refining of the drug, as well as shops authorised to sell it as part of that fee. The subsequent receipts constituted nearly one half of all government revenues for the Straits Settlements. Whilst publicly deplored for the deleterious effect in both moral and physical realms, the opium trade was tolerated in a two-faced way and the contradictions were well known at the time. In Logan's *The Journal* of 1856, the article, 'Gambling and Opium Smoking in the Straits of Malacca', estimated that the highly addictive practice of opium-smoking affected in Singapore, Malacca and Penang (including Province Wellesley) some 40,000 souls.

A phenomenon that deeply disturbed authorities and populace alike was 'amok running', when a Malay (or Bughis) armed himself with a large kris (dagger) in each hand, sought out a busy area and then stabbed and slashed his way through the crowd. A warning cry was raised throughout the area; women, children and the unarmed sought safety indoors whilst the man was hunted down, usually by the citizenry, and killed. Such acts were inexplicable; no apparent or even discernible motive could be established, nor did the perpetrators usually behave in a manner prior to the slaughter that would indicate the forthcoming mayhem.

The military strength in the Straits Settlements, aside from that supplied by the Royal Navy, was largely in the form of two regiments of sepoys, mostly from Bengal. Numbering some 1,000 bayonets; 400 were stationed in Singapore, 400, at Penang and 100 each at Labuan (on the NW coast of Borneo) and Malacca. Such a force would be wholly inadequate to stop any serious invasion, but its main purpose was to provide for the safety of the European population in the event of local insurrection. As it was, these troops, along with a handful of British artillerymen to man the guns in the forts, consumed roughly half of the Straits Settlements' annual budget.

Challenges aside, everyday life for Europeans in Singapore could be very pleasant as detailed in a delightful, eyewitness account by John Cameron FRGS in his book, *Our Tropical Possessions In Malayan India...*:

Morning Occupations

...nearly all, at least, are within hearing range of the 68-pounder gun on Fort Canning, the discharge of which each morning at five o'clock ushers in the day. ...six o'clock generally sees all dressed and out of doors, to enjoy a couple of miles walk or ride through the lovely country roads, in the delicious coolness of morning, before the sun's rays become disagreeably powerful.

...At no other hour of the day are the roads out of town so lively with Europeans. One can always depend upon picking up a companion, and getting and giving all the little gossip of the night before; or more seriously discussing the latest China or Europe mail news. During these walks, too, may be encountered pretty nearly the entire rising generation of European parentage – the heirs and heiresses, to be, of Singapore's merchants, who with their ayahs or native nurses are sent to "makan angin" – literally, "eat" the morning air.

Breakfasts – Drive to Town

...On coming home from these morning rounds, the custom is to get into loose, free and easy attire, generally baju and pajamas. A cup of coffee or tea, with biscuit or bread-and-butter and fruit, is then consumed, and the next two hours spent in reading, writing, or lolling about in the verandahs which front each apartment of a house...

At half-past eight the breakfast dressing gong or bell is sounded. A gentleman's toilette in this part of the east is not an elaborate one, and half an hour is ample time for its completion. The bath is its chief feature... Every gentleman has his native... body servant, whose sole duty it is to attend upon him personally. ...[they] lay out their master's apparel for the day; so that on coming from the bath a gentleman has little trouble to get himself attired. As to shaving the process is generally performed by itinerant Hindoo barbers, who for the small charge of a dollar or a dollar and a half per month come every morning to the residences of their customers. The charge is so small, and the saving in trouble so great, that almost all avail themselves of the convenience.

The universal breakfast hour is nine o'clock, and when the bell then rings the whole household assemble, and should there be ladies of the number this is the first time of their appearance. Singapore breakfasts... are rarely dwelt over long, half an hour, being about the time devoted to them. A little fish, some curry and rice, and perhaps a couple of eggs, washed down with a tumbler or so of good claret, does not take long to get through and yet forms a very fair foundation on which to begin the labours of the day. After breakfast the conveyances drive round to the porch or portico and having received their owners hasten in to town...

Tiffins – Commercial Exchange

Arrived in town, ten minutes or a quarter of an hour are usually spent in going the rounds of the square to learn the news of the morning. These commercial square gatherings are quite a characteristic of the place and of the community, and whatever channels they may open to the flow of local gossip, or it might even be scandal, yet they are so far useful that they serve the purpose of an open air and non-commercial exchange. Differences of position are in most cases left behind in office, and all meet here on a footing of equality, or if there is any ascendancy at all it is that which is obtained by the readiest wit or perhaps by the greatest measure of self-assurance. As scarcely a day passes without the arrival of a steamer with news from England, China, India, or from some interesting point in the neighbourhood...

This sort of congress takes place between the first arrival in town and ten or half-past ten o'clock. At that hour business has commenced and continues in full force till tiffin time, or one o'clock; and certainly it is gone through in quite as smart and active a manner as at home. The climate, though it may produce a greater languor in the evening, has apparently no such effect during the day. There is not much out-of-door bustle; but still when occasion requires the folks post about the square under the midday sun at a lively pace and with apparent impunity.

Tiffin time does not bring the luxurious abandonment to the table which it does in Java... a plate of curry and rice and some fruit or it may be a simple biscuit with a glass of beer or claret. Half an hour's relaxation too is generally indulged in, and as the daily newspaper comes out about this hour, there is a goodly flocking either to the exchange or the public godowns in the square for a perusal of it.

Two o'clock is the exchange hour, and though I do not think there is really much intercommunication on commercial subjects, yet as a rendezvous and a place where the leading men of the mercantile world can have an interchange of ideas even on irrelevant matters, it has the good effect of promoting and maintaining a more general intimacy than might otherwise prevail...

Business hours are not particularly severe, and by half-past four or five o'clock most of the mercantile houses have got through their work. But only a few proceed direct home at this hour; the greater number, at least of the younger members of the community, resort to the fives-court [a type of handball] or the cricket-ground on the esplanade... Cricket is of course precisely the same game in Singapore as it is at home.

Dinners

Dinner in Singapore is not the light airy meal which might reasonably be imagined from the nature of the climate... Soup and fish generally both precede the substantiate, which are of a solid nature, consisting of roast beef or mutton, turkey or capon, supplemented by side-dishes of tongue, fowl, cutlets, or such like, together with an abundant supply of vegetables, including potatoes nearly equal to English ones grown in China or India, and also cabbages from Java. The substantiate are invariably followed by curry and rice... accompanying them are all manner of sambals or native pickles and spices, which add materially to the piquancy of the dish.

...the usual beverage is beer, accompanied by a glass or two of pale sherry. The good folks of Singapore are by no means inclined to place too narrow restrictions on their libations, and it has been found in the experience of older residents that a liberality in this respect conduces to good health and long life.

...But it is in the luxuriance of the dessert perhaps more than anything else that the tables of Singapore are to be distinguished, and it is little wonder that it should be so; for there is no season of the year at which an abundance of fruit cannot be obtained. ...A cigar and a glass or two of sherry after the ladies are gone, and dinner is over.

Many of the residences have billiard-rooms attached which case the usual custom is to retire there after dinner. Where no billiard-room is within reach, a chat in the verandah, a little meditation, or perhaps a book passes the hours pleasantly enough until bedtime. And as dinner is seldom over before eight o'clock, and the usual hour for bed is ten, it is not a very long interval between them that has to be disposed of.

* * *

Now that the Earl family had settled in Singapore, 1850 would prove a productive year for George's scholarly pursuits. In addition to the publication of his paper on cotton in the Straits Settlements and the beginnings of an encyclopædic listing of 'The Trading Ports of the Indian Archipelago', two further chapters of 'On the Leading Characteristics of the Papuan, Australian & Malayu-Polynesian Nations' were to appear in the *Journal*. In the first of these, Earl takes up the long-standing problem of nomenclature for the island areas. No one had developed a generally accepted name for the large area containing more than 17,000 islands that lay largely to the east of Singapore, west of New Guinea and southwest of the Philippines. A confusingly wide range of terms had been employed over the centuries: the Indian Archipelago; the Archipelago; East-Indian Archipelago; Asiatic Archipelago; Eastern India; India Islands, Malayan India and even, the Asiatic Mediterranean, among a number of others including the far-fetched 'Hither Polynesia'. Earl wrote in the *Journal*:

> Nevertheless the time has arrived when a distinctive name for the brown races of the Indian Archipelago is required, and it should be made to accord as closely as possible with the terms by which that position of the world is most generally known, namely "Indian Archipelago". By adopting the Greek word for "islands" as a terminal, for which we have a precedent in the term "Polynesia", the inhabitants of the "Indian Archipelago" or "Malayan Archipelago" would become respectively Indu-nesians or Malayu-nesians. I have chosen the latter for several reasons. The first term would be too general, and might be thought equally applicable to the Ceylonese and to the natives of the Maldives and Laccadives. The latter, on the other hand, will show on the face of it that it is intended to apply only to the brown races of the Archipelago, and it would be some acknowledgement of the enterprise of the Malayans in having extended their voyage over the entire Archipelago previous to the arrival of Europeans.

In that same year, J.R. Logan took up this subject in *The Journal* in his article: 'The Ethnology of the Indian Archipelago: Embracing Enquiries into the Continental Relations of the Indo-Pacific Islanders':

> The name Indian Archipelago is too long to admit of being used in an adjective or in an ethnographical form. Mr Earl suggests the ethnographical term Indunesians but rejects it in favour of Malayunesians. ...I prefer the purely geographical term Ind*o*nesia... We thus get Indonesian for Indian Archipelagian or Archipelagic, and Indonesians for Indian Archipelagians or Indian Islanders. I have no affection for the multiplication of semi-grecian words, and would gladly see all the nesias wiped off the map if good Saxon equivalents could be substituted.

It would take many years of the usage of 'Indonesia' for the term to gain wide acceptance. In 1975, Dr Russell Jones, the eminent authority on East

Asian affairs, gave the second Anniversary Lecture of the Indonesia Circle which marked the 125th anniversary of the name 'Indonesia'. In this lecture, he noted that many encyclopædias still stated that the name Indonesia was given to the Archipelago by Adolf Bastian, a German ship's doctor who became a leading ethnographer.

In 1884, Bastian had published the first volume of a monumental work entitled *Indonesian oder die Inseln des Malayischen Archipel*, that did much to popularise, without discussing derivation, the appellations 'Indonesia/Indonesian'. Russell Jones established the links between George Earl, J.R. Logan, Bastian and the local nationalists who adopted the term in the early 20th century and concluded that: 'There can be no doubt about it: Earl coined Indonesia'.

* * *

In mid-October 1850, Singapore heard the news of the death of Dr José d'Almeida in his 66th year. The doctor was one of the longest inhabitants there (having arrived in 1825) and had been, perhaps, its most well-known and distinguished European resident. His house on Beach Road was long famous for the entertainment offered there.

Edward Hodges Cree, a Royal Navy surgeon, described an evening in 1844 at the d'Almeidas' mansion (José then had an estimated ten daughters and four sons):

> They [the d'Almeidas' daughters] are all very musical and get up delightful concerts in their house, twice a week, to which some of us have a general invitation... ...they sing and play various instruments divinely... It was a lovely moonlight night and the large room open to the verandah all round made it cool, so we were able to enjoy the quadrilles and waltzes and a little flirtation.

D'Almeida was a generous, hospitable and successful man whose charitable and benevolent activities had endeared him to most in the community. Charles Burton Buckley wrote in *An Anecdotal History of Old Times in Singapore*, 'that nearly every European in the community attended his funeral, the Governor being one of the pall-bearers, and the attendance of the Chinese and native merchants very large. He had been married more than once and had a large family of nineteen or twenty children.'

The doctor also had been the embodiment of the 'old Singapore', when the port's exotic charm and friendliness had grown out of a small community of Europeans. CM Turnbull wrote of these earlier settlers:

> They mixed freely with their Asian counterparts and were delighted to welcome strangers and visitors with news about Europe. Sailing ships took four months to reach Singapore from England and even mail coming by the expensive, uncertain 'overland' service, trans-shipped in Egypt and transported by camels across the Suez isthmus, seldom arrived in less than two months. Britons could not afford the time or money to visit Europe and expected to spend their whole working lives in the East.

Now, Singapore was in the steam age of sailing and the delightful aspects of both bustle and relative isolation had passed into nostalgia. For Earl, the doctor's passing must have been deeply felt. D'Almeida's generosity and support to the young George making his way in the East, and then the not-to-be-underestimated facilitation of a regular trading vessel for Port Essington from its earliest days, were acts of a true friend and perhaps even a father figure.

Shortly after Dr d'Almeida's death, George, Clara and Annie moved from their house in Armenian Street back to Kampong Glam where they were to stay for a little over a year. That year, 1851, saw life proceeding for George along recently established lines – his law agency, journalism and some committee work on behalf of the community. One matter relating to Port Essington did occupy his mind at this time. Earl tried to arouse interest in establishing steam-shipping services between Singapore and Sydney via the Torres Strait, calling at Port Essington as a coaling and general supply station. His papers, 'Steam routes through the Indian Archipelago: – established, proposed and prospective' and 'Sketch of the Steam route from Singapore to Torres Strait', both appeared in the 1851 *Journal*. Additionally, in July, he wrote to the Colonial Secretary in London, Edward Deas Thomson, about the matter and offered his services in establishing any settlement or coaling station should the proposal be adopted. Also in this letter, Earl essayed the probable effects of gold discoveries on colonial life; a subject of great contemporary interest as the news of a large strike in Bathurst, NSW had been announced by the government in May of that year. Taken at face value, George's letter to Thompson indicates that he was most willing to return to Port Essington or Northern Australia should the opportunity arise.

But Earl did not to know that the Colonial Secretary, Sir George Grey, had already made enquiries with the newly incorporated India and Australia Mail Steam Packet Company as to whether they had plans for such a refuelling station. Their response was that they had no such plans and that, because Port Essington was off the direct route, they could not see any other likely interest. Nevertheless, the subject of steamship routes in the region was to remain an important one and Earl would publicly be weighing in on the subject a few years later.

The year 1852 was to bring new developments. Abraham and James Richardson Logan decided, perfectly amicably, to divide their law practice. Abraham would remain in Singapore and, having bought the *Free Press* newspaper, would continue as editor whilst running the law agency as sole proprietor. James Richardson wished to return to Penang where he would again take over the editorship of the *Pinang Gazette* (which chair he had vacated ten years beforehand) and set up his own law agency practice there. He would also continue to edit and publish *The Journal of the Indian Archipelago*. For the time being, George would continue to work with Abraham at the law practice.

Earl was to make two contributions to *The Journal* in 1852, a translation from the Dutch of 'Contribution to the knowledge of the north and east coasts of New Guinea' by G.F. de Bruijn Kops, Dutch R.N. and, more importantly, the article 'Contributions to the physical geography of south-eastern Asia and Australia' (preceded by a one-page extract 'Land-locked harbours' from his 1846 book *Enterprise in Tropical Australia*). In 'Contributions...', (also published as a pamphlet in 1853) George was updating his earlier paper 'The physical structure and arrangement of the islands in the Indian Archipelago', published in the 1845 RGS *Journal* with research that had come to light during the preceding 17 years. Today, what is internationally known as the Wallace Line (so named by TH Huxley), had its origins in Earl's papers* (and subsequent pamphlet) on the subject as described by Alfred Russel Wallace in his 1869 book, *The Malay Archipelago: The Land of the Orang utan and the Bird of Paradise*:

> It was first pointed out by Mr. George Windsor Earl, in a paper read before the Royal Geographical Society in 1845, and subsequently in a pamphlet "On the Physical Geography of South-Eastern Asia and Australia", dated 1855, that a shallow sea connected the great islands of Sumatra, Java, and Borneo with the Asiatic continent, with which their natural productions generally agreed; while a similar shallow sea connected New

* Charles Darwin wrote to Wallace after reading a draft of the latter's paper on Malayan zoogeography: 'Are you aware that Mr. W. Earl published several years ago the view of distribution of animals in the Malay Archipelago in relation to the depth of the sea between the islands?' It is believed that it was this that first drew Wallace's attention to Earl's works.

> Guinea and some of the adjacent islands to Australia, all being characterised by the presence of marsupials.
>
> We have here a clue to the most radical contrast in the Archipelago, and by following it out in detail I have arrived at the conclusion that we can draw a line among the islands, which shall so divide them that one-half shall truly belong to Asia, while the other shall no less certainly be allied to Australia. I term these respectively the Indo-Malayan and the Austro-Malayan divisions of the Archipelago.
>
> ...he [Earl] maintains the former connection of Asia and Australia as an important part of his view; whereas, I dwell mainly on their long continued separation. Notwithstanding this and other important differences between us, to him undoubtedly belongs the merit of first indicating the division of the Archipelago into an Australian and an Asiatic region, which it has been my good fortune to establish by more detailed observations.

May 1852 marked the sixth anniversary of the Earls' marriage and departure from England, and the decision was made to return there for a visit. Clara was no doubt missing her Siborne family, now without a father, and George had not seen his mother and sister since the death of Percy. Annie would soon be five years old and better able to withstand a long voyage, and George would welcome a period of convalescence. Moreover, Earl wished to shepherd through to publication in London a major new book and also to defend there in person his professional integrity, which he felt had been grievously impugned.

Malay opium smokers

George Samuel Windsor Earl (1813-1865), photograph circa 1860. Noel-Paton

Print taken from an 1856 painting titled *Singapore at Sunrise from the Hills Westward* by Percy Carpenter. The lower frond on the right-hand side of the palm tree points towards the house on Erskine Hill which the Earls rented in 1857.

Sketches by Thomas Baines. The texts read: *Native canoe, which came alongside from Prince of Wales Island, off the tip of Cape York, August 27th 1855; Tom Tough and Monarch, Possession Island* (same date). George, Clara and Annie Earl were on this voyage (on the *Monarch*) and were later stranded on a coral reef off northwestern Australia for 10 days. NLA

View from Convalescent Bungalow, Penang (Prince of Wales' Island), aquatint engraved by William Daniell, after Captain Robert Smith, published in 1821. As recorded in their daughter Annie's 'Journal', the Earls stayed in the area for a month in 1863 whilst George convalesced on medical leave. Penang State Museum

View from Halliburton's Hill, Penang (Prince of Wales' Island), aquatint engraved by William Daniell, after Captain Robert Smith, published in 1821. In the distance, Province Wellesley on the mainland of the Malay Peninsula is visible. Penang State Museum

A male of the Outanta tribe from the south-west coast of New Guinea.
Chromolithograph from Earl's *The Native Races of the Indian Archipelago...*

Wedding procession in the valley of the Jalak in Ijang, eastern Java. Painting by the Dutch artist, Abram Salm, mid-19th century. Earl wrote in *The Eastern Seas*: *As few of the Europeans who visit Java proceed beyond Batavia, they are apt to judge of the natives of the island from those whom they meet at that port, and had I not penetrated farther into the country, I should, like them, have left the island with a very unfavourable impression.*

The graveyard at Victoria, Port Essington. Watercolour by Captain John McArthur, c. 1847. The obelisk marks the grave of Emma Lambrick and her two children. NLA

Mid-19th century engraving, depicting a Chinese opium den. Earl wrote of opium during his trip to Borneo in 1834: *This drug has much greater effect on the Malays than on the Chinese, whose constitutions are, perhaps, better able to support it.*

Aboriginal people at their camp, Port Essington, N. Territory. Photograph, November 1877.

View of George Town and Penang Hill from the harbour.
Anonymous artist, watercolour and pencil, 1854. Penang State Museum

Earl's tomb in the Northam Road Protestant Cemetery, George Town, Penang. Noel-Paton

Elizabeth (Annie) Alt, *neé* Earl, 1870. Noel-Paton

The Alt family: *Top row* (*l to r*): Kathleen; Elizabeth (Annie); Ethel Margaret (Madge); George Earl, William. *Seated* (*l to r*): Clara Earl; Mabel Edith; Anne (Nancy). *At bottom* (*l to r*): William Brian Lancelot; Pleasance; Phillis Innocent. Noel-Paton

William John Alt Noel-Paton

Clara Earl *née* Siborne, 1894. Noel-Paton

– Chapter Seventeen –

England

1853-1854

...more than even my patient nature can bear.

•

In September 1852, George, Clara and Annie boarded the barque *Thomas Arbuthnot* and set sail for England. She was a fine ship of 523 tons, built in Aberdeen for the London/Sydney run. We have a charming account of this voyage contained in Annie's memoir written 60 years or so later. Although only just five years old at the time, her recollections of a child's eye are vivid:

> I greatly enjoyed the voyage home, running the decks and climbing about in company with three little girls. We visited Cape Town, my sole impression being that it was very hot, very dusty, and that there were many flies. I was taken to see the plantations or vineyards where Constantia wine was grown, belonging to some people called Cloete, Dutch folk with whom my father was already acquainted. I remember tasting the sweet rich wine.
>
> ...After leaving the Cape we came in for a dreadful storm which dashed in the stern windows of the cabin next to ours where the Captain's wife was lying with her baby of a few days old. I recall the water washing backwards and forwards in our cabin also as the ship rolled, and in the middle of the night the sailors coming in to fasten up sails or cloths of some kind to strengthen our windows so that they should not be blown in too. The scene remains with me quite vividly, with the lights etc, but I wasn't in the least alarmed and quite happy... – in fact I played the piano on the person of my mother as she lay on the big bed. Next thing I recall was our lying off St Helena although we did not go ashore. ...St Helena seemed to be very high and black. It was pointed out where a rope ladder or something of that sort formed a means of communication between the sea and the top of the Island.
>
> ...My next recollection is arriving at my grandmother's house at Hampstead late in the evening and my cousin Rosa Earl (George's brother Percy's daughter) coming from behind the door and giving me a brightly dressed doll.

It was the winter of 1852/53 when they arrived back in London. Initially, they stayed at Wildwood but soon took their own lodgings nearby. Annie was enrolled at the local school where, having been taught by her mother to read and write, she felt immediately at ease. Her 'Memoir' contains many little recollections, one of which is revealing of class considerations:

> I was told not to play in a certain lane which ran at the back of the house and was frequented, as far as I can recall, by certain little Irish children of the lower class. My schoolmistress happened to pass by at the end of the lane and saw me thus engaged and reported the fact to my mother who asked her to punish me. On arriving at school the next day my little dress (brown Holland braided with red) was taken off then put on me again inside out. My hair was ruffled up and I was stood on a table in the corner for my companions to scoff at me. This cured me of the taste for low company.

With the family settled in, Earl's initial task was to put the finishing touches on a manuscript which had long been in preparation: *The Native Races of the Indian Archipelago. Papuans*. This was to prove to be one of his major works and it became the first volume of a new 'Ethnological Library' under the superintendence of Edwin Norris, the Secretary of the Royal Asiatic Society. Published in the latter half of 1853 by the firm of Hippolyte Baillière, the text of 239 pages was accompanied by four engraved plates (three of them full-colour chromolithographs), two wood engravings, two folding maps, a folding chart showing a range of head types, and a chart listing some dialects.

In his short preface to the work, Earl presents both his *raison d'être* for the discipline of ethnography and his debt to its prominent forerunner:

> The study of the Human Race, in its various phases, has become greatly extended since the late Dr. [James Cowles] Prichard, the father of the Ethnographical Science in this country, commended his researches into the physical history of mankind. The inaugural essay of the young physician in the year 1808, was expanded into a large volume in 1813, and further researches... extended the work until it became one of the most valuable contributions to modern scientific literature of which any nation can boast... The archæologist finds in it a clue to the mysteries connected with extinct nations... the philanthropist feels his sympathies enlarged as the habits and characteristics of untutored races become developed to his view; and even the statesman considers it necessary to refer to the pages

> of the ethnographer, that he may learn how collisions with the native races of distant possessions, which too often lead to desolating and expensive wars, may be best avoided...

London's *The Freemasons' Quarterly* (1853) reviewed the book and concluded:

> ...we can recommend this work with confidence to our readers, trusting that the remainder of the volumes may maintain the character and prestige with which Mr. Earl has decidedly opened the series.

The Native Races... would remain a standard reference work until into the early twentieth century on the subject of the Papuans and their diaspora across the region. It incorporated the writings of many others, mainly in translation, and it has to be noted that there is no record of Earl having ever visited Papua or New Guinea. *The Athenæum* of December 1853, while finding the selections contained from other authors on the subject 'judiciously made', also noted: 'For this work does not consist so much of the original observations of Mr. Earl as it does of the observations of those who have from time to time had intercourse with the Papuans.' Some three years later, in October 1856, a substantial review covering 26 pages was to appear in the *Quarterly Review of the Methodist Episcopal Church, South.* Although generally positive, the review perceptively noted:

> Mr. Earl has diligently, but unsystematically, compiled the present account of the Papuan tribes. ...He presents no theory: he has no system, ethnological, political, historical, to maintain. This produces some confusion in his statements and inferences, but it prevents him from either betraying or being betrayed into error. He proposes to collect, compare, and communicate information, fragmentary and incomplete at best, without contemplating any ulterior object. ...But the work is honest, intelligent and trustworthy, and furnishes, not only the fullest account which has been given of the Papuans, but the only adequate account of them contained in the English language.

Earl was also seeking out other opportunities whilst in London and one was to arise due to a public spat that had been developing between him

• Earl planned a sister volume, *Brown Tribes of the Moluccas, Timor and Celebes*, the text of which was probably never completed.

and one of the founders of the Royal Geographical Society, Roderick Murchison. George had of course heard in Singapore in 1851 of the discovery of gold in New South Wales. This exciting news had caused a worldwide gold rush to the area. It should be remembered that he had submitted a paper, 'On the physical structure and arrangement of the Islands of the Indian Archipelago', which was read to the Society in 1845. In it he had argued that while the islands of the eastern Archipelago differ in structure and elevation with those in Australia, there were patterns of similarity which, when taking account of relatively shallow seabed characteristics (compared to the great depths and trenches existing at the eastern rim), suggested an ancient connection between Australia and Asia. Moreover, he noted that the direction of the mountain ranges of the Malay Peninsula and Sumatra is identical to the ranges of Australia. Thus it was probable, Earl argued, that the Australian mountain ranges were as rich in mineral wealth as the Asiatic. George was not the first to suggest that Australia had once been linked to Asia, and that the Ural chain is an extension of the Malayan and Cambodian ranges to the north-west precisely as those of Australia are an extension to the south-east. But he refined the case in the context of mineral wealth (including gold), known to exist in the north-west Asiatic ranges and therefore to be anticipated in the Australian south-eastern extension.

Immediately after the reading, the paper's conclusions were disputed by Mr (later Sir) Roderick Murchison who argued that if such a connection had ever existed, fossil remains of flora and fauna would have been found in common throughout. An account of these proceedings was published in *The Athenæum* in June 1845 and read, in part:

> The existence of the Teak tree in Java as well as on the Asiatic continent, and the discovery of the Kangaroo in New Guinea, are adduced by Mr. Earl in further proof of the former connexion of these now dissevered lands; and the similarity of the direction and character of the Asiatic and Australian mountain ranges renders it probable that the latter may be found as rich in mineral wealth as the former are known to be. The paper being concluded, Mr. Murchison, the late president, took a decidedly opposite view of the matter, and maintained that nothing short of the discovery of similar ancient fossils in Australia and Asia could be admitted as proof of the former connexion of the two countries.

That the dispute had been, as Earl saw it, mishandled by the RGS (and the subsequent airing in print) caused George later to 'confess that I felt hurt at the time, that the usual practice of Scientific Societies (which requires that all opposition to papers read at general meetings be deferred to the next general meeting, and then produced on paper) should have been departed from on this particular occasion'.

Although Count Strzelecki's *Physical Description of New South Wales,* which tended to corroborate the basic thrust of George's paper, was not published until 1845, the similarities in the fossil flora of the Indian and Australian continents were known in the previous year as Strzelecki had brought back specimens to London.

Such would have remained a minor scholarly squabble except that Murchison, some eight years later in 1853, was now being given unequivocal credit in a London pamphlet by James Wyld as the first to have anticipated the existence of gold in New South Wales and Victoria. The paper, 'Notes on the Distribution of Gold throughout the World', was lavishly dedicated to Murchison who was then the President of the RGS. This raised George's long-standing private dissatisfaction over the entire matter to his public ire.

Although Murchison initially disavowed the attribution in Wyld's paper, he did little else generally to discourage the accolade. Indeed, in 1852 he had written without shyness, 'the *public men* think much more highly of me for having been the first who *worked out* mentally the Australian gold... and for dwelling on it in successive years until the diggers discovered it' [his italics].

Earl, while still in Singapore, had written to Lord Colchester (himself a Royal Navy Vice-Admiral and past President of the RGS) in a letter of April 10th 1852 that took up the Murchison matter. A series of letters between the two ensued and was published, with Lord Colchester's permission, in 1853 as a 16-page pamphlet issued in London by the firm Pelham Richardson entitled, 'A Correspondence relating to the discovery of gold in Australia'.

In Earl's final letter about the matter to Lord Colchester, written from Hampstead on the 14th of May 1853 (and contained in the pamphlet), he closes with the following sharp, not to say mordant, observations:

> I can assure your Lordship that in bringing this matter before the Council of the Geographical Society through the medium of your Lordship, I have not been influenced by any desire to "vindicate my character as a geographer." Whatever little credit may have been accorded to my labours in the cause of geographical research could scarcely be enhanced by any notice they may receive in this country, where the distinction

> would have to be shared with any gentleman who might feel disposed to use his influence with the periodical press in sounding his own praises, or in reciprocating compliments with friends and partisans. As regards other countries in which the Science of Physical Geography has become developed, I had already stated my views at length in the columns of a Journal [*The Journal of the Indian Archipelago and Eastern Asia*], which, although published in the far east, has a circulation on the continent of Europe scarcely less extensive than that of the Geographical Society's publications.
>
> Again thanking your Lordship for the unvarying courtesy I have met with in the course of a correspondence which must have been as disagreeable to your Lordship as it has been to myself...

The same year, Hippolyte Baillière, the publishers of *The Native Races...*, produced a 48-page pamphlet, 'Contributions to the Physical Geography of South-Eastern Asia', which reprinted (now with additional notes and a map) George's article that had appeared in Logan's *The Journal...* in May 1852.

Earl tackled the controversy in a substantially expanded Introduction, but neither this pamphlet nor the publication of the correspondence led to apologies or acknowledgements, the arguments having become bogged down with disputed dates and 'misunderstandings'. There was ever an air of superiority, not to say snobbery, from London-based metropolitan scholars, directed against those who were not.

In an 1852 letter on the Murchison matter to his old friend, Admiral (now Sir) Francis Beaufort KCB, George wrote: 'It was bad enough to be snubbed by the geologists, and to have my labours for years pronounced worthless by a set of quacks who had only a smattering of the science which they professed to lead, but to find them coolly appropriating the very theory they combined to upset, is more than even my patient nature can bear.'

The Earl/Wyld/Murchison/RGS contretemps concerning Australian gold caught the eye of some Americans in London who were looking for representatives to market a invention, the Berdan Pan, named after its inventor, Hiram Berdan. Designed for ore-crushing, it had been tested in gold fields in America, and the New York-based company were looking for export opportunities. George had been at a demonstration of the Berdan Pan in London in late-October 1853 and contact was soon established between the Americans and Earl. As Annie wrote in her 'Memoirs':

> My father determined to go again to Australia – a country to which he would always turn and would go to if he could. He was employed as an agent or something of that kind for a quartz crushing machine... Berdan was an American, and I remember we visited at the house or houses of Americans at Hampstead.... This was the time of the height of gold fever in Australia soon after the discovery of gold there.

Earl, given his long-standing interest in gold-mining and production in the Eastern seas, as well as his contacts in the area, was appointed the Australian (and perhaps region-wide) representative for the British company, Hyde Clarke & Associates, who had acquired the British and Imperial rights to manufacture and sell the Berdan Pan.

Donald Chaput in his paper, 'George Samuel Windsor Earl, Ethnologist as Hawker', wrote of the tool:

> The Berdan Pan averaged five feet in diameter. Two heavy cast[-]iron balls were placed in the pan. A drive shaft (horse or mule powered) moved the pan. Ore and mercury were placed in the pan, water added, then the horse was put into motion.
>
> The entire pan was set at an angle. The pan would go about 35rpm, the two iron balls sloshing and crushing, and the mercury would mix with the gold and sink to the bottom... There were dozens of modifications to the Berdan Pan but, from 1852 until 1930, the basic principle remained the same.
>
> The Berdan Pan was not the wonder of the ages, it was not even a good device. It was one of thousands of crushing machines, but it arrived early in the fields and held on longer than all the others. The Berdan was small, inexpensive, with few moving parts. However, it figures here because of the merchandising methods that involved a wandering ethnologist.

George Earl had been in England for around 18 months. It seems to have been a fallow period professionally, apart from the publication of *The Native Races...* He had been unable to complete its companion volume; he appears to have not written any papers or essays, or to have become involved creatively in any of the learned bodies or associations, with the sole exception of reading his paper, 'Progress of Discovery in the Western Portion of New Guinea, from 1828 to 1852', during the second week of September 1853 to a meeting in Hull of the British Association for the Advancement of Science.

There were also the perennial problems with his health. Perhaps he thought that both the Australian climate and the country itself would be salubrious. He certainly was deeply at odds with the intellectual climate in London in his disciplines and such may have fed a general dissatisfaction and a desire for new pastures. The groundwork he had laid in Singapore was now not to be furthered, at least for the time being. Perhaps he saw the Berdan Pan as a way to earn a substantial amount of money and decided to grasp the opportunity. Whatever the circumstances, at 41 years old, he, along with Clara and Annie, were booked for passage to Australia.

George had been able to be with his mother and sister for the first time since brother Percy had died. Sister Elizabeth's husband, John Loftus Hartwell, had died in Sydney in 1849, so no doubt there were family business matters to be settled. Living at Wildwood at the time was Percy's daughter, Rosa. She appears in the 1851 Census as 'Kate, aged 11, granddaughter'. Old Elizabeth Earl and her daughter seem to have gone on to bring up and educate Rosa. George was also able to be in touch with, but not see much of, Percy's widow, Ann, and the two boys. Sadly, they continued not to be recognised at Wildwood. Clara and Annie spent time with the Siborne family, precious months together in an age of separations. Clara's mother, now a widow, must have been saddened by their decision to leave England again for the far-off East as would have George's family.

– Chapter Eighteen –

Australia and Onward
1855-1857

I hate to leave the field when success is crowning my labours.

•

The family sailed from Liverpool in November 1854 on the *Golden Age*, a new American ship. Weighing nearly 3000 tons, she was a state-of-the-art paddle wheeler and, being a steamship, she offered a then new experience of open sea travel. Annie remembered:

> I recall the voyage to Australia very well. The ship seemed to me like a great floating Hotel... A large amount of gambling went on and I saw the green tables of an evening piled up with heaps of gold. I do not remember the places we stopped at on the way until we got to Melbourne, by which time I had come to know the ship so thoroughly that I very officiously showed over a party of successful gold-diggers and their women belongings who were dressed in the most gorgeously coloured silk raiment and who, appreciating my efforts, presented me with five shillings which my mother in great indignation made me return.

The voyage took circa three months and they arrived in Sydney during the early months of 1855. Soon, the family had temporarily settled in Parramatta, about 14 miles west of the city centre. The previous August, news of the formation of Hyde Clarke & Associates had reached Melbourne where it was announced to considerable interest that two models of the Berdan Pan were to be marketed, one with a seven-foot diameter and the other with a four-foot diameter. The larger pan required four or six horses/mules to work it and sold at £600; the smaller required just one animal and cost £100. In the same announcement it was reported that G.W. Earl had been appointed the Berdan agent for Australia.

One of George's first tasks was to secure storage and distribution for the pans, which he arranged with a Melbourne firm, Samuel and Co. These were relatively early days in the Australian gold industry and there were a number of competing devices in the marketplace. Once much of the surface alluvial gold had been captured, attention turned to quartz deposits which were known to contain considerable amounts of the metal. The Berdan Pan was initially promoted as a machine capable of crushing large amounts of quartz. The press was enthusiastic, calling it the 'only effective amalgamator'. Earl travelled widely and, although company records have been lost, it would appear that he made dozens of sales in Victoria and New South Wales. It was robustly built, relatively inexpensive, easy to operate, and would prove very well suited for small jobs, fine crushing, working black sands and for cleaning mill refuse that had a high mercury content.

During the first half of 1855, the Earl family was somewhat peripatetic, moving from Parramatta to Fernhill to stay with Annie's godfather, Edward Cox, and his family, and then to a hotel in Melbourne. That they didn't settle anywhere permanently may have indicated that George was taking a wait-and-see attitude as to whether he could support the family through sales of the Berdan Pan. Or there is a reasonable possibility that Earl was tasked to establish the basic network in Australia and then travel on to establish other centres of sales and distribution.

Not long after arrival, Earl did comment publicly on a current debate as to which route was most appropriate for steamships between London and Sydney/Melbourne. These cities wished communications to be via Singapore and hence the Torres Strait (the latter a 4,200-mile voyage), but an alternative was suggested for six months via the Torres Strait and six months via Cape Leeuwin. Earl favoured the latter and his memorandum arguing such was printed in the *Singapore Free Press* of May 3rd 1855 and prefaced with the remark, '...Mr G Windsor Earl, who has devoted a large share of attention to the subject, and whose practical acquaintance with both routes must enable him to discuss the matter with peculiar clearness and intelligence'.

On the 19th of July 1855, some seven months after their arrival from London, the Earls sailed for Singapore from Sydney on the barque *Monarch*, calling at Moreton Bay (Brisbane), Bali and Java. The *Monarch* was under charter to the Australian Government to carry AC (later Sir Augustus) Gregory and his team to the mouth of the Victoria River some 300 miles south-west of Port Essington. They joined the *Monarch* at Moreton Bay on 12th of August, where, along with the schooner *Tom Tough*, they also loaded 50 horses and two hundred sheep for the use of Gregory's expedition. Their plan was to travel inland from the Victoria River, crossing the Northern Territory and Queensland, then back to Moreton Bay.

Although George's co-presence on-board was probably a coincidence, he was nevertheless warmly greeted by the explorers and by a previous acquaintance, the German botanist, Baron Sir Ferdinand Mueller. Expedition member John Kent, in a letter to the Royal Geographical Society, wrote: 'Mr G. Windsor Earl is also a passenger on board the former vessel, and his experience in tropical Australia will be of great value to the expedition'. As the Earl family were bound for a different final destination, any help presumably would have been by way of advice. From Moreton Bay, the *Monarch* sailed through the Torres Strait and then past the entrance of Port Essington on September 1st 1855. At 10 p.m. on the following day she grounded on a reef in the entrance of Port Paterson. The *Monarch* was stranded for ten days, only floating off on a spring tide with the help of the *Tom Tough*, which had stood by throughout. Annie wrote:

> My father was extremely anxious during this time as it was discovered that there were no fire-arms on board, with the exception of one pistol, and we were lying in the midst of islands peopled by antagonistic natives; his anxiety every day for fear boats would come off and discover our helpless condition was very great. After we were able to move again a boat did come after us containing several savages who were anxious to barter fruit and some beautifully made baskets in exchange for bottles, pieces of old iron or anything they could get. My father noticed one of the savages had frizzy hair dyed red and was anxious to secure an example of it for his ethnological collection. Another savage took up a piece of hoop iron and sawed away until a piece of hair came off.

Both ships arrived safely at the mouth of the Victoria River on the 24th of September where Gregory and his team disembarked.* The *Monarch* then sailed on to Buleleng, on the north coast of Bali, arriving during the third week of October 1856. George decided she was in no fit condition to transport the Earl family any further. Indeed, the *Monarch* continued on to Singapore where she was broken up. Whilst in Bali, Clara fell ill, and Annie recalled: 'My mother was very ill of fever and nearly died. We had brought with us from Australia a very nice Irish servant, called Marjorie, who afterwards nursed my mother devotedly and was probably the means of saving her life.'

* The expedition spent eight months exploring and mapping a substantial area in North Australia. One of its findings was that a vast inland sea in the continent, the existence of which had been believed by so many [including Earl], almost certainly did not exist. The expedition also searched (in vain) for any sign of the lost Leichhardt party.

There was probably no better place to recuperate than beautiful and calm Buleleng. Six weeks passed before they were able to travel. On a small coastal vessel, they sailed up the north coast of Java first to Banje Wanje (Sweet Waters) and then to Batavia, first visited by George more than 20 years before. Here they spent the Christmas of 1855, and then made passage to Singapore. *The Straits Times* of 22nd of January 1856 reported that they had arrived on the *Koning der Nederlanden* on 15th of January 1856. Earl was to later write of the trip from Sydney that he had been 'so ill with dysentery that it was only by short stages that I got there at all'.

More than three years had passed since George and Clara had last left Singapore. Married now for just under ten years, Clara was only 27 years old, Annie eight-and-a-half, and George 43. They settled in a house next to the Magistrates' Court, Annie was enrolled in school, and Earl began the resumption of his legal career. The following month, he wrote a detailed report from Singapore to Henry Hyde Clarke of Hyde Clarke & Associates in London in which he was enthusiastic about the future commercial possibilities for the Berdan Pan. In reference to his activities in Australia on behalf of the company, he wrote: 'I hate to leave the field when success is crowning my labours.' It is unclear what compelling circumstances necessitated his leaving. In the same report he mentions ongoing health problems but that he was considering trips to Sarawak and Malacca to promote the product.

During the voyage to Singapore he had observed in Bali and Java that the Berdan Pan might be a far better machine than the ones presently in use throughout the region for extraction of oil from copra – the dried

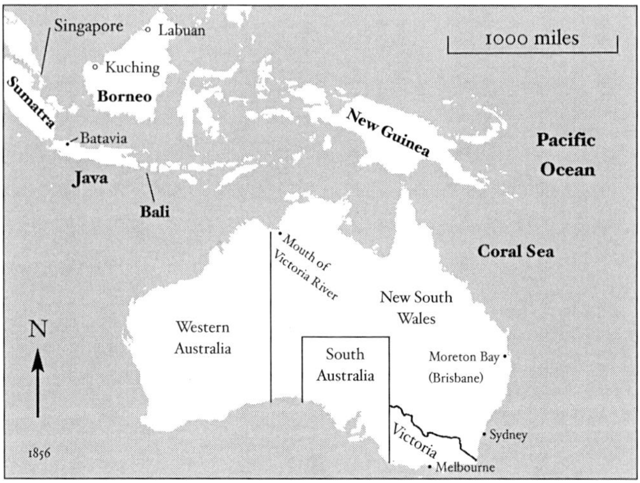

meat or dried kernel of the coconut. This, of course, was in addition to the Pan's more usual use for crushing quartz gold, tin and antimony.

The family soon journeyed to Malacca. Annie recalled:

> We went for a while to stay at Malacca, an interesting place more dead than alive, where there were the remains of both Portuguese and Dutch occupation... The inhabitants were nearly all half-caste and of Dutch descent. My father was practising as a lawyer; one of his clients was a rich old Chinese woman called Nonya Wong. I saw something of Chinese manners and customs... as we were living in the main street of Malacca... The great Mahommetan feast of 'Hussein Hassan' [Mohurrum] also took place while we were here and it was thought best we should remain indoors as they work themselves up into a great excitement over it.

In late April 1856, with Earl's health showing some improvement, the family made a visit to Sarawak on the north-west coast of Borneo to see George's old friend, Sir James Brooke. Earl had also been in recent negotiations with Brooke's newly formed Borneo Company for the purchase of a number of Berdan Pans, mainly for use in processing antimony, a major resource of the area.

Brooke, the Rajah of Sarawak, ruled from his capital, Kuching, and the Earls were honoured guests at his residence there. Brooke and Earl had come to know each other in London during the period when Earl was involved in the planning for the new settlement in Northern Australia. Brooke had sought Earl's advice on sailing in the Torres Strait amongst other information about the greater area. The two of them were kindred spirits with regard to the belief in the great potential of the East. Brooke had written in 1838: 'I go to carry Sir Stamford Raffles' views in Java over the whole Archipelago.' Earl's 1837 *The Eastern Seas* had had a significant effect on Brooke and he was determined to counter the influence of the East India Company and the Dutch, as well as combating the pernicious influence of endemic piracy in the area.

Some ten years older than Earl, James Brooke had served in the East India Company's Bengal Army, was wounded at the Battle of Rungpore Fort and was eventually invalided out on a pension of £70 per annum. He had become fascinated by the East, devoted much study to it, and financed a trading voyage, which was highly unsuccessful, to Macao. Brooke then returned to England, and on the death of his father in December 1835, inherited £30,000 (north of £25 million today). He purchased the *Royalist,* a 142-ton schooner (essentially a private warship with six 6-pounders) in 1836, and made preparations for an eventual return to the East, including the issuance of a prospectus for the voyage which again reflected the influence of *The Eastern Seas.*

Brooke arrived in the East in 1838 and, after successfully carrying out a mission to Kuching at the behest of Governor Bonham of Singapore, returned to Sarawak from Singapore in August 1840. There, he immediately became involved in the suppression of a revolt led by the local Malay chiefs against the rule of Sultan Omar Ali of Brunei. For his successful efforts, he was eventually appointed as the Governor of Sarawak by the Sultan and then, on August 18th 1842, the title of Rajah was bestowed on him by the Sultan – a position that gave him near imperial power.

The Earls stayed in considerable luxury at the Rajah's residence and Annie recorded with wonder her impressions of Kuching and Brooke:

> I was greatly interested in the visits of the Dyaks, the original inhabitants of Borneo, considered very savage and best known by their man-hunting expeditions. No Dyak was considered worth anything who had not killed one or more men and who was not able to exhibit their heads about his dwelling. They looked upon Rajah Brooke as an arbiter of their disagreements and had the greatest respect and awe of him… [they] seemed to look on the Rajah as a kind of demi-god…
>
> I went with my mother to the Court House and saw the Rajah hold his Court there; he dispensed justice with a great deal of shrewdness and apparently to the contentment of all.

In May 1856, George travelled inland from Kuching to the goldfields at Bau in hopes of selling Berdan Pans to the Borneo Company and to the Chinese prospectors. Annie also reported that her father, having gone up-country with a Mr. Fox, overheard (through his understanding of local languages and dialects) of a planned Chinese uprising against the Rajah. Hurrying back to Kuching, Earl passed on the information to Brooke who was then able to stifle the plot.

His business completed, George and the family took their leave and returned to Singapore, but serious trouble soon afterwards erupted in Sarawak. The Chinese, who for generations had been working the alluvial deposits of gold in Upper Sarawak, rose up, sacked Kuching, killed some of the English residents, and seized the government. The Rajah narrowly escaped with his life. The insurrection was put down by the Rajah's nephew (who would later succeed James) with a force of loyal Dayaks and Malays and the Brooke dynasty continued its rule of Sarawak, which was to last until the Japanese invasion in 1941.

In June, Earl wrote from Singapore to Hyde Clarke enclosing a report on progress made and detailing the negotiations with Brooke's Borneo Company, but by mid-August, in what was to be his last letter to Hyde Clarke, he asked for a settlement of all his accounts, credits and other related business to the Berdan Pan.

Reports from Australia had now firmly established that the larger Berdan Pan, at £600 (six times the cost of the smaller version), was in comparison to other machines now on the market woefully inadequate in the crushing of large amounts of ore. Earl may have felt that he could not achieve enough income from sales of the smaller model alone. He suggested that either Clarke himself or another should go to Australia to push sales; but this was to mark the end of Earl's involvement with the Berdan Pan, although eventually there were to be hundreds of the smaller machines in use in Australia and elsewhere in the region, some of them still working into the 20th century.

* * *

The year and a half since the Earl family had left London had been a period of incessant travel. Although his intellect and ambition remained undiminished, recurring bouts of malaria, dysentery and the lingering effects of rheumatic fever could no longer be brushed aside. Moreover, the life he had been leading for the previous 30 years had brought him some fame but at the price of being often on the move and a lack of financial stability. Earl needed to turn his attention to obtaining a reliable income to support the family.

By the beginning of 1857, he was focussing on his legal and advocacy practice. Now acting as an independent Law agent, he obtained the lease of premises in the High Street to serve as both office and residence. This was adjacent to the Court House and the town hall. Being in the centre of the city it offered everything which George and Clara needed, including a nearby school for Annie. We have few glimpses of the Earl's family activities at this time, but Annie did recall:

> One night at the Napiers[,] Captain Keppel (afterwards the Hon. Sir Henry Keppel) also dined with some of the officers of his man-of-war and he was very kind to me and I took a great fancy to him. He had known my father many years before and they were both friends of Rajah Brooke's.

> I remember being very naughty on one occasion and throwing a pair of stag's horns out of the window, which made my mother very angry as they had just been sent back from being set up in a very handsome way. My father was told of this on his return from the Court and he administered a sound whipping to me which did me a great deal of good and made me hesitate when I felt inclined to give way to temper on other occasions.
>
> ...We had pet animals of which I was very fond: such as mongooses, a bear and of course monkeys. My father liked having birds about so long as they were not in cages.

Keppel (who had commanded the 1849 evacuation of the settlement at Port Essington) would become the Admiral of the Fleet in 1872 to cap a long and distinguished naval career that saw action in South America, Europe, Africa, Borneo, China, Macao, the Crimea and Malaysia. In 1853, he had published *A visit to the Indian archipelago, in H.M. ship Mæander. With portions of the private journal of Sir James Brooke, K.C.B.* in which a significant part details the defence of James Brooke who had come under parliamentary criticism for his methods of fighting piracy and of his rise to being Rajah.

In this case, two parliamentarians, Mr Hume and Mr Cobden persistently raised loud questions in the House as to the propriety of the methods and means used by Brooke. In this, they were goaded on by the Eastern Archipelago Company who had received the coal concession in Labuan, off the coast of Borneo, from Brooke. In what was at its base a commercial dispute, Earl was quoted by both sides many times from his letters and *The Eastern Seas* in this serious controversy – selectively by Hume's faction in a misleading manner, and in a sober fashion by supporters of Brooke. Much hinged on establishing who were not and who were to be considered pirates (and therefore subject to punitive action) but Keppel was in no doubt of where the right lay. He dedicated his book to Brooke and wrote of Earl: 'The other gentleman [along with Brooke] is equally an authority; he is at this time an able contributor to colonial literature, and an ornament to the society of Singapore.' In the end, Brooke and his supporters carried the day and the Eastern Archipelago Company, in spite of perhaps having a legitimate commercial gripe, was eventually forced into liquidation a few years later.

George Earl seems to have had wind of his upcoming appointment for a government position and, in anticipation of having a steady income, plans were made to send Annie to school in England. A family friend, the Presbyterian minister of Singapore, The Reverend Mackenzie Fraser, was consulted and he recommended a Miss Truman on the Isle of Wight where Fraser's own two children were being educated. And indeed, Earl was appointed stipendiary Police Magistrate for Singapore (but not as an assistant to the Resident Councillor which would have put him much higher in the government hierarchy) as of June 1st 1857 at a salary of 600 rs per annum (£55,000 today).

Before Annie was to sail to England in the middle of 1857, news arrived of the outbreak of the Indian Mutiny. The revolt and accounts of atrocities there by the sepoy native troops shocked and unnerved the Straits Settlements. Annie wrote in her 'Memoirs':

> People can now scarcely realize how much the public was affected by this. Nearly every family had relations in India either amongst the residents or the Military and for a long time no one could know what was the fate of their relatives. Letters came only once a month; there was no telegraph... There was a very large number of convicts from all parts of India including the mutinous districts; their sole guard was a Sepoy Regiment... The fear was that this regiment might open the jails and let loose the prisoners...*
>
> My mother went on a visit to Mrs. Napier who was staying at Abou Bakr's house at Tanjongpagar. He had put his house at her disposal; but my father sent for her back as it would have set so bad an example for an official's wife to have done this.

The sepoys were to remain loyal and the government could depend on the continued support of the Chinese and Malays. But the worry and uncertainty that swept through the Straits Settlements during the troubles in India became a contributory factor in the process which would see Singapore, along with Malacca and Penang (including Province Wellesley), become a Crown colony a decade later.

Around the time of George taking up the duties of Magistrate, the Earls moved from the High Street to a bungalow (as can be seen in Percy Carpenter's painting of 1856) on Mt. Erskine, a low hill overlooking Singapore. Its elevation would have provided slightly cooler temperatures and welcome breezes and it was a most desirable place to live. The residence would come to provide some domestic stability after the travelling and uncertainty of recent years.

* Calcutta's long-standing policy of transporting convicts to the Straits Settlements was deeply resented there.

Annie Earl sailed on a P&O steamer bound for England in July 1857, just after her tenth birthday. For George and Clara to bid farewell to their only child could not have been easy. Nevertheless, to do so was both a mark and an obligation for parents of a certain class and standing. It would be a number of years before George and Clara were to be reunited with Annie as a young woman.

Unsurprisingly, Earl seems to have worked little on his scholarly researches during 1857. He continued with his legal work and public duties, and was laying the ground for developments in what would prove to be a pivotal 1858.

Southern Plains, Pinang from the Great Tree Pass,
print from watercolour by John Turnbull Thomson, 1848.
PENANG STATE LIBRARY

– Chapter Nineteen –

Penang and Province Wellesley
1858-1863

The suggestion that the Straits Settlements should be separated from India and transformed into a crown colony was first mooted in print by George Windsor Earl.
CM Turnbull

•

The Indian Mutiny was largely suppressed by early 1858, but the decision had already been reached in London that the governance of India should be taken over by the Crown and that the East India Company, who were found wanting, should be liquidated. The provisions of the Government of India Act 1858 would commence on the 1st of November of that year. The Straits Settlements would still come under the suzerainty of the office of the Governor-General of India, and little would change with regard to administrative policies.

Calcutta had not made adequate provision for Straits' authorities to cope with a population that had now almost quadrupled since 1830, and civil servants posted there by Calcutta often possessed little knowledge (including languages) of the area and therefore were prone to creating unproductive or damaging policies.

Moreover, the number of administrative posts was woefully inadequate and Calcutta objected to senior positions being filled by the 'uncovenanted'. EIC-covenanted civil servants (as distinct from military, maritime and ecclesiastical organisations) occupied senior positions that required £500 bonds in insurance of their duties, and for the most part the occupants had jobs/pensions for life. Charles Burton Buckley's book *Old Times in Singapore* quotes a Mr J. T. Thomson writing in 1865, who captured the long-standing popular, if unduly harsh, sentiment:

> To live in it [the East India Company's Civil Service] for 21 years and to do nothing, either good or bad... was all that was necessary for the attainment of fortune, pensions and honour...once nominated, the Civil Servant had no further care in the world for had he not talents for the political or revenue department, he was always fitted for the sacred office of a Judge. ...He could always draw his monthly salary bill and take his pension in due course.

In 1857, Governor Blundell had applied to Calcutta for official permission to appoint uncovenanted officials to the key posts of Resident Councillors (a *fait accompli*), because the shortage had been so acute that at the end of 1856, the Assistant Residents at all three stations in the Straits Settlements were European-born but locally appointed, uncovenanted, men. Calcutta refused; but this was ignored and as an effect of this locally determined policy, an 'uncovenanted' George Windsor Earl was appointed in the latter half of 1858 to the post of third (Deputy) Assistant Resident at Singapore.*

Earl's appointment was a substantial promotion (it put him in the top 15 or so of the government hierarchy); posts were few and those available much sought-after in an age of political patronage. It seems odd that Governor Blundell, whose autocratic navigation between the demands of his superiors in India and the wishes of the local population had made him unpopular, would choose to appoint Earl. In *The Eastern Seas* of 1837, George had advocated the separation of the Straits Settlements from the Government of India and having the former administered by the British Government. In 1855, *The Straits Times* had called for the formation of a Reform League to agitate for political change led by a break from rule by India. Among the leaders of the Reform League were William Read, Abraham Logan (*Singapore Free Press*), Robin Woods (*The Straits Times*) and Joaquim d'Almeida (son of José). George Earl was very much part of this circle and their aims could have hardly endeared any of them to the Governor. Indeed, the *Singapore Free Press* of February 4th 1858 opined about rumours of a Blundell' resignation: '...a hope is expressed that this report may be true, and that Mr Blundell may be accompanied on his retirement by some of his sons[-]in-law'. Perhaps it was the replacement in August 1859 of Edmund Blundell by William Orfeur Cavenagh as Governor of the Straits Settlements that had secured the path for Earl's appointment.

George continued with his duties in Singapore as Magistrate, but towards the end of 1858, at his own request, he was transferred to Penang in replacement of the Assistant Resident Councillor and Acting Police Magistrate, J. B. Alexander. It is unclear why Earl requested the posting, as his situation in Singapore was more than satisfactory with a senior rank

* After the demise of the EIC, the structure of the government was changed in 1858 with the creation of an overseeing commission headed by the Governor. Now, under the Governor (appointed by Calcutta), the administrative areas of the Straits Settlements (Penang, Malacca and Singapore) would be headed by a Resident (essentially a Lieutenant-Governor) and assisted by an Assistant and a third (Deputy) Resident.

in society, a charming house on Mount Erskine and in a locale considered one of the most salubrious in the East. A *Straits Times* article of December 25th 1858 announcing Earl's posting described the duties faced by his successor on the Singapore bench as being 'arduous and onerous, and far too heavy for one Justice to discharge'. Penang would offer little in the way of respite, but the variety of duties there were probably more to Earl's desire.

Thomas Bradell held the post of Senior Assistant Resident of Penang, but had returned to England on long-term sick leave. J. B. Alexander had acted for him in his absence, but after a few months he, too, became ill, and died. So, George was to assume the post *pro tem* of Senior Assistant Resident at Penang, which included the duties of Police Magistrate for Province Wellesley. Both Malacca and Province Wellesley had recently been instructed to hold courts in the interior of these areas in an attempt to bring 'the advantages of British Justice within the reach of almost every one of our subjects' and to 'materially... weaken the pernicious influence of those illegal tribunals... that the settlements of disputes amongst the peasantry is often referred'. The measure was directly aimed at 'counteracting the power of the Secret Societies', as the *Singapore Free Press* put it on September 13th 1860 in their 'Annual Report on the Administration of the Straits Settlements 1859-1860'. Earl's combined responsibilities would now necessitate extensive travel in the region, a requirement that he would make good use of, but one that would come to tax his precarious health.

George and Clara sailed for the capital of Penang, George Town, on February 4th 1859 on the local steamer *Hooghly*. The island of Penang (then officially referred to as Prince of Wales' Island) is situated at the north-west entrance to the Straits of Malacca and is some 13 by 10 miles in area. In 1859, its population was comprised mostly of Chinese, Malays and Tamils. Possessing an excellent harbour, there was a thriving shipping business, which included the valuable exports of natural produce, especially *penang* (betel nut), rice, sugar, timber, coconut and a variety of spices including nutmeg and cloves. Along with Province Wellesley – some two miles east across a narrow channel, on the Malaysian Peninsula – constituted a substantial percentage of Straits Settlements trade, in addition to being its breadbasket.

Initially, George and Clara had houses in both George Town and Province Wellesley. Of the two areas, George Town was the more cosmopolitan and salubrious. Graced by Penang Hill, which rises to 2700ft just a few miles behind the port, it offered significantly cooler temperatures and was famed as far away as India for its sanatoria.

Earl was now reunited with his close friend James Richardson Logan, again editor of the *Penang Gazette*. Logan was to publish only three final series of *The Journal of the Indian Archipelago* from 1859 through 1863 and George would have the honour of occupying the entirety of the final issue. It was also during this time that he decided to bury the hatchet with the Royal Geographical Society over his displeasure regarding the Murchison affair and, perhaps, over his own feelings about the tensions between metropolitan and colonial scholarship. In a letter from Penang dated 16th of May 1859 written to Dr Norton Shaw, Secretary of the Society (whom he addressed as 'My dear Dr Shaw'), George expressed that 'I am glad to see that your Society is progressing so favourably, for although I felt a little sore at something which happened a few years ago, I have always highly appreciated the value of the Society's labours'.

One of George's early and testing assignments was to investigate the trouble in the Krian district of the Malay state of Perak on the southern border of Province Wellesley. A local chief had attacked and wounded Penang's Deputy-Commissioner of Police during investigations about complaints by Chinese traders from Penang of ill-treatment there. Governor Cavenagh in Singapore instructed Earl to proceed to Krian to investigate, but a month went by before W. T. Lewis, the Resident Councillor of Penang, supplied him with the necessary police report and instructions.

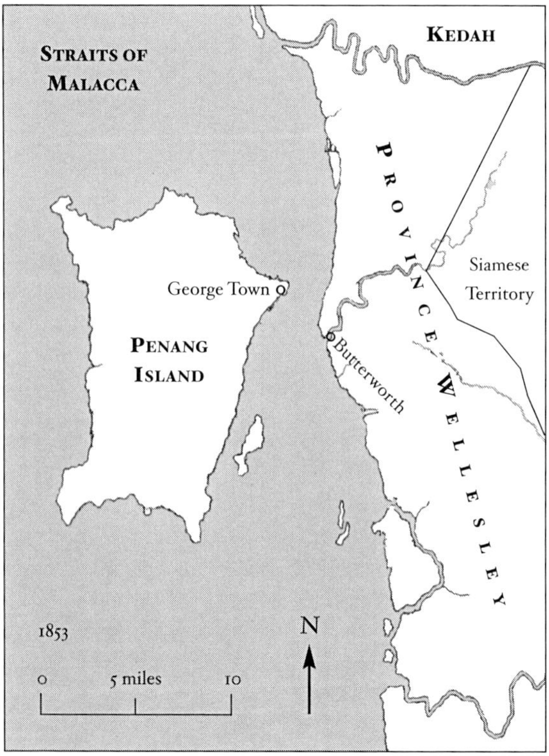

Cavenagh's sharp annoyance about the delay led to an acrimonious correspondence in which Earl's complaints concerning the Resident Councillor's inefficiency were not well received by the Governor, who demanded loyalty among officials and did not fully grasp the situation.

Lewis latterly had a record of poor judgement: two years before Earl arrived, the Resident Councillor had mishandled the disturbances among the Chinese community in Penang and discredited the whole Administration. CM Turnbull described the state of affairs:

> By 1859, a sick old man, Lewis had retreated into seclusion in his hilltop residence and virtually abdicated responsibility to his subordinates. Lewis clung to his post because he could not afford to retire, but he had been so long in the Straits that no one else suspected that he was not a regular covenanted official and when he was compulsorily retired in 1860 on the grounds of senility and gross inefficiency, the authorities were astounded to discover that Lewis was in fact an uncovenanted official ineligible for an adequate retirement pension.

However, Governor Cavenagh expressed concern for Councillor Lewis who had served in the civil service in the region for some 52 years and he aided the successful attempt to secure Lewis some sort of adequate pension. The early confusion and conflict between Cavenagh and Earl over the Perek matter was soon forgotten and George was to gain Cavenagh's respect.

* * *

Out of the thousands of cases that Earl was to hear from the bench, few transcriptions of these may survive, but one was printed in *Straits Law Reports*, 1877, and gives a fair example of the everyday working of the courts and those before it, and might have been chosen for the anthology due to the unusual circumstances of complainant, defendant (a police official) and verdict. The contemporary problems of perjuring witnesses and lawbreaking police officials are also present. The case is given here in full:

> No. 704
>
> Friday 4th November, 1859.
>
> The Examination of *Peter Duggie, Frederick Bowen, Joseph Burgess, Ooee Ah Hoon, Tamby* P. P. 144, and *John Scott* M.D., taken on this 4th day of November in the year of our Lord one thousand eight hundred and fifty nine, in the Police Magistrate's office at P. W. Island aforesaid, before

the undersigned Magistrate of Police for Prince of Wales' Island aforesaid, in the presence and hearing of Inspector Frederick Gibbons, who is charged this day before me with assaulting and beating the said Peter Duggie, in Chulia Street, on the evening of the 30th October instant, at about 5 o'clock.

Peter Duggie [Complainant], sworn states ;—I am a seaman of the ship "Sanderson" now lying in the harbour. On Sunday last I came on shore about 1/2 past four o'clock and went to the Crown and Anchor, public house, where I had two glasses of grog. While I was sitting there another Frenchman commenced quarrelling with a Chinese, and a police peon came up and interfered to prevent them from fighting. I was standing some distance off, looking on, when I received a blow on the head which knocked me down senseless. I do not know how I received the 2nd blow on my eye and cheek (complainant exhibits a wound on the upper part of the head, and a contusion on the cheek and left eye which is black) when I recovered I was taken to the Station house, and brought before the Magistrate next morning on a charge of being drunk and disorderly. I will swear that I only took two glasses of grog that afternoon.
Taken before me,
(Sd.) George Windsor Earl,
Police Magistrate.

Frederick Bowen [Witness for the Complainant], sworn states ;—I live in Chulia Street, I lately left the ship "Princess Royal" and have had no employment since. I was Steward of that ship. On Sunday afternoon about 5 o'clock I was talking with defendant at the Pitt Street Station when a peon brought information that there was a disturbance in Chulia Street, defendant immediately went in that direction—I followed and on the way defendant received a policeman's staff from a peon whom he met. He had nothing in his hand when he left the Station—when we arrived near the Crown and Anchor we saw four Europeans struggling with six or seven peons who appeared to be endeavouring to take them into custody. Defendant in the first instance endeavoured to pacify the Europeans, but afterwards he struck at them with the Policeman's staff, and knocked down three of the 4 men. Prosecutor was one of the three that were knocked down. He was the first that was struck. I did not see any one of the four men strike at defendant before he knocked them down. The three that were knocked down were taken to the Station-house.

By defendant [Inspector Frederick Gibbons].—I did not see any person strike the three men besides yourself. I did not see any brick-bats thrown. I did not see any of the peons strike the Europeans.
Taken before me.
(Sd.) George Windsor Earl,
Police Magistrate.

Joseph Burgess [Witness for the Complainant], sworn states;—I am living at the Crown and Anchor, public house, in Chulia Street. On Sunday last about 1 o'clock I do not remember the time exactly but it was in the afternoon, a crowd collected about the house to look at some French and Italian seamen, about fifteen altogether, who were drinking and amusing themselves in the front room; complainant was one of the number. One of the foreigners who is not present ran out brandishing a rattan, apparently for the purpose of driving away the crowd, who all retreated except one Chinaman who stood his ground, on which the foreigner struck him on the back with a rattan. The foreigner was not sober. The Chinaman abused the foreigner in English on which he struck him again and a fight commenced between them. Several peons came up to quell the disturbance. Complainant was present, and endeavoured to separate the combatants. He was perfectly sober, and had nothing in his hand—while this was going on defendant came running up with a Policeman's truncheon in his hand, with which he struck complainant a blow on the head, and while he was falling defendant struck him a second blow with the truncheon on the side of the face, defendant then struck another of the seamen and knocked him down also. About a dozen peons then dragged complainant and some of the other seamen towards the Station, and I saw one of the peons strike complainant with his fist several times while he was being dragged away insensible. The other man who was knocked down got up almost immediately.

By Defendant,—I saw the man who struck the Chinaman with a rattan running along the road with a peon on his back; the peon was endeavouring to pinion him and would not let him go.
Taken before me,
(Sd.) George Windsor Earl,
Police Magistrate

Inspector Gibbons—states in defence :—On Sunday last about 5 p.m. some peons came running to the Pitt Street Station and reported that there

was a disturbance in Chulia Street. I immediately went to the spot and on arriving near the Crown and Anchor, I saw an European seaman running about with a peon on his back, I saw two or three other seamen trying to wrest a truncheon from a peon and the complainant striking right and left at the natives, who had collected, I went up to him and put my hand on his breast, on which he struck at me, and I struck him with the truncheon, and some of the peons took him to the Station. Several other of the European seamen were also arrested.
[Taken] Before me,
(Sd.) George Windsor Earl,
Police Magistrate.

Defendant Calls.
OoeeAhRoon [Witness for the Defendant], sworn states;—I live in Bishop Street; am a Carpenter; On Sunday last about 5 p.m. I was, in Chulia Road when an European who is not present struck me with a rattan, and complainant struck me on the side of the head with his fist—defendant was not present then. Some of the peons tried to take the man up, who struck me with a rattan, into custody—defendant then came up, and complainant seized him by both hands, and struck at him, but I cannot say whether he hit him. The peon then ran for assistance and returned with some more peons. I did not see defendant strike complainant.
Defendant had nothing in his hand.
Taken before me
(Sd.) George Windsor Earl.,
Police Magistrate.

Tomby [Witness for the Defendant], H. P. 144—Sworn States;—I was present on this occasion and saw complainant there. Complainant took my coat and tore it, —I then took hold of complainant's companion and complainant; they assaulted me and struck me on the side of the nose (no mark). Defendant then came and took some of the Europeans into custody—I did not see defendant strike any of the Europeans. My eyes were dark—(*mata glap*).

By Defendant.—My coat was torn by the complainant. Complainant was drunk.
Taken before me
(Sd.) George Windsor Earl,
Police Magistrate.

John Seott, M. D., sworn states;—I have attended Complainant for the last three days and have dressed a wound on his head which seems to have been inflicted by a blunt instrument, such as a piece of wood; the scalp was divided, but the bone uninjured,

Taken before me,
(Sd.) George Windsor Earl,
Police Magistrate.

Sentence.—To pay a fine of 50 Rupees, all to be given to complainant as compensation for injury received.

Defendant, stating his inability to pay the fine, is sentenced two months' imprisonment in the House of Correction.
(Sd.) George Windsor Earl
Police Magistrate.

By the end of 1859, there were changes afoot for Straits Settlements' Civil Service personnel. George could have returned to Singapore with, probably, a promotion, but Governor Cavenagh noted in a letter to Captain MacPherson (then *ex officio* member of the Commission) that 'Earle [sic] does not wish to leave Penang at present'. In fact, George seems to have settled in and along with official duties was again taking up his scholarly researches. In April 1860, during a working tour of the northern boundaries of Province Wellesley, he heard reports of the existence of large mounds of shells which the locals believed to be natural deposits. On a return trip in August of that year, he 'came unexpectedly on a dome-shaped mound of cockle-shells, eighteen[-]feet high, and nearly two hundred paces in circumference at its base, lying about five furlongs to the north of the bridge that crosses the Leher Ikan Mati Lagoons'.

In what seems to have been his only serious venture into archaeology, Earl excavated part of the mound and ascertained that it was a man-made midden of great historical antiquity. It also contained some human remains; which he subsequently shipped to the Ethnological Society in London. The result of his investigations would later lead to the publication of an article that he had completed by the end of 1860, 'On the shell-mounds of Province Wellesley, in the Malay Peninsula'. It was to be read before the Ethnological Society in London on March 4th 1862, and as such provided the first description in print of any prehistoric (Neolithic) site in Malaya.

* * *

George and Clara's near two-year stay in the area seems to have suited them very well and they were not, uncharacteristically, looking for a change of scenery. In December 1860, a vacancy arose for the important position of Police Magistrate in Singapore. However, in writing on December 31st 1860 to Captain MacPherson (later the first Colonial Secretary when the Straits Settlements became a Crown colony in 1867), Governor Cavenagh noted:

> I had intended sending Earle [sic] to Singapore and bringing Smith here but Earl has begged to be allowed to remain in the Province even though he would receive higher pay by the change and under these circumstances of course I will not move him.

Stay they did and 1861 seems to have been a relatively quiet year for George and Clara. Now residing in Butterworth, Province Wellesley (across the narrow channel from George Town), Earl was cementing his career in the civil service. Also, through his working travels throughout Province Wellesley during this period, he compiled a series of notes which were assembled and published in a small volume by Pinang Gazette Printing in 1861 under the title *Topography and itinerary of Province Wellesley*.

Earl began collecting material in 1862 from his days in Port Essington to form the basis of a new work which would appear the following year both in Logan's *The Journal* and as a book. In his Introduction to *Handbook for Colonists in Tropical Australia*, George stakes out the territory:

> The arrangement of these notes for publication has not been altogether a labour of love. But it happened that during my official connection with Port Essington, which lasted from the first formation of the establishment in the year 1838 until within a few months of its abandonment in December, 1849, the chief duty assigned to me was that of collecting information which might prove useful to colonists in the event of the settlement being thrown open to private enterprise by the sale of Crown Lands. A portion of this information, more immediately relating to commerce, navigation, and the resources of neighbouring countries, has already been published, but I was permitted to withhold the details that could be interesting only to pastoral and agricultural settlers until a prospect arose of their being turned to a practical use. That time has at

> length arrived, the stock stations of the Queensland colonists having extended northward nearly to the parallel of the head of the Gulf of Carpentaria, while a movement has taken place which looks like a general advance along the whole line of southern colonies into the Tropical Region; – and my friend Mr. J. R. Logan having placed at my disposal the columns of the Journal of the Indian Archipelago, I can no longer plead any reasonable cause for hesitation. My materials are arranged in the form of a "Handbook," as being most convenient for reference, and at the same time best suited for keeping the Author strictly within the bounds of practical utility. I think it will be found to contain every well ascertained fact relating to the Tropical Region that is likely to prove acceptable to colonists, who may rest assured that these facts have been recorded without the slightest inclination on the part of the writer to make matters appear more favourable than they really are.
>
> Geo. Windsor Earl.
>
> Province Wellesley,
>
> *January 8th*, 1863.

There is a hint of defensiveness in Earl's Introduction that obliquely addresses previous public criticism of him due to his occasional penchant for excessive optimism. The work may have been assembled not only for the stated reasons, but also because, since the abandonment of Port Essington some 13 years before, scholarship and broad information in this field had lagged. *Handbook for Colonists in Tropical Australia* seems to have been, in part, written to reinforce his position as an expert on the topic, and to address a rising contemporary interest as well as offering 'every well[-]ascertained fact relating to the Tropical Region that is likely to prove acceptable to colonists...'

* * *

It was also during 1862 that George and Clara arranged for Annie to return after her schooling in Ryde on the Isle of Wight. She sailed from Southampton around the beginning of December under the care of a cousin of Governor Cavenagh's wife. The voyage took her via Gibraltar, Malta, Cairo, the Red Sea and Ceylon (Sri Lanka). In her 'Journal', Annie recalled her reunion as a 15-year-old in early 1863 with her parents:

> When we arrived in Penang my father came off to meet me and was very much moved at seeing me again after six years' absence. He then took me to Province Wellesley, which is on the mainland opposite Penang and

where he was Magistrate... My mother of course was waiting to receive me and equally of course made me welcome.

Other members of the Earl family had also made their way to the Straits Settlements. Sometime in 1862, the son of George's late brother Percy, William Percy Earl, arrived in Penang. William had been born in 1834 or early 1835 and became a certified second mate in 1858. It is not known why he decided to come to the Straits Settlements but once there he was to rise through a succession of posts and eventually was to hold the position of Commissioner of Police in Penang. He married Flora Anthony, a daughter of Anthony Aratoon Anthony in 1867, but died there in 1871.

William Percy Earl's younger brother, Alfred Huntley, also made his way to Penang. He had married an Elizabeth Bowers in 1856 when he was nineteen but was widowed a few years later. He was to marry Sarah Anthony, sister of Flora, in Penang in February 1868 and was listed as the Commander of the 147-ton brig *Lalla Rookh*. Little seems to be known of him and he was to die in 1869 and be buried in Penang.

Oddly, there is no mention of her cousins, William and Alfred, in Annie's 'Memoirs', but she does gives her impressions of her new home:

> Although it was a very quiet place I rather enjoyed my life at Province Wellesley. My day began very early while it was yet dark when I used to start out before sunrise for a ride with my father. Later on, when he was not so strong, I used to be accompanied by our head Syce, an old and trusted servant. No one who has not experienced it can understand the delight of this early ride while all is fresh and cool, on roads free from dust winding about through large cocoanut [sic] groves, past Malay villages where the early morning fires were being lighted for the morning meal; or on raised roads lifted up above the mangrove swamps, the trees coming very near on which frequently large troops of monkeys were established who took great exception to my appearance and more especially to that of Don, the great Cuban bloodhound who always accompanied me on these rides. There were two kinds of monkeys that I noticed: the small active ones like those seen on barrel-organs in England who chattered vehemently, and a larger more sedate kind not nearly so active, many of them with grey beards, but who also swore in their more emphatic fashion when they saw the dog. Once or twice on these rides we came across the footmarks of a tiger; those of wild boar were more often seen and, in Province Wellesley at least, they were the more dangerous beasts. My father used to dislike the killing of tigers there as they were

never man-eaters* and used to keep down the numbers of wild pig which did much harm amongst the sugar plantations and other native produce, and had been known wilfully to attack and gore to death human beings. While we were at Province Wellesley the marks of the tiger were seen in the verandah of our house where one had evidently passed the night!

We also had occasional visits from snakes, an enormous boa constrictor had been found in the building next to ours and its skin, when dried, stretched from one side of our big hall to the other. It had been mistaken by one of the native chemists for a pile of gunny bags, and only sitting down on it and feeling it move did he realize what he was sitting on. My mother also used to kill snakes in the garden.

During my rides I sometimes used to visit one of the Malay houses with my father. These houses are built on piles and a very open ladder has to be climbed to reach the door which is rather small. After creeping in all seems at first very dark as there are no windows. The floor is uncomfortable to walk across as it bends and rocks with each footstep, being made of some kind of matting – all very cool and airy no doubt. The interior of the house seemed, as far as I can recall, one large room with open compartments down one side – or both...

My father was fond of the Malays who had an implicit trust in him. He used to take lengthy journeys to hold long Courts in different parts of the Province, sometimes going thirty miles and back in one day. Once or twice my mother and myself accompanied him but the journey was rather an arduous one and the courthouse was generally a hot place in which to spend the day.

By the middle of 1863, Earl's accumulated medical afflictions necessitated a stay at a sanatorium. As a government officer he was entitled to the use of a bungalow on Penang Hill for a month and the family decamped from Province Wellesley. Annie wrote that, 'the change from the heat was delightful and the vegetation was so beautiful. I recollect riding up in the afternoon and feeling the temperature getting cooler as we got higher and higher. (My mother was carried up in a chair; she never rode.) It was sufficiently cool for us to find the oil frozen in the morning and it had to be melted in the sun before being poured into the lamps.'

A few months after the recuperative stay on Penang Hill, on the 29th of August, Earl was to make his weekly visit to the Court in Bukit Tambun in the south of Province Wellesley. Whilst steering a small boat on

* Annie was mistaken about the lack of danger from tigers to the local inhabitants.

that excessively hot day he felt a giddiness during the 3- or 4-hour journey but continued onward, presided over the court cases but was, as he wrote later, 'conscious of slightly unusual effort in guiding the pen and thinking, and of something wrong with the sight of [my] right eye, the field of vision of which did not correspond with that of [the] left, compelling [me] to keep one eye closed'.

George returned home to Butterworth that night, slept soundly, and saw a doctor the next morning who noted (in addition to Earl's temperament being 'sanguine' and his habits 'temperate'):

> There was an unnatural stare about the right eye... There was slight loss of power down the whole of the right side, which drooped as he walked, the right shoulder hanging lower than the left, and the point of the right foot being apt to catch in being lifted over small elevations... The mouth was a little down to the left side. There was slight thickness in his speech, scarcely perceptible when he had not been talking for some time, but more noticeable when he had been speaking enough to fatigue his tongue. There had been some numbness in the right arm, but it had passed off.
>
> By my advice, he kept away from his work for a week, during which the above symptoms slightly improved. ...in the meantime [he] returned to his work, merely attending the office close to his house, for 2 or 3 hours a day, and giving up journeys of all kinds.

Although he did not know it, the 50-year-old George Windsor Earl had suffered a stroke.

– Chapter Twenty –

Respite, Romance and Recognition

1864

...a change of air is essentially necessary to his health...

•

In December 1863, George, Clara and Annie boarded ship in Penang for Singapore from where they were to sail to the Cape of Good Hope and, possibly, onward to England. Earl had partially resumed his duties in September after being taken ill in late August, but soon was experiencing psychological disturbances.

The President of the Standing Medical Committee in Penang, Dr J. B. King, examined him and while finding that 'His appetite and general health have continued good'. also noted: 'There has however been a steady gradual decline of nervous power and balance. He flushes deeply under slight emotion. He is easily worried. The noise of people talking, as of natives outside his house, irritates him. The visit of a friend to dinner, with some after dinner conversation of a commonplace nature, so excites him that he cannot sleep, but is restless in and out of bed, and walking about the house all night.'

Medical science of the time would not have attributed Earl's physical and mental symptoms as consequences of a stroke (in this case involving the left motor-cortex and brain stem). Nor would George's bout with rheumatic fever 20 years before and its effects over time have been considered a possible contributory factor to his health. Rather, it is likely that any wide range of physical (especially those specific to the tropics) and concomitant psychological ailments would be deemed to have been caused by the local environment. Annie wrote that he had had a 'stroke of the sun'.

Governor Cavenagh expressed in a letter of the 10th of October to Colonel MacPherson that he was sorry to hear that Earl was not improving. Then, on the 9th of November 1863, Dr King certified that Earl:

> ...is in a bad state of health and I solemnly and sincerely declare that according to the best of my judgment, a change of air is essentially necessary to his health and do therefore recommend that he may be permitted to start for the Cape of Good Hope (and afterwards to England if it

> should be found advisable) by the 'Pluto' Steamer, on or about the 15th November via Singapore on sick leave for 12 months to date from the day of his embarkation.

The Earl family were to stay in Singapore for about a month. Annie remembered it as 'a very gay place and we were invited a great deal by all my parents' old friends, especially as not being many girls there[,] a fresh one coming, like myself, was made very much of'.

Whilst there, the Earls, as well as an astounding number of locals both native and European, turned out to see the celebrated Confederate raider, the sail-and-steam-powered CSS *Alabama*. In port for a few days from December 21st to the 24th to re-supply, the ship's presence was a public sensation as she was renowned throughout the world for her daring and for her destruction of ships flying Union colours.*

The local press downplayed the visit for reasons of neutrality, but John Cameron in *Our Tropical Possessions...* reported the spectacle:

> Captain Semmes [of the *Alabama*] caused a notice to appear in the newspapers that visitors could not then be received, as his ship was coaling, but that all who chose to inspect her on the following day would be gladly welcomed on board.
>
> New Harbour is three miles distant from the town by the road, and next day carriages were at a premium, for natives of all classes, as well as the European residents, had determined to avail themselves of the opportunity to inspect a ship that will possess some place in the history of the present age. The excitement among the natives was the more remarkable... Seven years ago, at the time of the Chinese war, the town batteries were constantly saluting the arrivals of important plenipotentiaries in the finest ships of the British Navy, and yet seldom was even an inquiry ventured by the natives as to the cause of these unusual proceedings. All however, from the smallest boy to the greyheaded old patriarchs, could tell that the Alabama was in. They had learned her name, and flocked in crowds to see her... Some had doubtless learned her story,

* The *Alabama* captured, sank or burned 82 Union ships from 1862, until her sinking off of Le Havre by the USS *Kearsarge* in June 1864. It is said that during her raiding career she took more than 2,000 prisoners without a loss of life to them or to her crew. She had been built in ambiguous international legal circumstances in Birkenhead, launched in 1862, and HM's Government eventually was to pay an indemnity of 15 million dollars to the USA.

> and flocked in crowds to see her... Some had doubtless learned her story, but the great mass must have been ignorant of it. Perhaps a clue to the interest they displayed might be found in the often repeated exclamations,— 'Hantu, Kappal Hantu' – 'Ghost – ghost ship.'

The Earls were friendly with Hugh Rowland Beaver, a local English agent who facilitated the refuelling and revictualing of the *Alabama* and was later to be given in gratitude by Captain Semmes the only surviving relic from the ship – its battle ensign. Annie described her impressions:

> We went on board... I much admired the Confederate officers in their long grey coats and gold bands. They were most charming young men and the risk they were running shed a good deal of romance about them...
>
> We saw a good deal of Mr. Beaver. One evening, after my mother and I had been dining at the same house with him... [he] offered to drive us home in his American buggy; it was a bright moon-light night and we went for quite a long drive which was one of the most delightful I ever took in my life. My mother and I were rather alarmed once or twice when, by taking a wrong turning, we had to drive under the porticoes of some of our friends' houses, for fear of anyone looking out of the windows and recognizing us!

The ladies' good reputations intact, the family sailed from Singapore during January 1864, bound not for the Cape of Good Hope but for Adelaide via Galle (Ceylon) and King George Sound (Albany). Whilst in Singapore, George had seen Surgeon Major J. Rose to report that he was unable to find ready passage to the Cape. Rose wrote on the 30th of December: 'Considering it of importance that he [Earl] should leave these parts without delay, I have advised him to proceed to Australia instead of to the Cape...'

Before departure, Earl took the opportunity to address the contents of a letter he had received from the Under Secretary of State for Colonies in London. (His reply is addressed to the Secretary of State at the Colonial Office, the Duke of Newcastle.):

> Penang [probably written from Singapore]
> January 1864
>
> My Lord Duke,
> I had the honour to receive a letter from the Under Secretary of State for Colonies dated on the 2nd of January, 1862, in reply to an application

I had made to your Grace for promotion in the Straits Civil Service, informing me that it would be borne in mind and considered in common with the claims of other candidates, should occasion arise.

I have now the honour to inform your Grace that I have obtained Leave of Absence for a year under a Medical Certificate (copy of which I enclose) and that I proceed this day in the homeward mail steamer to Point de Galle [on the southern tip of Ceylon] for the purpose of embarking in the Australian mail steamer for South Australia, where I purpose remaining during the winter season, returning to the Straits towards the end of the year.

It will be seen from the Medical Certificate that the complaint which has obliged me to seek change of climate is not of a character calculated to impair my efficiency as a public servant:- and I shall take the opportunity of obtaining a practical acquaintance with the routine of public duties in Colonies under the control of Her Majesty's Colonial Department, which might prove useful in the event of the contemplated transfer of the Straits Settlements taking place.

I have the honour to be
Your Grace's most obedient servant,
Geo. Windsor Earl

Earl might have been putting on a brave face to the Colonial Office with regard to his health, for it would be difficult to cast more positively a year's medical leave. More likely was that he saw his ailments as but a short-term impairment and wished to make it very clear to London that he still sought promotion – especially so should the Straits Settlements become a Crown colony; for in such case its civil service would come under the direct and full control of the Colonial Office.

Clara and Annie were greatly disappointed with the destination for both had hoped that George would return to England for convalescence. Annie wrote that her father 'wished to get into cold weather and besides that there was always his passionate love for Australia'.

Annie's disappointment was soon forgotten during the voyage to Galle when she met a handsome young man of 23 making his way to England from Japan on business. William Alt had travelled from Nagasaki where he had been a general commission agent since 1860 as one of the few Westerners engaged in international trade with Japan. One of Annie's daughters was to write of her father that 'he fell heels over head in love with the beautiful Elisabeth Earl'.

It is not known what George and Clara made of this shipboard romance lasting a week or so; but rare is the father of a daughter – especially one at the tender age of sixteen – who doesn't cast a scrutinising eye over her suitor and his potential son-in-law. If George did so, he may have approved of what he saw. William John Alt was born in Greenwich, England, on April 4th 1840, the son of a soldier, Lieutenant Daniel Allt. At the age of twelve, after the death of his father, William entered the merchant navy under a kindly Captain who aided the boy, a willing pupil, in his education. By 1859, William was serving in the Customs Service in China, monitoring British trade there, and he then moved on to Nagasaki after Japan opened the port to foreigners. Within two years he was the proprietor of Alt & Co., one of the most successful foreign trading-houses in Japan, and he had already made a fortune from the import of ship and military equipment and the export of various commodities, especially tea.

The relationship between young Annie and William developed during the voyage to the extent (at least in William's view) that he considered himself to be engaged. Since the Earls were to stay in Adelaide until late in 1864, he told Annie (as recorded in her 'Journal') that 'she was free to engage herself to another man if she met one she cared for better before [my] return to the East'; but otherwise he would come back for her. They said their farewells in Galle on the 27th of January 1864 and William Alt sailed on to England.

* * *

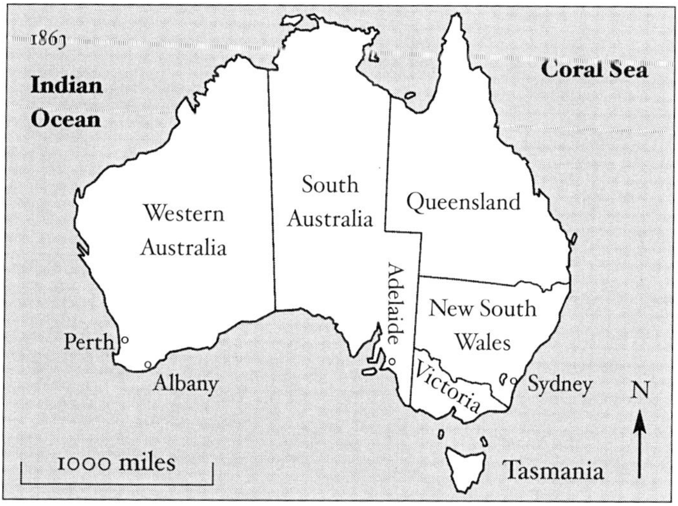

The Earl family arrived in Adelaide on the 10th of February 1864 from Albany on-board the steamer *Alexandra*. Although George had journeyed there mainly for rest and cure, it may not have been entirely a coincidence that excitement and debate were in the air there concerning plans to develop the recent acquisition of a vast stretch of land called the Northern Territory. The areas combined, the State now stretched from the Southern to the Northern shores of the continent. A letter to the *South Australian Register* (signed K.W.W.) was published on the 23rd of February:

> Sir – At a time when we are about to make an attempt to colonize a portion of our new territory, I think it is our duty to seek out and gladly avail ourselves of all possible information on the subject of colonizing, so as to avert the humiliation of a failure such as resulted from the attempts to settle Port Essington, in Northern Australia, and Port Augusta, in Western Australia.
>
> Now, Sir, we have at the present moment sojourning with us a gentleman – I allude to Mr. G. W. Earl – who was personally and actively engaged in both the before-named experiments. Here is an opportunity for gaining information on the subject which may be useful, as he could doubtless point out many obstacles likely to arise in the effort we are about to make, which could thereby be removed.
>
> You will naturally ask how this information is to be obtained. I would suggest that if the gentleman I have mentioned were asked by the members of the Philosophical Society, or some other influential body, to read a paper on the subject, he would gladly give the benefit of his experience, which would, by means of the press, be made public throughout the colonies.
>
> Mr. Earl has, I know, strong South Australian sympathies, and would, I believe, do anything in his power to advance the interests of the province.

Plans were being made for a new regional capital, some 1,600 miles North of Adelaide and an expeditionary party under the command of Colonel Boyle Travers Finniss was formed in early 1864. One of the purposes of this 'Great Central State', as it was projected to be called, was to tap 'The Unlimited Asian Market' in the Indian Archipelago, Dutch East Indies, Malay states, India and, most importantly, China. There was no one who had essayed this subject in greater breadth or in greater detail during the past 28 years than George Windsor Earl, and most recently in

Handbook for Colonists in Tropical Australia. Moreover, the Government of South Australia had issued the title *The Northern Territory of South Australia* during the previous year, in which Earl had been copiously quoted from a number of his works, presumably with his foreknowledge.

The participants in the debate over the future for the Great Central State provide a microcosm of the interests involved in the history of colonization of Australia: HM's Government and financial powers in London; the land-sellers (usually governmental), land-buyers (immigrants and speculators), agriculturists, pastoralists, and regional business interests keen for trade in products and foodstuffs. The prospect of running a telegraphic cable to the northern shore of the continent from Timor and then to Adelaide came under consideration with its tantalising promise of control and profit from that flow of information. Because of his hydrological knowledge of the area, Earl was to be cited in newspaper reports later in the year as to which route he believed the best to lay the underwater cable. A north-south rail link was also envisioned.

The Gregory expedition of 1855-56 to the Victoria River (which the Earls had accompanied on its journey there) reported of having discovered 'at least 3,000,000 acres of available grazing land' in the area. This caused great interest from pastoralists seeking new lands for their flocks (especially sheep). The Royal Geographical Society and British Government had jointly financed the expedition, and Sir Dominick Daly, the Governor of South Australia, now wanted to act on its promising findings. Daly saw settlements in the Victoria River area as a springboard for the growing of cotton (supplies of which had been disrupted by the civil war in America), agriculture in general, and the opening up of, as he wrote, 'this vast and magnificent expanse of country... where the greatest advantages exist for speedy communication and uninterrupted trade with the East Indies'.

Chief Secretary Henry Ayers, then Minister without Portfolio of the South Australia Government, was in charge of the planning for the forthcoming Finniss expedition. But there was dissention over the expedition's aims, especially from the government's Treasurer, John Hart. Ayers wished the new capital to be in the tropical area of the Arnhem Peninsula which he, and many others, believed would become a magnet for attracting native labour from across the crowded Indian Archipelago as well as from India and China. Hart adamantly favoured the sub-tropical Victoria River area and he set about attempting to persuade Finniss to that point of view. The pastoralists and the mercantile-agriculture camps were at loggerheads over the site of the new capital and the path of development for the territory. On the 1st of April, the sale of land in the north, as authorised by the parliament in Adelaide, became law and of the 125,000 acres offered, 81,000 had been applied for. Sceptics saw 'something like the South Sea Bubble, and a vent for land jobbing and gambling', as the *South Australian Register* was to later write; for the value of the land would be largely determined, at least during the formative years, by the siting of the new capital.

Ayers commissioned Earl to prepare a memorandum on locations suitable for the establishment of an anchor settlement in the region. The *South Australian Register* of the 26th of March covered his findings:

> The choice of a locality at which to attempt the first settlement has engaged a great deal of attention. The Government were at first disposed to give the preference to the Victoria River, whilst others advocated a situation more to the north-east, in the neighbourhood of Van Diemen's Gulf. It happened fortunately that whilst this matter was being discussed, Mr. G. W. Earl, the well-known writer on the climate, ethnology, and resources of Tropical Australia, arrived in Adelaide on a visit, and was thus enabled to give the Government much information which would otherwise have been quite unobtainable. From having resided eleven years at Port Essington, besides having visited many other parts of North Australia, Mr. Earl was able to speak authoritatively on many matters about which the Government were in doubt. The information which he has supplied to the colonists will be found in other columns, and will, we have no doubt, be perused with interest by many English readers. It will be seen that the locality fixed upon for the first settlement is in the neighbourhood of Van Diemen's Gulf, and near to the mouth of the Adelaide [Adam Bay], which river Mr. Stuart descended in his last expedition. The harbour recommended is Port Darwin, which is easily accessible, roomy, and well sheltered. The country around, too, has the advantage of being high, and is considered to be salubrious. The expedition, however, will not be tied to this particular spot if they should find a better one in the neighborhood.

On Saturday, the 16th of April 1864, a luncheon was given by the Government for some 150 prominent guests to celebrate the imminent departure of the Finniss expedition. Colonel Finniss had been appointed Resident Councillor for the new territory (at a salary of £1000 per annum) and the *South Australian Register* of the 18th inst. reported the event and gave a précis of Governor Daly's speech that included the following:

> Then there had been several advantages in getting up the expedition at the present time. They were in prosperous circumstances at home – that is, in this colony – and they had had the benefit of the advice and assistance of one whose name, if he was not present, he would mention. It was Mr. Earl – (applause) – who he hoped was not absent from ill health. He had come to the colony for the recovery of his health, and he trusted that would be restored. (Hear, hear.) His amiable and friendly disposition was evinced on all occasions; and his services – which had been placed at their disposal – had been most valuable. To this he was happy to accord his testimony. (Applause.)

That Earl had recommended a site at Adam Bay is somewhat perplexing for he admitted that he didn't know the geography there well – it was as he put it, 'confined to a passing view' – and his choice was made largely on the basis of what he called the 'salubrity' of the area. Given the record at Port Essington, the healthiness of an location considered for settlement had become a topic of general concern and no doubt was, given his own experiences, a salient consideration to Earl. His advice may have swayed Governor Daly and Chief Secretary Ayers slightly in the direction of favouring a tropical northern site for the new capital, but such a recommendation was but one of many in circulation waiting to be tested on the ground.

Hence, a measure of flexibility was given to the Finniss expedition and this was embraced by Earl as was mentioned in the *Empire* (Sydney) on May 7th:

> ...and that unanimous opinion [of the quality of the land east of Arnhem Land] is well summed up by Mr. G. W. EARL, in the course of some valuable information recently published by him, for the use of intending colonists proceeding with Colonel FINNISS to the north-west coast; for it should be mentioned that this expedition has instructions, in the unlikely event of failing to find a suitable port, either at Victoria River or Van Diemen's Gulf, to proceed to the western shore of Carpentaria, and search the country about Limmen Bight. Mr. EARL then says :– "The south-west coast of the Gulf, which runs in an almost straight line from the Roper to the Flinders, a distance of four hundred miles, is probably more favoured by nature than any other piece of land of equal extent within the tropics. With the exception of the mangrove forests at the mouths of the numerous rivers, there appears to be scarcely an acre of that does not afford good pasturage.

For a man meant to be convalescing, George Earl had been quite busy during the two months since his arrival. After his reading of his paper 'On the shell-mounds of Province Wellesley, in the Malay Peninsula' at the Adelaide Philosophical Society on April 19th (printed in full in *The South Australian Advertiser* on April 23rd) he seems to have slackened the pace a bit, although his opinions on a wide variety of subjects pertaining to the North were to be aired in the press across Southern Australia during the ensuing months. *The Sydney Morning Herald* of June 14th reported:

> Mr. G. W. Earl, who was familiar with the Port Essington experiment, strongly recommends a position on the peninsula which forms the southern headland of Clarence Straits, and which lies between the Adelaide River [Adam Bay] and Shoal Bay [15 miles NE of present-day Darwin]. The position is sufficiently sheltered, and admits of easy access by sailing vessels, besides being well posted as a port of call. He strongly deprecates the selection of any land-locked harbour, all such places within the tropics being invariably found unhealthy.

During the family's stay, George, Clara and Annie became friendly with Governor Sir Dominick Daly and his wife, Lady Caroline. Daly was an Irishman, fifteen years older than Earl, who had seen many years of overseas service, most recently as Governor of Canada's Prince Edward Island. A fine administrator, he was appointed Governor in October 1861 and was

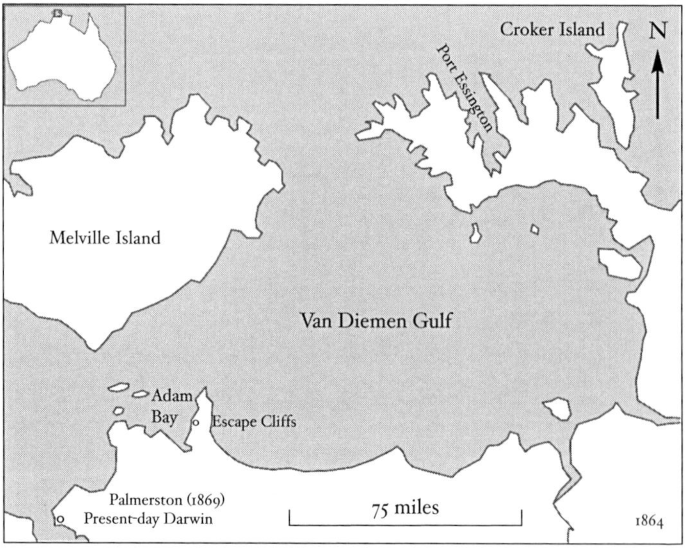

to become greatly admired in South Australia for his accessibility, impartiality and wisdom. A most convivial and amiable man; his praise of Earl at the luncheon for the Finniss expedition had not been gratuitous and George was to hope in the future to work closely with him.

Earl continued with his convalescence during the winter of 1864 and this season was enlivened when William Alt arrived in Adelaide, probably in August, to claim his seventeen-year-old bride. Unfortunately, Annie's 'Journal' does not record the occasion or the events that led up to her marriage. But we do have a description of her from one of her daughters: 'She had brown curly hair with dark auburn tints... Her skin was fair and her colouring bright; her blue eyes danced when she was animated... The nose was well-shaped and the mouth also. She had beautiful bones, therefore lovely lines in the way that the face was shaped, with eyes set deeply, and eyebrows drooping a little at the corners.'

George and Clara certainly approved of the match but may have had some pause over the prospect of seeing their young daughter move to one of the most isolated countries in the region and one with a tiny Western community. On September 16th 1864 the *South Australian Adviser* carried the following announcement:

> On the 15th September, at Trinity Church, Adelaide, by the Very Rev. Dean Farrell, William John Alt, Esq., of Japan, to Elizabeth Christiana Fernhill, daughter of George Windsor Earl, Esq., of Province Wellesley, Straits of Malacca.

Mr. and Mrs. Alt sailed to Japan and George and Clara now had to consider their return to Province Wellesley as his year's medical leave would soon expire. A notice appeared in the *South Australian Registe*r on October 17th that the Earls, who had been residing at No. 6, Pybus-buildings, North Terrace, would be auctioning a number of household items. On the same day, the *South Australian Register* reported that Earl had been scheduled to read his paper, 'The Productive Resources of Tropical Australia', before the Adelaide Philosophical Society but, the meeting postponed to the 18th, he would be unable to do so as he was 'about to take his departure immediately'.* (However, the Earls did not sail until November 7th on the barque *Omagh*.)

* On September 5th, Earl's paper, 'On the Meteorology of Northern Australia' had been read before the Society by the Chairman. A version was subsequently printed in the *South Australian Register* on December 28th 1865.

1864 was a bountiful year for George Windsor Earl. The fruits of more than three decades of living in and writing about the East and Australia had ripened into public acknowledgment of his achievements and a stature that commanded respect for his opinions at the highest levels. In his personal life, his daughter had been married to a fine and successful young man, and perhaps most important, as a friend and colleague in Adelaide later wrote, 'whilst here his health became so good, that he considered his constitution completely renovated'. As the Earls made their way back to the Straits Settlements, George no doubt felt the sap rising as the future promised new, challenging and rewarding opportunities.

The west side of King William Street, Adelaide.
On the left is the old General Post Office.
Photograph from 1860s.
STATE LIBRARY OF SOUTH AUSTRALIA

– Chapter Twenty-One –

ONCE MORE SOMETIME IN NOVEMBER
1865

...I am likely to be in better health in a week or two than I have been in for some years.

•

Around the beginning of January 1865, George Earl resumed duties in the Straits Settlements. Clara and he initially resided in Penang and from there George keenly followed reports that slowly made their way to him on the activities of the Finniss expedition. By the middle of May, the climate in Penang of which George wrote 'does not suit me' had taken a toll on his health. The Earls moved back to 'dear old' Province Wellesley, as he put it, and George resumed his former tasks there, including travelling to the circuit courts. He and Clara were receiving news almost every month from Annie and William in Nagasaki, and had recently learned that the Alts were expecting their first child.

A letter Earl wrote to South Australia's Governor Sir Dominick Daly on June 6th 1865 amply displays his continuing passion and undimmed vision for the development of Australia's Northern Territory. Reports from there and Adelaide, as well as rumours from Java that had filtered in to George, were not encouraging. The Finniss expedition had embarked in April 1864 and arrived at Escape Cliffs, Adam Bay, on the 21st of June. From the outset, the enterprise was beset with internal discord arising from its wide, not to say ambiguous, remit from the government in the South. Moreover, there were tales of organisational incompetence and of the serious mishandling of relations with the local Aborigines. Earl was alarmed for the very existence of the enterprise and wrote to Sir Dominick:

> ...to remind your Excellency of an offer I made to you at one of our last interviews, namely of my services to assist in resuscitating the enterprise if ever abandonment should be thought of. I sincerely hope that such assistance may never be required, as it would be of so much importance that the colony itself should overcome the difficulties without assistance from outsiders. But we cannot tell what may happen, and I now renew my offer with a promise that no disaster that can happen, even if it

> should amount to the total loss of the party now there, shall deter me from carrying it out. But under such circumstances it would be necessary that the entire responsibility should devolve upon me, and, above all, that I should have the privilege of selecting every individual of the relief party.

This letter of some 2,700 words is a tour de force covering the essential elements of planning, financing, outfitting, manning, deploying, building and defending a viable settlement and port. From experience, Earl wrote, 'and if I appear to go too much into details, please remember how important these details are to the success of an enterprise, and how utterly ruinous the neglect of apparently insignificant matters may sometimes prove.' The proposal places a permanent settlement on the western bank of the Upper Adelaide River in Arnhem Land and a port at Salt Water Arm (near to present-day Darwin).

Pertaining to the financing of the expedition, Earl wrote:

> I have now gone through all the essential points of the project, and must enter into a few personal matters. I shall have to resign the Straits Civil Service and 720 per annum with allowances, for I should not have the face to ask the Indian Government to take me back after having been used up in another service. Nor shall I care to remain at the fore in the N.T. a moment longer than is necessary to put things into proper train, which will require 18 months at most. But a suggestion made during a conversation with Mr. Ayers (whether by Mr. A. or myself I cannot distinctly remember) helps to a solution. A Judge is likely to be required in the Northern Territory before long, and there could be no office better suited to my taste and training. My standing as an advocate, solicitor, proctor &c of the Queen's Courts in the Straits Settlements since 1848 would, I think, render me admissible under the S.A. Act. In such an office, I could still be useful without being in the way; – and a pension of 300 per annum in the event of my becoming altogether unfit for work, to be continued to my wife if she survives me, would compensate me for retiring from this service before I have served long enough for pension. By the way, Mrs. Earl would accompany me if I go, so that she will have fairly earned a claim for consideration.

It is barely conceivable that this letter would have been written without some bidding from Governor Daly's government as it states: 'And as dollars or rupees would be required for disbursement, the sum placed at my disposal should not be less than 5000. This should be placed to my credit with Messrs Paterson Simons & Co. of Singapore, a firm well known in your colony...' Given Earl's age, health and secure position in life, it is somewhat surprising that he was eager to undertake such a speculative and taxing enterprise. But such challenges had been the pattern of his life and such was his love for Australia.

Before signing off, he mentioned to Governor Daly that Province Wellesley was, 'remarkably like the N. Territory both as regards soil and climate, but of course is not so invigorating. Nor will I leave it again willingly except to go to the N. Territory if required, and I think it equally certain that if I were once there I would become a fixture also'. Earl could not expect a reply to this audacious proposal (which would have him succeed Colonel Finniss as Resident Councillor) for another three months or so.

It was now the middle of the rainy season in Penang and Province Wellesley, and George's health was once again causing concern. Although he thought himself fully recovered from the attack of 'heatstroke' in August 1863; his chronic 'bloody flux' had flared up to an alarming degree. He wrote on the 24th of July 1865:

> My dearest Mother,
>
> I have had a dreadful attack of dysentry [sic] since I wrote last, so violent that everybody wonders how I could have got through. But I am thankful to say I have rallied, and the doctors say that if I get away to sea immediately I am likely to be in better health in a week or two than I have been in for some years. My passage direct to London has been taken in the "Shantung" to sail on Saturday the 29th – five days more. She is a small ship, only 311 tons, but a fine vessel, and the Captain a gentleman. As the passage home will be a stormy one, and Clara suffers dreadfully from seasickness, it would be a sin to allow her to accompany me. She therefore joins Annie in Japan.
>
> That I may see you and my dearest sister once more sometime in November is the earnest prayer and hope of your ever affectionate son,

Earl had seen the medical officer in Penang and the doctor wrote that only George's 'wonderfully sanguine and buoyant spirit' was keeping him alive and that no medical treatment could now save him if he chose to remain in the tropics. He was given a year's medical leave and began preparations for his departure and the arranging of Clara's passage to

Japan. Governor Cavenagh, writing on July 21st to the Resident Councillor at Penang, Lieutenant-Colonel Henry Stuart Man, expressed his fears that it would be difficult to fill up Earl's berth. *The Singapore Free Press* carried a note on the 3rd of August, 'We regret to learn that Mr. Earl, Assistant Resident Councillor and Magistrate of Police at Pinang, has again been forced to quit his post on account of ill health.'

The *Shantung* did not sail from Penang on the 29th of July as planned, and Earl signed his final will and testament on the 2nd of August. *The Shantung* embarked on the 7th but during the 8th, George had an attack, probably dysenteric, and died that day or in the early hours of the 9th of August 1865. The *Singapore Gazette* on August 12th 1865 reported:

> By private advices received from Penang per Mail steamer Orissa yesterday we regret to learn of the death of GW Earl Esq, the late Magistrate of Province Wellesley and Assistant Resident of Penang on 9th instant. He sailed from Penang for London in the Barque Shantung on the 7th instant, and died shortly after leaving. His remains were brought back by the ship's boat at 2pm on the 9th and interred at 6am the following day.

He was laid to rest, aged 52, in the Northam Road Protestant Cemetery in George Town, Penang. Later, a rectangular stone tomb about four-feet high with a flat top was erected. On one side the inscription reads:

IN MEMORY OF

GEORGE SAMUEL WINDSOR EARL

ASSISTANT RESIDENT COUNCILLOR, PENANG.

AUTHOR OF EASTERN SEAS AND OTHER WORKS
YOUNGER SON OF THE LATE PERCY EARL ESQ. SENIOR OF HAMPSTEAD ENGLAND
BORN FEBRUARY 10 1813, DIED AUGUST 9 1865

And on the other side is carved:

THIS STONE IS RAISED BY HIS AFFECTIONATE MOTHER.

Envoi

•

George Windsor Earl's death was noted in newspapers in Penang, Singapore, Sydney and Adelaide; *The South Australian Advertiser* of the 12th of October 1865 carried the following:

> ...In him Australia loses one who took a deep interest in her welfare and prosperity. North Australia and the Islands of the Eastern Seas especially were objects of his attention, and his published remarks upon them are in the hands of every one possessing any knowledge of the subject. In private life Mr. Earl was a man of great general information, a kind and warm friend, and one of whom we may truly say that all who knew him loved him. His death will be a matter of great and general regret, and amongst his own immediate friends a deep and heartfelt loss...

No significant public mention was made in England of his passing nor would he be mentioned in the obituaries read for the past year by his old antagonist, Sir Roderick Murchison (once again President of the Royal Geographical Society), at their annual meeting in July 1866.

In his will, Earl left his entire estate, largely made up of two insurance policies totalling 10,000 East India Company Rupees (£115,000 today), to Clara. He did not die an affluent man. As an uncovenanted civil servant, he was not entitled to a pension for his services and therefore Clara could not receive a widow's benefit. A number of government officials in situations akin to George's would be taken on in covenanted roles when the Straits Settlements became a Crown colony two years after his death.

The Alts had their first child, Mabel Edith, on July 2nd 1865 and she is believed to have been the first Western baby born in Japan. It is not known if George ever heard the news that he was a grandfather. William and Annie would have a further five daughters and two sons. The family (then with four children) returned to England in 1871 due to William's health problems exacerbated by life in the East and he entered into semi-retirement. Both were to die in London, William in 1908, aged 68, and Annie (Elizabeth Christiana Fernhill), in 1923 at the age of 76.

Clara Earl, a widow and a grandmother at age 35, would not re-marry and would outlive George by 40 years, dying in London in 1905 at the age of 76. Her granddaughter, Mabel Edith, wrote of her: '...she had a very sweet voice which had also been much admired in her youth. It was a joy to hear her sing even as quite an old lady. She was much loved by her grandchildren and was very indulgent. She had a keen sense of humour... She herself used to feel that her figure detracted from her good looks – but it did not; her stoutness was so motherly... Of brains she had plenty, and she was a great reader... a keen admirer of Sir Walter Scott, as a writer and a man; also of Thackeray – being less interested in Dickens.'

Clara's mother-in-law, old Elizabeth Earl, died nine years after she had buried her last son and George's sister, Elizabeth, passed away at Wildwood in 1890 at the age of 73, having never re-married after John Loftus Hartwell's death in 1849.

Of Earl's close colleagues and friends, Sir Francis Beaufort had died in 1857 at the age of 83, and was succeeded in his post of Hydrographer of the Navy by John Washington, who passed away with the rank of Rear-Admiral in 1863, aged 62. The stoical Captain John McArthur had died aged 71 in England in 1862, having never written his memoirs of Port Essington despite Earl's earnest hope that he would do so. As for the Straits Settlements, Sir William Orfeur Cavenagh, the last Governor before it became a Crown colony, died aged 71 in 1891. Annie wrote in her 'Journal': 'We retained our friendship with the Cavenaghs for many years – until their death.' Edward Cox of Woolloomooloo, Annie's godfather, would die in 1868. James Richardson Logan, aged 50, joined George in Penang's Northam Road Protestant Cemetery in 1869. James' brother, Abraham, would also come to rest there in 1873, aged 57.

It would appear that the ambitious proposal* written to Governor Sir Dominick Daly (who was to die in office at the age of 69 in 1868) went unanswered; news of George's death may have precluded that. But a substantial obituary, strongly believed to have been penned by the Governor himself, appeared in the *South Australian Register* on November 27th 1865. Largely a retrospective of Earl's travels and involvement in the attempts to develop Northern Australia, it noted that his first voyage in 1827 as a midshipman on the EIC's *Lady Holland* 'seems to have given him a distaste for a seafaring life as a profession'. Also mentioned, with regard to Port Essington and Earl's anticipated return to there in 1849: '...news got abroad that the settlement would be abandoned, as the funds appropriated for its maintenance were required for the new settlement of Labuan,

* Colonel B. T. Finniss, the man Earl had hoped to succeed, was to be relieved as Resident Councillor in 1866 after his expedition to the north had proved calamitous. Three further expeditions were to be mounted before Palmerston (now Darwin) was established in 1869 as the site for the new capital.

on the north-west coast of Borneo'. Imperial tactics were ever shifting, and Earl ever beat a drum in the midst of those vicissitudes for the establishment of a thriving entrepôt in Northern Australia to emulate, and perhaps even surpass, Singapore.

However, a dynamic development of Northern Australia has not yet come to pass – let alone Earl's vision of a vibrant, mercantilist, multicultural trading centre underpinned with agricultural plenty produced by labour from across the islands to the north and beyond. Shipping had soon come to prefer the southern route to the continent and the north remained isolated. Today, the Northern Territory – comprising an area twice the size of France – has only 250,000 residents. The pristine and ruggedly-beautiful Garig Gunak Barlu National Park, covering all but the entirety of the Cobourg Peninsula, now encompasses the abandoned settlement at Victoria, Port Essington, and a permit is required to visit the site.

Today, Earl is sometimes rightly mentioned as having been in the same vein as others who had a belief in and a vision of Empire, such as Raffles and Brooke, although he lacked their overweening audacity, financial risk-taking and willingness to upset the status quo and create new orders. Rather, he chose to work through and in existing structures and systems. Perhaps this is why late in life Earl described himself as 'an essentially practical man', but it is difficult to divine what this self-reflective observation fully meant to him. A truly practical man would have, perhaps, stayed in Hampstead and not spent his health and life on the other side of the world in the varied roles of settler, trader and sea captain, explorer, hydrographer, acquirer of languages, pioneer, travelling scholar, polemicist, mining equipment representative, Singapore Law agent, government official in the Straits Settlements and, finally, aspirant for the position of Resident Councillor of the Northern Territory of Australia.

During Earl's life, he was chiefly and widely known to the public as the author of *The Eastern Seas*. Published in 1837, when he was 24 years old, it soon became the book for a generation on the subject when it supplanted John Crawfurd's 1820 work, *History of the Indian Archipelago.* The distinguished Crawfurd, President of the Ethnological Society (1861-63), was not known for his sunny appraisals of others in that field. However, he truly respected Earl, although icing that particular cake by perennially referring to him as 'Mr. Windsor East'. *The Native Races of the Indian Archipelago. Papuans.* would keep George's name before those interested in the subject for more than 50 years; and his belief that ethnology could serve to lessen ignorance and misunderstandings between races 'which too often lead to desolating and expensive wars' is as valid today as it was then. This belief was not mere armchair idealism, in many cases he spoke their language(s), spent time with them in their homes and showed them a respect based on true understanding that was sincerely reciprocated.

The controversy with Roderick Murchison, an argument that George thought was 'more than a patient soul can bear', as to whom first predicted the presence of gold in Australia has long been forgotten. Today, Earl is chiefly remembered in geographical circles for his contributions to the formulation of the Wallace Line and, prominently, for coining the name (albeit his second choice) for an area of the world that would come to be known as Indonesia. These achievements would be acknowledged posthumously and he would have had no inkling of any lasting recognition for them during his lifetime.

Earl's substantial body of published work is largely of an empirical nature. His prose style is straightforward, clear, precise and highly competent; well suited to its informative purpose. But even when using a first-person narrative, as in *The Eastern Seas*, his text is curiously impersonal, adhering no doubt to the scholarly (and societal) norms of the time. Emotionally, he keeps his awe, wonder and undoubted love of the East to himself in his professional writings and one can look there almost in vain for truly personal, even unwittingly shown, revelations.

He could be sharply opinionated in his writings, as when making clear his abhorrence of slavery, hatred of piracy, indignation at the social and economic policies of the Dutch, and distaste for the opium trade. But these outspoken judgements were usually subsumed by his larger purpose, that of seeing the Empire grow and prosper both in the economic and moral spheres. As early as 1837, in *The Eastern Seas*, he called for the governance of Singapore to be taken over from the East India Company by the British Government as an 'act of justice to the peaceable portion of the natives of the Indian Archipelago', whereby piracy would be destroyed, order maintained, the city improved and properly defended, agriculture and commerce enhanced, and, as he saw it, the relative impartiality of British justice be extended throughout a region sorely in need of such mediation.

Within his disciplines, Earl addressed a large variety of subjects, and strove to be encyclopædic about them. He occasionally fell into the trap of giving opinions or stating what he believed to be facts on matters he thought he knew or thought he ought to know, but did not. In his youth, this could partly be put down to the enthusiasm of one searching for a path in the world. After his visit to Port Essington in 1843, Captain Home described Earl to Vice-Admiral Sir William Parker: '...a more zealous, acute, or intelligent gentleman I have scarcely ever met…' George's energetic optimism, restless striving, outward self-assurance and, one suspects, his loquaciousness in his younger days were impressive to some and an annoyance to others. As he grew older and a few wounds accumulated, he could be a little brittle over a perceived slight or a challenge to an aspect of his unparalleled knowledge on a substantial array of topics pertaining to the region. These are minor blemishes on a wide-ranging and substantial scholarly career, even if it was not one in the scientific realm to compare with those who conceived and established great systems such as Darwin and Wallace.

Earl was, of course, not in the public eye only for his books, research papers and newspaper articles relating to the East. During the last seven years of his life he served as a Magistrate and then, additionally, as an Assistant Resident Councillor in the Straits Settlements. Both were prestigious positions and he was certainly aware of the dignity of the offices and the social honour accruing from them. By accounts, he fulfilled the posts with vigour, diligence, moderation and probity, and proved to be a fine colleague. Earl could be very firm in his judgements from the bench, but made these without undue personal regard or arrogance. He would, on a matter of principle, contest other powers-that-be at the risk of his prestige, as when he prominently stood with a few others (including James Richardson Logan) in opposing the calls of European merchants in the Straits Settlements for punitive measures against the Chinese secret societies. Such actions, they reasoned, would do greater harm to the Chinese community as a whole, and Earl showed here his deep and sensitive understanding of the ethnic fabric in the Straits Settlements.

However, in the broadest sense, Earl was not a reformer, rebel or social philosopher. Rather, he appears to have been fundamentally comfortable in the pursuit of his many occupations (although seemingly not fully so with just any one of them) throughout his life and perhaps, in his approach to these and his other concerns, he was 'an essentially practical man'.

Of his private life, little is revealed in the few personal documents that have come to light. Beyond horse riding in the morning, his other leisure pursuits are unknown. He possessed a fine ear for languages, a talent for near-forensic writing, and a perceptive eye for the canvas of the East, but any tastes he may have had in music, literature and art went unrecorded, as have any beliefs that he may have held in the political or religious spheres. The inner life of this 'wonderfully sanguine and buoyant spirit' who was capable of forming many deep and lasting friendships remains undiscovered, as does the precise cause and full nature of his Eastern calling.

But there can be no doubt that a vibrant part of George Windsor Earl lived for the prospect of fulfilling a visionary future for Northern Australia. Nothing but death could stay this desire. His adult life was beset by grievous chronic illnesses, borne with fortitude and stoicism, but he was able to muster on the cusp of death a mental vitality to attempt a re-invention of himself through a new and taxing career in Australia in pursuit of that vision.

George and Clara's only child, Annie, may well have observed more than she fully understood when she wrote of her father that 'he liked having birds about so long as they weren't in cages'.

References

•

Chapter 1: Roots: The Beginnings • 1813-1828

History of local land transactions, Hampstead Manorial Court records.

Hampstead Parish Church: The Story of a Building through 250 Years, Michael Port and the Vicar and Churchwardens of St. John-at-Hampstead Parochial Church Council, John-at-Hampstead Parochial Church Council, 1996.

Hampstead One Thousand, John Richardson, Historical Publications Ltd, Whitstable, Kent, 1985.

'Minutes of the Hampstead Sunday and Day School Society 1800-1825', Metropolitan Archives, London.

The King's Nurseries: The Story of Westminster School, John Field, James & James (Publishers) Ltd, 1987.

The Convict Ships, 1787-1868, Charles Bateson, Brown, Son and Ferguson, Glasgow, 1959.

Chapter 2: The Swan River • 1829

'The Swan River Venture', W. Charnley, *History Today*, Vol X (March 1960).

Western Australia: A History from its Discovery to the Inauguration of the Commonwealth, J.S. Battye, University of Western Australia Press, 1978.

'Eating and drinking at early Swan River Colony', Bob Reece, *Early Days*, Vol. 13, No. 4, 2010, pp 462-477.

Metropolitan Archives, London.

Chapter 3: Landfall and Thereafter • 1830-1832

James Stirling: Admiral and Founding Governor of Western Australia, Pamela Statham-Drew. University of Western Australia Press, 2003.

Extracts from the Letters and Journals of George Fletcher Moore, Esq.: Now Filling a Judicial Office at the Swan River Settlement, Martin Doyle, editor, Orr and Smith, London, 1834.

'Out of the Shadows: George Windsor Earl in Western Australia', Russell Jones, *Indonesia Circle*, No. 64, 1994.

Georgiana, Molloy: Portrait with Background, Alexandra Hasluck. Oxford University Press (1976).

Public Record Office, Colonial Office, British Library and Greater London Record Office.

Chapter 4: The Eastern Seas • 1832-1833

The Eastern Seas; or Voyages and Adventures in the Indian Archipelago in 1832-33-34; Comprising a Tour of the Island of Java–Visits to Borneo, the Malay Peninsula, Siam, &c.; Also, an Account of the Present State of Singapore, with Observations on the Commercial Resources of the Archipelago, George Windsor Earl M.R.A.S., Wm. H. Allen & Co., 1837.

'George Samuel Windsor Earl'. C.A. Gibson-Hill, *Journal of Malayan Branch of the Royal Asiatic Society*, Vol XXXII, pt. 1, 1959.

Hampstead Manorial Court records.

Chapter 5: Captain Earl • 1833-1834

Metropolitan Archives, London.

Chapter 6: Into the Fray • 1835-1836

History of the Indian Archipelago. Containing an account of the Manners, Arts, Languages, Religions, Institutions, and Commerce of its Inhabitants, John Crawfurd, A Constable and Co., Edinburgh, 1820.

Chapter 7: The Case for a New Settlement • 1837

The Origins of Australia's Capital Cities, edited by Pamela Statham, Cambridge University Press (Melbourne), 1989.

Maritime Empires: British Imperial Maritime Trade in the Nineteenth Century, edited by David Killingray, Margarette Lincoln and Nigel Rigby, Boydell & Brewer, Woodbridge, England, 2004.

Chapter 8: Journey to a New Settlement • 1838

Letters from Port Essington, 1838-1845, Compiled and edited by J.M.R. Cameron, Historical Society of the Northern Territory, Darwin, 1999.

Voyages of the Dutch Brig-of-War Dourga through the southern and little-known parts of the Moluccan Archipelago, and along the previously unknown southern coast of New Guinea, performed during the years 1825 and 1826, D.H. Kolff. Jun., trans. G. W. Earl., James Madden & Co., 1840.

Chapter 9: First Steps • 1838

Forsaken Settlement, An illustrated history of the settlement of Victoria, Port Essington, North Australia 1838-1849, Peter G. Spillett, Lansdowne Press, NSW, 1972.

Letters from Port Essington, 1838-1845, Compiled and edited J.M.R. Cameron. Historical Society of the Northern Territory, Darwin, 1999.

Chapter 11: Storm Clouds Gather • 1843-1845

Forsaken Settlement, Peter G. Spillett, as above.

Chapter 12: A Change of Circumstances • 1845

Notes on the Siborne family by Lt. Col. Kenneth Henderson, DSO (son-in-law of Major General Herbert Siborne). Contained within Annie's 'Memoirs'. See references for Chapter 14.

Metropolitan Archives, London.

Chapter 13: Percy William Earl • 1846

'The Introduction of Railways into New South Wales 1846 – 1855'. G. J. Abbott, *Journal of Royal Australian Historical Society*, Vol. 52, March 1966.

Records of the Canterbury Museum (New Zealand), Vol. 26:1-19, 2012.

'A naturalist of the very first order? Percy William Earl (1811-1846) in New Zealand', R. Paul Scofield, Joanne H. Cooper, Samuel T. Turvey, *Records of the Canterbury Museum* (New Zealand), Vol. 26: pp 1-19, 2012.

Metropolitan Archives, London.

Chapter 14: New Horizons • 1846-1848

Forsaken Settlement, Peter G. Spillett, Lansdowne Press, NSW, 1972
'Some Memories of Elizabeth Christiana Fernhill Alt (née Earl), Dictated to one of her Daughters. Also Six Chapters written by Herself', Elizabeth Christiana Fernhill Alt, unpublished typescript, 169pp.

Chapter 15: Singapore and Port Essington • 1848-1849

Owen Stanley R.N., 1811-1850, Captain of the 'Rattlesnake', Adelaide Lubbock. William Heinemann Ltd., Melbourne (& London), 1968.

T. H. Huxley's Diary of the Voyage of H.M.S. Rattlesnake, sdited from the unpublished ms., J. Huxley ed., Chatto & Windus, 1935.

Life and Letters of Thomas Henry Huxley, Leonard Huxley. Appleton & Co. New York, 1901.

Port Essington, 'Archaeology and the history of Port Essington'. Thesis by F. J. Allen in partial fulfilment of requirements for the Degree of Doctor of Philosophy in the Australian National University, 1969.

Port Essington, The historical archaeology of a north Australian nineteenth century military outpost, Jim Allen, Studies in Australasian Historical Archaeology Volume 1, Australasian Society for Historical Archaeology, Sydney University Press, NSW, 2008.

Chapter 16: Singapore • 1850-1852

A History of Modern Singapore 1819-2005, C.M. Turnbull. National University of Singapore Press, Singapore, 2009.

Our Tropical Possessions In Malayan India: Being a descriptive Account of Singapore, Penang, Province Wellesley, and Malacca; their Peoples, Products, Commerce, and Gov-

ernment. (Three volumes), John Cameron F.R.G.S., Smith, Elder and Co., London, 1865.

One Hundred Years of Singapore, Volume 1, Walter Makepeace, Gilbert E. Brooke and Roland St John Braddell, Oxford University Press, Singapore, 1991.

An Anecdotal History of Old Times in Singapore, Volume II, Charles Burton Buckley, No publisher listed, printed by Frasier & Neave Limited, Singapore, 1902.

The Native Races of the Indian Archipelago. (Papuans.), Book Review *Quarterly Review of the Methodist Episcopal Church, South*,. Volume X, New Series, No. 4, October 1856, pp 481-507.

The Malay Archipelago: The Land of the Orang-utan and the Bird of Paradise: A Narrative of Travel, with Studies of Man and Nature. (Two volumes), London, Macmillan & Co., 1869.

Quarterly Review of the Methodist Episcopal Church, South, Volume X, New Series, No. 4, October 1856, pp 481-507.

Chapter 17: England • 1853-1854

Physical description of New South Wales and Van Diemen's Land: Accompanied by a Geological Map, Sections, and Diagrams, and Figures of the Organic Remains, P. E. De Strzelecki. Longman, Brown, Green, and Longmans, London, 1845.

'George Samuel Windsor Earl, Ethnologist as Hawker', Donald Chaput, *Journal of the Royal Australian Historical Society*, Vol. 70, pt 1, June, 1984.

Chapter 18: Australia and Onward • 1855-1857

A visit to the Indian archipelago, in H.M. ship Mæander. With portions of the private journal of Sir James Brooke, K.C.B., Captn. the Hon. Henry Keppel, R.N., illustrations by Oswald W. Brierly, R. Bentley, London, 1853.

Chapter 19: Penang and Province Wellesley • 1858-1863

Straits Law Reports, Being a Report of Cases decided in the Supreme Courts of the Straits Settlements, Penang, Singapore and Malacca: also a few Judgments of the Indian and English Cases, printed at the Commercial Press, Penang, 1877.

Chapter 20: Respite, Romance and Recognition • 1864

Great Central State, The Foundation of the Northern Territory, Jack Cross, Wakefield Press, Kent Town, South Australia, 2001.

Chapter 21: Once More Sometime in November • 1865

Letter to Daly: South Australian Archives, A101 (C1).

Envoi

Foreign Bodies, Oceania and the Science of Race 1750-1940, edited by Bronwen Douglas and Chris Ballard, Australian National University Press, Canberra, 2008.

Introduction by C.M. Turnbull to *The Eastern Seas*, G.W. Earl, Oxford University Press, Singapore and Kuala Lumpur, 1971.

Descendants of George Windsor Earl

Papers by Robert Hellyer, Associate Professor of History, Wake Forest University, USA.

General 'Boy': The Life of Lieutenant General Sir Frederick Browning, Richard Mead, Pen and Sword, Barnsley, 2010.

It's Been a Lot of Fun, Brian Johnston, W. H. Allen, London, 1974.

Bibliography of Works by G. W. Earl

•

Books & Pamphlets

Observations on the Commercial and Agricultural Capabilities of the North Coast of New Holland and the Advantages to be Derived from the Establishment of a Settlement in the Vicinity of Raffles Bay, Effingham Wilson, London, 1836. Pamphlet.

Sailing Directions for the Arafura Sea, Compiled from the Narratives of Lieuts. Kolff and Modera, of the Dutch Navy, Hydrographic Office, London. [One map], 8vo, 16pp, Introduction by Earl (ii), 1837. Also reprinted by Australian Office, Sydney, 1839.

The Eastern Seas; or Voyages and Adventures in the Indian Archipelago in 1832-33-34; Comprising a Tour of the Island of Java–Visits to Borneo, the Malay Peninsula, Siam, &c.; Also, an Account of the Present State of Singapore, with Observations on the Commercial Resources of the Archipelago, Wm H. Allen & Co., London, xii, pp. 461, four folding leaves of plates, maps: no preface: dedicated to Dr José d'Almeida of Singapore], 1837.

Voyages of the Dutch Brig-of-War Dourga, through the southern and little-known ports of the Moluccan Archipelago, and along the previously unknown southern coast of New Guinea, performed during the years 1825 & 1826, Lt D. H. Kolff, Jun., R.M.W.O. Translated from the Dutch [*Reize door der weinig bekenden Zuidelyken Molukschen Archipel*, Amsterdam, 1828] by George Windsor Earl, James Madden & Co., London. [Two maps, one being from *The Eastern Seas*, the other from the *Sailing Directions for the Arafura Sea*, both with the date changed to 1839. [Translator's preface not signed or dated, but located on HMS *Alligator*, Sydney. Author's preface wrongly dated November 1838 (for 1828)]. pp. xxiv, 365., 1840.

Enterprise in Tropical Australia, Madden and Malcolm, London, vii, 177pp, dedicated to Sir J. J. Gordon Bremer, 1846.

The Native Races of the Indian Archipelago. Papuans. (Volume I of Ethnological Library, conducted Edwin Norris, Secretary of the Royal Asiatic Society), Hippolyte Baillière, London (& New York), 239pp, four engraved plates (three of them full-colour chromolithographs), two wood engravings, two folding maps, a folding chart showing a range of head types, and a chart listing some dialects, 1853. (Also: J.B. Baillière, Paris; Bailly Baillière, Madrid.)

Contributions to the physical geography of south-eastern Asia and Australia, Hippolyte Baillière, London. pp. 48, folded map, 1853. [See also, *JIA*, Vol. 6, 1853].

A Correspondence Relating to the Discovery of Gold in Australia, Pelham Richardson, London, 16pp., 1853. Pamphlet.

The native races of the Indian Archipelago: Brown tribes of the Moluccas, Timor and Celebes. Announced by the Ethnological Society, but not published.

Topography and itinerary of Province Wellesley, Pinang Gazette Press, George Town (Penang), Straits Settlements, 33p, 1861.

Handbook for Colonists in Tropical Australia, Pinang Gazette Press, printed by Matthew Gregory Sr., i-x, 3 folding maps, 1 plate, 1863. See under *JIA*, NS Vol. 4, (1), below.

Contributions to Learned Journals

Journal of the Royal Asiatic Society of Great Britain and Ireland (*JRAS*) (London, 1834-continuing).

'A Narrative of a Voyage from Singapore to the West Coast of Borneo, in the Schooner Stamford in the Year 1834, with an Account of a Journey to Montradok, the Capital of a Chinese Colony in possession of the principal Gold Mines', by George Earl. Read before the Royal Asiatic Society in London on July 4th 1835 by Earl and printed in *JRAS*, Vol. 3, pp. 1-24, 1836.

'Sketch of the Island of Borneo (Communicated in a Letter to the Right Hon. Sir Alexander Johnston)'. Read before the Royal Asiatic Society in London on February 4th 1837 and printed in *JRAS*, Vol. 4, pp. 174-86, 1837.

Journal of the Royal Geographical Society of London (*JRGS*) (London, 1830/31-92).

'Reize door der weinig bekenden Zuidelyken Molukschen Archipel, door Lieut. D. H. Kolff, Jun. Amsterdam, 1828'. ('Voyage through the southern, or little known part of, the Archipelago of the Moluccas, &c.'), by G.W. Earl, *JRGS*, Vol. 7, pp. 369-74, 1837.

An account of a visit to Kisser, one of the Serawatti group in the Indian Archipelago', by G.W. Earl, *JRGS*, Vol. 11, pp. 108-17, 1841.

'Notes on northern Australia & the neighbouring seas', by G. W. Earle [*sic*]. *JRGS*, Vol. 12, pp. 139-41, 1842.

'On the physical structure & arrangement of the islands of the Indian Archipelago', by W. Earle [sic]. *JRGS*, Vol. 15, pp. 358-65, 1845.

'On the aboriginal tribes of the northern coast of Australia', by G. Windsor Earl. *JRGS*, 16, pp. 239-51, 1846.

Journal of the Indian Archipelago & Eastern Asia (*JIA*)
(Singapore, 1847-63).

'Specimens of the dialects of Timor & of the chain extending thence to New Guinea', by Geo. Windsor Earl, M.R.A.S. *JIA*, Vol. 2, pp. 695-704, 1848.

'On the leading characteristics of the Papuan Australian & Malayu-Polynesian nations', by G. Windsor Earl. *JIA* Vol. 3, 1849, pp. 682-689. *JIA*, Vol. 4, pp. 1-10, 66-74 & 172-81, 1850.

'The island of Mindoro', extract from *Diario de Manila*, translation by Earl. JIA, Vol. 3, pp. 756-66, 1849.

'The Molucca Islands', [translated from the French of Count van Hogendorp's *Coup d'Oeil sur Ille de Java &c.*, 1830], *JIA*, Vol. 3, pp. viii-xv, 1849.

'The trading ports of the Indian Archipelago' by G. Windsor Earl M.R.A.S. *JIA*, Vol. 4, pp. 238-51 (Abai-Ambong), 380-99 (Albay-Ampanan), 483-95 (Analabu-Ayer Raja) & 530-51 (Baba-Banda Is): series not continued, 1850.

'On the culture of cotton in the Straits Settlements', by G. Windsor Earl. *JIA*, Vol. 4, pp. 720-27, 1850.

'Steam routes through the Indian Archipelago: – established, proposed and prospective, by G. Windsor Earl. *JIA*, Vol. 5, pp. 441-50: one map, 1851.

'Steam route through Torres Strait', by G. Windsor Earl, *JIA*, Vol. 5, pp. 489-97: one map, 1851.

'Sketch of the steam route from Singapore to Torres Strait', by G. Windsor Earl, *JIA*, Vol. 5, pp. 613-24, 1851.

'Steam routes from Torres Strait to Sydney', by G. Windsor Earl. *JIA*, Vol. 5, pp. 671-76: one map, 1851.

'Land-locked harbours' from *Enterprise in Tropical Australia* (1846). *JIA*, Vol. 6, p. 242, 1852.

'Contributions to the physical geography of south-eastern Asia & Australia', by George Windsor Earl. *JIA*, Vol. 6, pp. 243-77, 1852. *JIA*, NS 2, pp. 278-86, 1858. [Expanded version of Earl's article 'On the physical structure & arrangement of the islands of the Indian Archipelago' published in *JRGS* Vol. 15, 1845. See also under books.

'Contribution to the knowledge of the north & east coasts of New Guinea', by G. F. de Bruijn Kops, Lieut. Dutch R. N. [translated from the *Natuurkundig Tijdschrift voor Nederlandsch-Indië*.] *JIA*, Vol. 6, pp. 304-48: one map, 1852.

'The Kei & Arm Islands', notices by J.F.B. (Francis J. Bernard) from *Singapore Chronicle*, 1826, and by G.W.E. (George Windsor Earl) from *Parliamentary Papers*, Port Essington, 1843. *JIA*, Vol. 7, pp, 64-69 & 69-72, respectively, 1853.

'Book Review: *A visit to the Indian Archipelago in H.M.S.* Mæander, by the Hon. Henry Keppel, R.N.', 2 vols, Bentley, 1853 [not signed]. *JIA*, Vol. 7, pp. 247-59, 1853.

'Bima & Sumbawa' by H. Zollinger (translated from the *Verhandelingen van het Bataviaasch Genootschap van Kunsten en Wetenschappen*, **23**, 1850). *JIA*, NS (New Series) Vol. 1, pp. 233-65, 1856.

'Handbook for Colonists in Tropical Australia', by George Windsor Earl, M. R.A.S, Corresponding Member of the Ethnological Society; Commissioner of Crown Lands at Port Essington..., *JIA*, NS Vol. 4, (1) pp. 1-187: one map, 1863. [This is the last part of the journal to be issued: NS Vol. 3, 1859, also consists of part 1 only, with no second part: the two first parts are, therefore frequently bound together to make one volume, designated NS Vol. 3, 1859-63.]

Transactions of the Ethnographical Society of London (*TES*) (London, 1850-75)

'On the shell-mounds of Province Wellesley, in the Malay Peninsula', by G. Windsor Earl. TES II, pp. 119-129, 1863.

JOURNAL

OF THE

INDIAN ARCHIPELAGO AND EASTERN ASIA.

EDITED BY

J. R. LOGAN

OF PINANG.

SINGAPORE, 1847 TO 1862. TWELVE VOLUMES. 8°. PRICE £20.

Vol. I. 1847. pp. 508, with 12 Illustrations and 2 Maps.

I. The present condition of the Indian Archipelago, by J. R. Logan, Member of the Asia ic Society, &c.—II. Gutta Percha, by T. Oxley, A.B.—III. Some Remarks on the Dyaks of Banjarmassing.—IV. Annual Remittances by Chinese Immigrants to their families in China.—V. Shair Bidasari: a Malay Poem with an English Translation and Notes, by Logan.—VI. Details respecting Cochin China, by Mgr. Le Fevre, Bishop of Isauropolis, &c.—VII. Some Contributions to the Natural History of the Rafflesia Patma, by the Heer Zollinger, M.B.S. &c.—VIII. A Glance at Rhio, by J. T. Thomson.—IX. Contributions to the Statistics of the Population of Java, by P. Bleeker, Mem. Dir. and Sec. Bat. Soc. &c.—X. Notes on the Geological Features of Singapore and some of the Islands adjacent, by Lieut.-Col. James Low, C.M.R.A.S., &c.—XI. Description of Karrang Bollong (in Java) and of the Bird's Nest Rocks there.—XII. Narrative of the events connected with the arrest of the Rt. Rev. Mgr. Le Fevre, by the Cochin China Government in 1846.—XIII. Temminck's general view of the Dutch Possessions in the Indian Archipelago.—XIV. Notes on the Coal deposits which have been discovered along the Siamese Coast, from Pinang to the vicinity of Junkceylon, by Lieut.-Col. Low.—XV. Discovery of Coal in Ligor and Kedah on the West Coast of the Malay Peninsula, by Logan.—XVI. Introductory Remarks to a Series of Contributions to the Ethnology of the Indian Archipelago, by Logan.—XVII. A few Remarks on Conchology and Malacology, by Will. Traill, M.D.—XVIII. The Orang Binua of Johore, by Logan.—XIX. Physical Characteristics of the Mintira, by Logan.—XX. The Orang Sabimba of the extremity of the Malay Peninsula, by Logan.—XXI. The Orang Bidnanda Kallang of the River Pulai in Johore, by Logan.—XXII. The Orang Sletar of the Rivers and Creeks of the Old Strait and Estuary of the Johore, by Logan.—XXIII. Table of Measurement illustrative of the physical peculiarities of the Mintira Biduanda, &c., by Logan.—XXIV. The Superstitions of the Mintira, by Logan.—XXV. Visit of a Party of Orang Mintira to Singapore, by Logan.—XXVI. The Ethnology of the Johore Archipelago, by Logan.—XXVII. Remarks on the Sletar and Sabimba Tribes, by J. T. Thomson.—XXVIII. Examination of the Coast of the Peninsula from P. Mutiara to P. Panjang in search of Coal deposits in November 1847, by Capt. Congalton.—XXIX. The Laws of the Indian Archipelago and Eastern Asia, by Logan.—XXX. The Laws of Muung Thai or Siam, by Lieut.-Col. Low.—XXXI. Miscellaneous Notices. Contributions and Correspondence. Malay Pantuns.—Index. I. General Index. II. Index of Names, and Glossary.

Miscellaneous

A General View of the Fields of Commerce in the Islands and Countries of Eastern Asia. Announced by the publishers Madden and Malcolm in 1846, but seemingly never produced.

'Progress of Discovery in the Western Portion of New Guinea, from 1828 to 1852', paper read before the British Association for the Advancement of Science at their meeting in Hull during the second week of September 1853. Not found.

Enterprise, Discoveries, and Adventures in Australia. George Windsor Earl, Madden and Malcolm, London, 8vo, two engraved plates, two folding maps, no date [circa 1852?]. Not seen.

'On the Submarine Plateaus of the East Indies', *The American Journal of Science and Arts* (*Silliman's Journal*), Second Series, Vol XXVI, No. 77, to November 1858, pp. 442-444. (Extract from *JIA* article, Vol. 6, 1852.)

'Notes on the bovine animals of the Malay Peninsula', *Annals and Magazine of Natural History*, Series 2, Vol 14, pp. 318-319, 1854.

'On the Meteorology of Northern Australia', Adelaide Philosophical Society, 2pp, 1864. Not seen. (Perhaps the same text as it appeared in 'Contributions to the meteorology of northern Australia', *South Australian Register*, December 28th, 1864.

DESCENDANTS OF GEORGE WINDSOR EARL

•

Annie and William Alt arrived in Nagasaki in November 1864. She was seventeen and he twenty-four. Annie's daughter, Phillis, wrote that 'when she discovered on her arrival that there was no fresh milk ever to be had, she wept'. Nevertheless, they were to spend the next seven years in a country just emerging from its isolation as well as one undergoing profound internal political change.

William deftly negotiated a commercial path in Japan as the country moved towards diminishing the power of the princes under the Shogunate in favour of the spiritual Emperor, the Mikado. In 1867, as business grew, William Alt brought his nephew Frederick Hellyer to Nagasaki to help him manage Alt & Co., followed shortly afterwards by his other nephew, Thomas Hellyer.

In 1868, the Meiji Restoration, which brought the Mikado and his supporters to power, set Japan on the road to industrialisation. Alt & Co. helped fill the needs of the Emperor's cause by selling them steamships, rifles, ammunition and uniforms, in addition to the company's usual trading activities. William also became a close friend of the young Iwasaki Yataro, a Tosa Domain samurai who would found the Mitsubishi organisation in 1870.

William and Annie were to live in Japan until 1871, first in Nagasaki (1864 to 1868) and thereafter in Yokohama, where William's proximity to the Mikado was important. The first four of their children were born in Japan: Mabel Edith, Nagasaki, 1865; Ethel Margaret (the writer's grandmother), Nagasaki, 1866; Kathleen, Nagasaki, 1868; and George Earl, Yokohama, 1870.

In 1871, William Alt's ill health forced him to leave the East, by which time he had made his fortune. Alt & Co. was sold to his two nephews and the family returned to England where William took a large house, Woburn Park (today St. George's College) in Surrey. Three more children were born there: Anne, 1872; Phillis Innocent, 1874; and William Brian Lancelot, 1877. Pleasance, the last child, was born in London in 1872.

Woburn Park was an ideal family home remembered by the Alt children with much happiness. Their grandmother, George Earl's widow, Clara, spent much time there with the family. This idyllic life came to an end after six years when William decided to move as he had lost a large amount of money in a project, grand even for the Victorian age, to build a railway connection between London and Calcutta via Constantinople, Baghdad and Karachi. The (still affluent) Alt family moved from Woburn Park to Cranbrook in Kent, and then to various neighbourhoods in London.

Here are the stories of the grandchildren of George and Clara Earl:

Mabel Edith

Mabel Edith married Bertram John Mitford in 1894. They had two children, Elisabeth, who married Richard West, and John Bertram (Jack), who married Marjorie Hutton and had two children, Susan and Bertram. Mabel Edith died in 1947, aged 82.

Ethel Margaret (Madge)

At the age of sixteen Madge met and fell in love with Frederick, the second of eleven children of Sir Joseph Noel Paton and Lady Paton. Joseph Noel Paton was a distinguished artist and citizen of Edinburgh, member of the Royal Scottish Academy, Queens Limner for Scotland, and friend and associate of the Pre-Raphaelite movement and its members. William Alt, who is reputed to have liked neither Scotsmen nor artists, did not welcome the friendship of the couple. Proposals of marriage were not approved of and for years every obstruction was made to her friendship with Frederick. After thirteen years, they decided to marry against William's wishes, and he disavowed his daughter.

The couple went to India where later Frederick was appointed by Viceroy Curzon to be the first Director-General of Commercial Intelligence for the Government of India. He died after an operation in Edinburgh in 1914, leaving Madge, who had remained fiercely loyal, with three children. She died in 1963 aged 97. After an 'engagement' of nine years and nineteen years of marriage, she had survived her husband for nearly 50 years.

The children of Frederick and Madge Noel Paton

Of their three children, Peggy remained unmarried and spent her life looking after her mother, as well as being a writer. Lora married Josselyn Hennessy, a journalist and writer; they had three children. Victor married Joane, elder daughter of Sir Gilbert Wiles KCIE, a distinguished member of the Indian civil service. For over thirty years Victor had a successful business career in India, being a director of various companies and a keen soldier in the Auxiliary Forces (Bombay Light Horse). For some years he was Chairman of Killick Industries in Bombay before retiring to Scotland in 1951.

In 1958, Victor was ennobled by The Queen as Baron Ferrier of Culter. This was a life peerage; he was in the first batch of ten to be selected for this new rank of the peerage. He served the House of Lords diligently for the rest of his life, both as a member of committees and as a Deputy Speaker. He was also a member of the Royal Company of Archers. Victor died in 1992, aged 92; Joane had predeceased him in 1962. He and Joane had three daughters and one son (the writer of this book), each of whom has children and grandchildren.

Kathleen and Phillis

Born in Nagasaki and England, respectively, Kathleen and Phillis did not marry. After their father's death, they lived with and looked after their mother, Annie, at her house at 41 Cadogan Street in London. It was to Phillis that Annie dictated her memoir. Kathleen died at age 73 in 1941 and Phillis in 1951, aged 76.

George Earl

Born in Yokohama and educated in England, George Earl was encouraged by his father to join the Army. This was not a success and in 1894, at the age of 24, he went to America. Settling in Missouri, he managed an estate there owned by his father, with the help of Frederick Hellyer who had earlier worked for Alt & Co. in Japan. In 1895, he married Virginia Cahoon. So devoted was George to his mother-country that he returned to England from America at the outbreak of the First World War and, as a volunteer, rejoined his old regiment, the King's Own Yorkshire Light Infantry (KOYLI). He was killed at Hill 80, Ypres, on 18th of April 1915. Captain Alt, mentioned in dispatches, at the age of 44 was one of the oldest men to be killed on the front line. He is buried at Oosttaverne Cemetery in Belgium. Virginia died in 1957.

The children of George Earl and Virginia Alt

There were two sons, Daniel and George. Daniel died in boyhood. George trained as an architect, married late in life and died without issue.

Anne (Nancy)

The Alt's fifth child was always known as Nancy. She was educated privately and married Frederick Henry Browning at the age of 22 in 1894. Frederick had been educated at Wellington College, possibly with the thought that he would go into the Army. He was a clever boy and excellent sportsman. He did not follow two brothers into the services or a third brother into the Church. Instead, he joined the family firm of Twiss and Browning where the partners were his father, two uncles and two cousins. In 1905 he became senior partner of the firm whose main business was, as sole agent, the importation into the UK of Hennessy brandy. He and Nancy were an elegant, much-sought-after couple in London society. Arguably the most beautiful of the Alt daughters, Nancy fitted in well with her husband's social and sporting life. They lived in Hans Road (just off the Brompton Road) in London. Frederick died in 1929 and Nancy in 1957.

The children of Frederick and Nancy Browning

There were two children, Grace born in 1895 (who did not marry) and Frederick Arthur Montague born in 1896, known as Tommy to family and friends.

Taking after his father, Tommy was a great sportsman, a strong, rather dominating character, and at Eton was considered to be highly intelligent if academically average. He entered Sandhurst in 1914 and later served with distinction in the First World War, earning as a young officer the DSO and the Croix de guerre. After the war he was both a professional soldier and an athlete. In addition to being a first-class hurdler, he was a member of the British bobsleigh team at the 1924 Olympic Games in Chamonix. His reputation as a top-class soldier grew apace. He was a marked disciplinarian, demanding the highest standards in all things, and was completely dedicated. He gathered the sobriquet 'Boy' Browning because it reflected his youthfulness, enthusiasm and always immaculate appearance.

In 1932, at the age of 36, Tommy Browning married the novelist, Daphne du Maurier. In some ways they were not obviously well suited; he, the successful Army officer, smart, organised, disciplined, competent, gregarious; she, antisocial, shy, romantically intellectual, imaginative, brilliantly talented, unconventional. Yet they had a deep love for each other which carried them through the strains of long separations and war.

He was a most distinguished soldier who, during the Second World War, confronted difficulties and challenges with skill, dedication and honesty. Of particular credit, he was the founder and first Commander of the Airborne Division which played such a critical role in that war. He had his critics but, in a time of war, this is hard to avoid.

In 1946 he was awarded the KBE. Lt. General Sir Frederick Browning held, over the next ten years, positions of great importance: with Mountbatten in Singapore 1946/47; Comptroller and Treasurer to the Household of The Princess Elizabeth 1948-52; Treasurer to The Duke of Edinburgh 1952-56. He also had many extramural responsibilities and duties. Having already been appointed KCVO, in 1959 he was made a GCVO, a sign of particular esteem by Her Majesty The Queen. He died after a period of some ill health in 1965, aged 69. Daphne died at the age of 81 in 1989. They had three children: Tessa, the Viscountess Montgomery of Alamein; Christian, a film director; and Flavia, Lady Leng.

William Brian Lancelot

William was the second son and seventh child. Born in 1877, his early years were spent in London before education at Clifton College and New College Oxford. Influenced by his father, he became an Amy Volunteer and left Oxford to join the City of London Imperial Volunteers, raised at the time of the South African wars. At age 22, Lt. Alt was the company's youngest officer. After arriving in Cape Town during February 1900, he served in the north of Cape Colony and then at Bloemfontein. William took part in the advance to Pretoria and his regiment was then at the attack on Diamond Hill, where he was wounded in the arm. He had it dressed and returned to the front line. Later, when he was about to have it re-dressed, he was shot in the head. He is buried at the foot of the kopje where he fell on the 12th of June 1900, not far from van der Merwe Farm on the Delagoa Railway. He was the only officer of the City of London Imperial Volunteers to lose his life during that war.

Pleasance

Pleasance was the last child born to Annie and William Alt. As with her brother Brian, the only homes she knew were Holland Park Gardens and Airlie Gardens in London. In 1905, three years before her father's death, she married Charles Evelyn Johnston, a City merchant in a well-established, prosperous coffee business. The family firm had been created in 1842 in Santos, Brazil, by his grandfather. Pleasance's father-in-law, Reginald E Johnston, became Governor of the Bank of England in 1909. Charles had served in the Great War as a lieutenant-colonel and had won a DSO and MC.

In 1922, tragedy struck the family while they were on holiday at Bude in Cornwall. An old family friend, Marcus Scully, who had been badly wounded in the war, was staying with them. Scully was swept away by a strong current while swimming in the sea and, Charles, himself a strong swimmer, went to his aid but was caught by the current and drowned. Scully was rescued by other swimmers.

Pleasance, strong character that she was, held her family together helped no doubt by the support of the wider Johnston family. An unusual aspect of this sad event was that two years after the tragedy, Pleasance married Marcus Scully, but later divorced him and reverted to the Johnston name. She died in 1957, aged 88.

The children of Charles and Pleasance Johnston

Pleasance and Charles had four children, three boys and a girl. Kathleen (who married John Carter and had four children); Reginald and Christopher who both married and had children, and the youngest son, Brian.

Brian Johnston, 'Johnners', won an MC for his actions in the war, and joined the BBC in 1946, initially as cricket commentator. He married Pauline Tozer at St. Paul's Knightsbridge on the 22nd April 1948. They had three sons and two daughters.

'Johnners' branched out into light entertainment as well as becoming the broadcasting voice of English cricket, and became one of the best-known and best-loved men in public life during a long career in which he also authored more than a dozen books, including two autobiographies. He died on January 5th 1994, aged 81, and his memorial service at Westminster Abbey was attended by more than 2,000 people.

George and Clara Earl had one child, eight grandchildren and thirteen great-grandchildren.

INDEX

Folios in italics refer to map locations.

First published in the U.K. by

Ashgrove Publishing

an imprint of:

Hollydata Publishers Ltd
27 John Street
London
WC1N 2BX

ISBN 978 185398 186 9

Book design by Brad Thompson

Printed and bound in the U.K.